Weekly Assessment

Bothell, WA • Chicago, IL • Columbus, OH • New York, NY

www.mheonline.com/readingwonders

Send all inquiries to:
McGraw-Hill Education
Two Penn Plaza
New York, New York 10121

Printed in the United States of America.

7 8 9 10 RHR 18 17 16 15 14
D

Table of Contents

Table of Contents - Cont'd.

Weekly Assessment

Weekly Assessment is an integral part of the complete assessment program aligned with ***McGraw-Hill Reading Wonders*** and the Common Core State Standards (CCSS).

Purpose of *Weekly Assessment*

Weekly Assessment offers the opportunity to monitor student progress in a steady and structured manner while providing formative assessment data. As students complete each week of the reading program, they will be assessed on their understanding of key instructional content. The results of the assessments can be used to inform subsequent instruction.

The results of ***Weekly Assessment*** provide a status of current achievement in relation to student progress through the CCSS-aligned curriculum.

Focus of *Weekly Assessment*

Weekly Assessment focuses on two key areas of English Language Arts as identified by the CCSS—Reading and Language. Students will read two selections each week and respond to items focusing on Comprehension Skills and Vocabulary Strategies. These items assess the ability to access meaning from the text and demonstrate understanding of unknown and multiple-meaning words and phrases.

Administering *Weekly Assessment*

Each weekly assessment should be administered once the instruction for the specific week is completed. Make copies of the weekly assessment for the class. You will need one copy of the Answer Key page for each student taking the assessment. The scoring table at the bottom of the Answer Key provides a place to list student scores. The accumulated data from each weekly assessment charts student progress and underscores strengths and weaknesses.

After each student has a copy of the assessment, provide a version of the following directions: **Say:** *Write your name and the date on the question pages for this assessment.* (When students are finished, continue with the directions.) *You will read two selections and answer questions about them. Read each selection and the questions that follow it carefully. For the multiple-choice items, completely fill in the circle next to the correct answer. For the constructed response item, write your response on the lines provided. When you have completed the assessment, put your pencil down and turn the pages over. You may begin now.*

Answer procedural questions during the assessment, but do not provide any assistance on the items or selections. After the class has completed the assessment, ask students to verify that their names and the date are written on the necessary pages.

Overview of *Weekly Assessment*

Each weekly assessment is comprised of the following

- 2 "Cold Read" selections
- 10 multiple-choice items assessing Comprehension Skills
- 10 multiple-choice items assessing Vocabulary Strategies
- 1 constructed response item assessing Comprehension

Reading Selections

Each weekly assessment features two selections on which the assessment items are based. (In instances where poetry is used, multiple poems may be set as a selection.) The selections reflect the unit theme and/or weekly Essential Question to support the focus of the classroom instruction.

Selections increase in complexity as the school year progresses to mirror the rigor of reading materials students encounter in the classroom. In Units 1–3, the Lexile range for selections is 700–800; in Units 4–6, it is 800–900.

Comprehension—Multiple-Choice Items

Each selection is followed by five items, for a total of ten items in a week, that assess student understanding of the text through the use of Comprehension Skills—both that week's Comprehension Skill focus and a review Comprehension Skill. The review skill is taken from a week as near as possible to the current week and aligns with the instruction, i.e., skills that are more suited to Reading for Information will not be used to assess Reading for Literature even though they are in the closest proximity in the program scope and sequence. In Unit 1, Week 1 no review skills are featured, and during the course of the year some weeks feature additional review questions to best assess student comprehension of the text.

Vocabulary—Multiple-Choice Items

Each selection is followed by five items, for a total of ten items in a week, that ask students to demonstrate the ability to uncover the meanings of unknown and multiple-meaning words and phrases using Vocabulary Strategies—both that week's Vocabulary Strategy focus and a review Vocabulary Strategy. The review strategy is taken from a week as near as possible to the current week and aligns with the instruction, i.e., strategies used to identify and gain meaning from figurative language may not be readily available for use in an informational text. In Unit 1, Week 1 no review strategies are featured, and during the course of the year some weeks feature additional review questions to best assess student language knowledge.

Comprehension—Constructed Response

At the close of each weekly assessment is a constructed response item that provides students the opportunity to craft a written response that shows their critical thinking skills and allows them to support an opinion/position by using text evidence from one or both selections.

NOTE: Please consider this item as an optional assessment that allows students to show comprehension of a text in a more in-depth manner as they make connections between and within texts.

Scoring *Weekly Assessment*

Multiple-choice items are worth one point each, for a total of twenty points in each assessment. If you decide to have students complete the constructed response, use the correct response parameters provided in the Answer Key along with the scoring rubric listed below to assign a score of *0* through *4*.

Score: 4
- The student understands the question/prompt and responds suitably using the appropriate text evidence from the selection or selections.
- The response is an acceptably complete answer to the question/prompt.
- The organization of the response is meaningful.
- The response stays on-topic; ideas are linked to one another with effective transitions.
- The response has correct spelling, grammar, usage, and mechanics, and it is written neatly and legibly.

Score: 3
- The student understands the question/prompt and responds suitably using the appropriate text evidence from the selection or selections.
- The response is a somewhat complete answer to the question/prompt.
- The organization of the response is somewhat meaningful.
- The response maintains focus; ideas are linked to one another.
- The response has occasional errors in spelling, grammar, usage, and mechanics, and it is, for the most part, written neatly and legibly.

Score: 2
- The student has partial understanding of the question/prompt and uses some text evidence.
- The response is an incomplete answer to the question/prompt.
- The organization of the response is weak.
- The writing is careless; contains extraneous information and ineffective transitions.
- The response requires effort to read easily.
- The response has noticeable errors in spelling, grammar, usage, and mechanics, and it is written somewhat neatly and legibly.

Score: 1
- The student has minimal understanding of the question/prompt and uses little to no appropriate text evidence.
- The response is a barely acceptable answer to the question/prompt.
- The response lacks organization.
- The writing is erratic with little focus; ideas are not connected to each other.
- The response is difficult to follow.
- The response has frequent errors in spelling, grammar, usage, and mechanics, and it is written with borderline neatness and legibility.

Score: 0
- The student fails to compose a response.
- If a response is attempted, it is inaccurate, meaningless, or completely irrelevant.
- The response may be written so poorly that it is neither legible nor understandable.

Evaluating *Weekly Assessment* Scores

The primary focus of each weekly assessment is to evaluate student progress toward mastery of previously-taught skills and strategies.

The expectation is for students to score 80% or higher on the assessment as a whole. Within this score, the expectation is for students to score higher than 6/8 on the items assessing the particular week's Comprehension Skill; higher than 6/8 on the items assessing the particular week's Vocabulary Strategy; and "3" or higher on the constructed response, if it is assigned.

For students who do not meet these benchmarks, assign appropriate lessons from the Tier 2 online PDFs. Refer to the weekly "Progress Monitoring" spreads in the Teacher's Editions of ***McGraw-Hill Reading Wonders*** for specific lessons.

The Answer Keys in ***Weekly Assessment*** have been constructed to provide the information you need to aid your understanding of student performance, as well as individualized instructional and intervention needs.

This column lists the instructional content for the week that is assessed in each item.

Question	Correct Answer	Content Focus	CCSS	Complexity

This column lists the CCSS alignment for each assessment item.

This column lists the Depth of Knowledge associated with each item.

14	G	Main Idea and Key Details	RI.5.2	DOK 2
15	B	Main Idea and Key Details	RI.5.2	DOK 2
16	I	Context Clues	L.5.4a	DOK 2
17	A	Prefix *re-*	L.5.4b	DOK 1

Weekly review items are shaded in for clear identification.

Comprehension 1, 2, 4, 6, 7, 10, 12, 14, 16, 17	/10	%
Vocabulary 3, 5, 8, 9, 11, 13, 15, 18, 19, 20	/10	%
Total Weekly Assessment Score	/20	%

Scoring rows identify items associated with Reading and Language strands and allow for quick record keeping.

Read the passage "Maddie and the Homeless Pets" before answering Numbers 1 through 10.

Maddie and the Homeless Pets

Maddie lives in New Bern, a city near the coast in North Carolina. She likes living in New Bern except when a hurricane moves up the coast. Then she worries.

One day her school is closed because of an ominous weather forecast that a hurricane is on the way. The torrential rain of a hurricane often causes flooding. That day almost ten inches of rain falls on North Carolina. The power is out for hours, but Maddie's family feels lucky. Their home is on high ground, so it isn't flooded. When the power is back the next day, Maddie turns on the television for news of the storm. She hears that many dogs and cats got separated from their families and were found wandering around loose after the storm.

The reporter says, "Volunteers and the Humane Society have opened an emergency shelter for lost pets at the county fair grounds. Anyone who had to leave a home and needs a safe place for a pet can bring it to the shelter to stay for now. The people at the shelter need help from the community and are requesting donations of pet food."

GO ON →

Because Maddie really wants to help, she resolves to find a way. She wonders what she can do. She might open a lemonade stand. Then she remembers she did that once. She sold a total of ten glasses of lemonade and made $2.50. It would not be enough to buy much food.

Next, Maddie thinks about asking her parents for money. Yet, asking them may not be a good idea. She has heard them talking about saving on expenses. Mom lost her job arranging flowers at the floral shop when it went out of business, and Dad's company cut his hours last week. Asking them for money is definitely not a good idea.

Finally, Maddie gets a good idea. Almost everyone likes pets. If she can convince her classmates to donate food, she might collect enough to make a difference. Right away Maddie makes a poster. At the top, it says, "Help the Pets." She adds a newspaper article about the emergency shelter and then draws pictures of cats and dogs. She also gives some examples of kinds of pet food. In the garage, Maddie finds a big cardboard box. She decorates it with pictures of animals.

In the morning, Maddie takes her poster and box to school. She asks her teacher, Ms. Jones, if she can put them in the hall near the door to the room. Ms. Jones says, "This is a great poster and great idea!" She helps Maddie find the best place for the poster and box. She suggests that Maddie make a card to deliver with the food so that all the students who collaborate to help the shelter by donating food can sign their names. Finally, Maddie ties three colorful balloons to the box.

After the first day, four cans of cat and dog food are in the box. The next day, there are more cans and several bags of food. Maddie already needs to find another box.

On Saturday, Maddie's dad drives her to the shelter and helps her carry the boxes inside. The people at the shelter are delighted. Their supplies are unusually low because there are so many homeless pets. They invite Maddie to visit with the pets. She even gets to hold a kitten on her lap for a few minutes.

Driving home, Maddie has a new thought. Maybe she can find a permanent animal shelter that needs donations. It would be fun to have another food drive, especially if everyone pitches in to help.

GO ON →

Name: ______________________________ Date: ________

Now answer Numbers 1 through 10. Base your answers on "Maddie and the Homeless Pets."

1 Which event happens first in the passage?

Ⓐ Maddie turns on the television for news.

Ⓑ Ten inches of rain falls on North Carolina.

Ⓒ Maddie gets her classmates to donate food for pets.

Ⓓ Maddie's school is closed because of the weather report.

2 Read this sentence from the passage.

One day her school is closed because of an ominous weather forecast that a hurricane is on the way.

What does *ominous* mean in the sentence above?

Ⓕ false

Ⓖ hopeful

Ⓗ possible

Ⓘ threatening

3 What happens after the storm but before Maddie decides not to open a lemonade stand?

Ⓐ Maddie's teacher likes her idea.

Ⓑ Maddie holds a kitten on her lap.

Ⓒ Dogs and cats are wandering around loose.

Ⓓ Maddie collects pet food from her classmates.

4 What happens at the end of the passage?

Ⓕ Maddie worries about lost pets.

Ⓖ Maddie holds a kitten for a few minutes.

Ⓗ Maddie thinks about having another food drive.

Ⓘ The reporter says animals at the shelter need food.

GO ON →

Name: ______________________ **Date:** ________

5 Read this sentence from the passage.

The torrential rain of a hurricane often causes flooding.

What does *torrential* mean in the sentence above?

Ⓐ gentle

Ⓑ heavy

Ⓒ unexpected

Ⓓ welcome

6 Read this sentence from the passage.

Mom lost her job arranging flowers at the floral shop when it went out of business, and Dad's company cut his hours last week.

What does *floral* mean in the sentence above?

Ⓕ best

Ⓖ designer

Ⓗ flower

Ⓘ pastry

7 What happens after Maddie watches the news report but before she gets a good idea?

Ⓐ She makes a poster.

Ⓑ She draws pictures of cats and dogs.

Ⓒ She drives to the shelter with her dad.

Ⓓ She thinks of asking her parents to help.

GO ON →

Name: ______________________________ Date: ________

8 Read this sentence from the passage.

Because Maddie really wants to help, she resolves to find a way.

What does *resolves* mean in the sentence above?

Ⓕ weakly tries

Ⓖ works again

Ⓗ firmly decides

Ⓘ hopelessly wishes

9 Read this sentence from the passage.

She suggests that Maddie make a card to deliver with the food so that all the students who collaborate to help the shelter by donating food can sign their names.

What does *collaborate* mean in the sentence above?

Ⓐ think of other ideas

Ⓑ work together

Ⓒ refuse

Ⓓ vote

10 What happens before Maddie ties balloons to the box but after she makes a poster?

Ⓕ Maddie talks to her teacher.

Ⓖ Maddie hears about the flooding.

Ⓗ Maddie thinks about ways she can help.

Ⓘ Maddie's classmates bring food to donate for pets.

GO ON →

Read the passage "Something to Do" before answering Numbers 11 through 20.

Something to Do

Ever since school let out for the summer, Kyle O'Hara had been spending his afternoons being passive as he sat around watching television shows. His dad would tell him to turn off the TV set now and then. Each time Kyle would protest, and his dad would reply, "I'm not sorry for you; I'd have more sympathy if you worked as hard as I do!"

One afternoon Kyle lingered in the lobby of his apartment building, feeling sad. Mr. Jackson, the custodian for the building, stopped to chat and find out what was wrong. At first Kyle didn't want to admit how bored he was. But he considered Mr. Jackson a friend, and finally he told him.

The custodian thought about Kyle's problem for a moment. "Well," he began, "several elderly residents in this building can't get outside much anymore. Maybe you could run errands for them during the day."

"That's a great idea! It sounds like fun!" exclaimed Kyle. Later that afternoon Kyle posted a flyer on the bulletin board in the lobby and told his father about his plan. Several days went by, and he didn't receive a single phone call in response to the flyer. He found this bewildering and wondered what the problem was. In the flyer he had listed really low prices for his services. One day Kyle

GO ON →

left his apartment in search of Mr. Jackson. The custodian was delivering a package to a resident. Kyle told him he had not received any phone calls.

"That's really strange," Mr. Jackson told Kyle. "I know that Mrs. Kim's dog needs exercise, but she can't take her on long walks every day. And Mr. Castelli has an injury, so it is hard for him to get around. He needs someone to pick up his prescriptions at the store. Maybe they just don't have money to spare to pay for someone else to do the jobs."

Kyle could hardly believe his ears. He simply couldn't comprehend that the people living in his building's luxurious apartments were struggling to make ends meet.

Mr. Jackson must have read his mind. He said, "Some of the residents have lived in this building a long time, and it's hard to pay rent that keeps going up when your income stays the same."

Kyle hesitated and then said, "You know, I'm mainly looking for something to keep me busy until school starts. The pay isn't the main consideration for me."

"It is for them, Kyle," Mr. Jackson said.

Kyle understood what he meant. He rode the elevator to the third floor, walked down the hall, and knocked on a door. Mrs. Kim opened it. But before she could say anything, Kyle asked, "Would you like me to walk your dog? There's no charge."

A little dog peeked at Kyle from around the door. "Oh, Kyle!" said Mrs. Kim. "That would be so nice. Trixie is a little shy, but she'll take to you quickly. And maybe in the future I can find a way to return the favor."

As Trixie bounded down the street ahead of Kyle, he made sure to keep a tight grip on her leash. When they rounded the corner, they passed Kyle's father, who was coming home from work. Without hesitation, he quickly gave Kyle a broad grin as he walked by.

GO ON →

Name: ______________________________ Date: ________

Now answer Numbers 11 through 20. Base your answers on "Something to Do."

11 What event happens first in the passage?

Ⓐ Kyle decides that getting paid to help others isn't important.

Ⓑ Kyle posts a flyer on the bulletin board in the lobby.

Ⓒ Kyle tells Mr. Jackson that he is bored.

Ⓓ Kyle walks Trixie for Mrs. Kim.

12 Read this sentence from the passage.

"I'm not sorry for you; I'd have more sympathy if you worked as hard as I do!"

What does *sympathy* mean in the sentence above?

Ⓕ sad feelings

Ⓗ respect

Ⓖ interest

Ⓘ time

13 What happens after Kyle makes a flyer to get jobs but before he decides that pay isn't the main consideration?

Ⓐ Mr. Jackson tells Kyle that he could run errands for people.

Ⓑ Kyle offers to walk Mrs. Kim's dog for her for no charge.

Ⓒ Kyle learns that people may not have enough money.

Ⓓ Kyle watches television shows.

14 What happens last in this passage?

Ⓕ Mr. Jackson delivers a package to a resident.

Ⓖ Mrs. Kim tells Kyle that Trixie is a little shy.

Ⓗ Kyle's dad tells him to turn off the TV set.

Ⓘ Kyle's dad gives him a broad grin.

GO ON →

Name: ______________________________ Date: __________

15 Read these sentences from the passage.

Kyle could hardly believe his ears. He simply couldn't comprehend that the people living in his building's luxurious apartments were struggling to make ends meet.

What does *comprehend* mean in the sentences above?

Ⓐ wonder

Ⓑ seek out

Ⓒ hear clearly

Ⓓ understand

16 Read these sentences from the passage.

When they rounded the corner, they passed Kyle's father, who was coming home from work. Without hesitation, he quickly gave Kyle a broad grin as he walked by.

What does *hesitation* mean in the sentences above?

Ⓕ delay

Ⓖ explanation

Ⓗ happiness

Ⓘ thinking

17 What happens right before Mr. Jackson tells Kyle that he could run errands for the residents?

Ⓐ Mr. Jackson stops to talk to Kyle to find out what is wrong.

Ⓑ Mr. Jackson tells Kyle that some residents can't get outside much.

Ⓒ Kyle decides that he is mainly looking for something to do rather than a paid job.

Ⓓ Mrs. Kim tells Kyle that in the future she may be able to find a way to return the favor.

GO ON →

Name: ______________________________ Date: ________

18 Read this sentence from the passage.

He found this bewildering and wondered what the problem was.

What does *bewildering* mean in the sentence above?

Ⓕ amusing

Ⓖ confusing

Ⓗ embarrassing

Ⓘ exciting

19 Read this sentence from the passage.

Ever since school let out for the summer, Kyle O'Hara had been spending his afternoons being passive as he sat around watching television shows.

What is the meaning of *passive* in the sentence above?

Ⓐ busy

Ⓑ naughty

Ⓒ not active

Ⓓ considerate of others

20 Which tells the events of the passage in order?

Ⓕ Kyle tries to get jobs for pay. He realizes he is bored. He walks Trixie.

Ⓖ Kyle is bored. He tries to get jobs. He helps people in his apartment building.

Ⓗ Kyle walks Trixie. He tells Mr. Jackson that he is bored. He posts a flyer on the bulletin board.

Ⓘ Kyle helps people in his apartment building. He tells Mr. Jackson that he is bored. He tells his father about his plan.

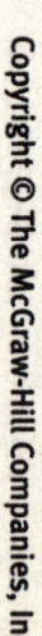

STOP

Name: ______________________ Date: ________

21 In the passages "Maddie and the Homeless Pets" and "Something to Do," how do the characters achieve their goals? Explain how their processes of change are similar. Use clear text evidence in your response.

Answer Key

Name: ______________________

Question	Correct Answer	Content Focus	CCSS	Complexity
1	D	Character, Setting, Plot: Sequence	RL.3.3	DOK 1
2	I	Context Clues: Sentence Clues	L.5.4a	DOK 2
3	C	Character, Setting, Plot: Sequence	RL.3.3	DOK 1
4	H	Character, Setting, Plot: Sequence	RL.3.3	DOK 1
5	B	Context Clues: Sentence Clues	L.5.4a	DOK 2
6	H	Context Clues: Sentence Clues	L.5.4a	DOK 2
7	D	Character, Setting, Plot: Sequence	RL.3.3	DOK 1
8	H	Context Clues: Sentence Clues	L.5.4a	DOK 2
9	B	Context Clues: Sentence Clues	L.5.4a	DOK 2
10	F	Character, Setting, Plot: Sequence	RL.3.3	DOK 1
11	C	Character, Setting, Plot: Sequence	RL.3.3	DOK 1
12	F	Context Clues: Sentence Clues	L.5.4a	DOK 2
13	C	Character, Setting, Plot: Sequence	RL.3.3	DOK 1
14	I	Character, Setting, Plot: Sequence	RL.3.3	DOK 1
15	D	Context Clues: Sentence Clues	L.5.4a	DOK 2
16	F	Context Clues: Sentence Clues	L.5.4a	DOK 2
17	B	Character, Setting, Plot: Sequence	RL.3.3	DOK 1
18	G	Context Clues: Sentence Clues	L.5.4a	DOK 2
19	C	Context Clues: Sentence Clues	L.5.4a	DOK 2
20	G	Character, Setting, Plot: Sequence	RL.3.3	DOK 1
21	see below	Comparing Across Texts	RL.5.9	DOK 4

Comprehension 1, 3, 4, 7, 10, 11, 13, 14, 17, 20	/10	%
Vocabulary 2, 5, 6, 8, 9, 12, 15, 16, 18, 19	/10	%
Total Weekly Assessment Score	/20	%

21 To receive full credit for the response, the following information should be included: Maddie and Kyle both figure out ways to help others in need. Maddie delivers food to the shelter to help the pets, and Kyle offers to run errands for no charge to help his neighbors.

Read the passage "On the Trail" before answering Numbers 1 through 10.

On the Trail

My name is Luis. Two weeks ago on Saturday, my friend Justin and I were biking along Riverside Trail when all at once Justin shouted, "There's something sparkling under those bushes. Let's see what it is!"

We got off our bikes and started poking around under the bushes. I spotted something shining and exclaimed, "Oh my gosh! It's a wallet with jewels on it." I picked it up, and we saw that the wallet had sparkling imitation jewels.

"Let's see if there is identification inside," I said. "We should try to find the owner."

We found photos, some money, and a library card for Mary Johnson. Justin said, "We can try to find Mary Johnson's phone number on the Internet."

We headed for the computer at Justin's house and searched for "Johnson" in a directory for our town. We found eight Mary Johnsons and two M. Johnsons. That was too many Mary and M. Johnsons!

GO ON →

Justin asked, "Should we throw in the towel?"

I said, "No, we shouldn't give up. We could start calling, but what if she lives in another town and only comes here to bike, or what if she has an unlisted number? We should look for other clues first."

Next, we examined the snapshots. One was very old, and another was of a boy about two years old with "William, 2011" written on the back. The third showed a girl about seven in front of Mount Rushmore, and "Annalee, 2011" was written on the back.

Justin guessed, "William and Annalee might be Mary Johnson's children. On Monday, we could see if she goes to our school. But that's a long time for Mary Johnson to wait for her wallet, so let's look for other clues."

We went through the wallet again and found, tucked in back, an appointment card for an eye examination at a mall in town. The appointment was for two o'clock—that same day!

I said, "If we want this plan to succeed, we have to get to the mall before two o'clock, and we have no time to lose."

Justin said, "My mom probably will drive us. I'll ask her."

So that is how we got to the mall at exactly three minutes before two. We hurried into the waiting room at the doctor's office. Almost immediately a worried-looking woman came in. She said, "I have a two o'clock appointment. My name is Mary Johnson."

When Justin and I introduced ourselves and showed her the wallet, her eyes lit up. She said, "What a relief! I have been beside myself!"

Mrs. Johnson thanked us repeatedly. She was elated to have back her money and the photos of her children and great-grandparents.

After we explained where we found the wallet, she said, "I took the children for a bike ride this morning. William was in a cart that I attach to my bike. He must have found the wallet in my bag and tossed it from the cart."

She added, "You two deserve a reward" and handed each of us five dollars. It was worth missing the rest of our Saturday bike ride, and it was fun using clues to solve the problem!

GO ON →

Name: ______________________________ Date: ________

Now answer Numbers 1 through 10. Base your answers on "On the Trail."

1 What is the main problem in the passage?

Ⓐ The boys want to find the owner of the wallet.

Ⓑ Mary Johnson has a very common last name.

Ⓒ There are too many elementary schools to check.

Ⓓ The boys must find a way to get to the mall quickly.

2 Read this sentence from the passage.

> **Two weeks ago on Saturday, my friend Justin and I were biking along Riverside Trail when all at once Justin shouted, "There's something sparkling under those bushes."**

What does the idiom *all at once* mean?

Ⓕ fearfully

Ⓖ happily

Ⓗ loudly

Ⓘ suddenly

3 Read these sentences from the passage.

> **Justin asked, "Should we throw in the towel?"**
>
> **I said, "No, we shouldn't give up."**

What does the idiom *throw in the towel* mean?

Ⓐ start calling

Ⓑ ask for help

Ⓒ admit defeat

Ⓓ toss the wallet

GO ON →

Name: ______________________________ Date: ________

4. Which evidence from the text explains why Luis spots the wallet?

Ⓕ It is visible under bushes.

Ⓖ It has imitation jewels that sparkle.

Ⓗ The boys are biking on Riverside Trail.

Ⓘ Mary Johnson took her children for a bike ride.

5. What is a reason the boys give up the plan to call the owner of the wallet?

Ⓐ There is not enough time.

Ⓑ Justin's computer has broken down.

Ⓒ They would rather finish the bike ride.

Ⓓ There are too many M. or Mary Johnsons.

6. How do the boys compare as problem solvers?

Ⓕ Justin is a better detective.

Ⓖ Luis is more ready to give up.

Ⓗ Both like to follow clues to solve a problem.

Ⓘ Both want to make all the decisions about what to do.

7. Read this sentence from the passage.

I said, "If we want this plan to succeed, we have to get to the mall before two o'clock, and we have no time to lose."

What does the idiom *no time to lose* mean?

Ⓐ not enough time

Ⓑ barely enough time

Ⓒ more than enough time

Ⓓ to find out what time it is now

GO ON →

Name: ______________________________ Date: ________

8 What happened right before Justin asked his mother for a ride to the mall?

Ⓕ They found a wallet in the bushes.

Ⓖ They found an appointment card in a wallet.

Ⓗ They found photographs of children in a wallet.

Ⓘ They looked up "Mary Johnson" on the Internet.

9 Read these sentences from the passage.

She said, "What a relief! I have been beside myself!"

What does the idiom *beside myself* mean?

Ⓐ busy

Ⓑ careless

Ⓒ nearby

Ⓓ worried

10 Read this sentence from the passage.

She was elated to have back her money and the photos of her children and great-grandparents.

What does *elated* mean in the sentence above?

Ⓕ very happy

Ⓖ quite confused

Ⓗ somewhat surprised

Ⓘ extremely disappointed

GO ON →

Read the passage "A Saturday Morning Adventure" before answering Numbers 11 through 20.

A Saturday Morning Adventure

"These new video games are really cool!" Rasheed exclaims. He and his friend Jami play video games almost every weekend. Without a doubt, their favorites are the ones that take place in outer space. They put on spacesuits and climb into a spaceship. Then they begin a journey in which they fight battles against other spaceships and aliens. The games are very realistic. They are also challenging and require Rasheed and Jami to use their problem-solving skills.

On this particular Saturday, the two kids are playing "Space Attack." In this game, blazing hot meteors zoom from outer space into Earth's atmosphere. Attack ships try to collide with the players' ship. Players try to avoid the meteors and destroy the attack ships. The game requires quick thinking and lightning-fast reflexes. This is one of Jami and Rasheed's favorite games, as it presents unusual challenges and is never the same game twice.

"Look," Jami says. "I just reversed course. Maybe if we go the opposite direction, our spaceship won't get smashed by a meteor or an attack ship. It's good we have our spacesuits on. If our ship gets hit by a meteor, we can just float through space until a robot rescues us. I think we're lucky that this is just a game and not real life."

GO ON →

"To continue playing for an additional minute, please pay 100 more tokens at this time," says the robot running the game room. "Otherwise, your game will terminate in 10 seconds."

Rasheed hands the tokens to the robot, which looks almost like a real person. "These new robots can do anything," he says. They're so much better than the outdated ones of the last century."

"You can say that again," says Jami. "My grandpa told me stories about the robots that people used when he was young. They couldn't walk as well as they do now. They were jerky, and they talked funny. My grandpa makes me laugh when he imitates them."

Suddenly, Rasheed screams, "Look out! The attack ship just rotated and turned around. Now it's headed right toward us! We'd better do something quick!"

Realizing that the ball is in her court, Jami calmly pulls up on her joystick. "This is easy," she says, laughing. But her laugh is cut off by the gasp she makes when the joystick fails to respond. "This joystick is broken!" she yells. "The attack ship is gaining on us quickly!"

Rasheed rushes over and adjusts the game dials to increase their speed, but the ship still can't move fast enough to avoid the attack. With a sickening thud, the attack ship hits theirs. Jami is thrown forward and then staggers back into her seat. Suddenly, Rasheed is thrust into the air and finds himself dangling from the ceiling. He holds tightly onto his seat belt, and sways slowly back and forth.

Something has gone wrong in the game. But Jami doesn't get bent out of shape. She carefully checks to make sure that her spacesuit hasn't been damaged. Next, she asks Rasheed if he's hurt and tells him to examine his spacesuit. Then, she calmly takes out her tools. She repairs the joystick and adjusts the dials. "All fixed," she announces. She calmly steers the ship into the dock.

When the kids climb out of their spaceship, Rasheed makes a suggestion. "Maybe next week we can go laser-bowling instead of playing video games. After all, variety is the spice of life!"

"No way!" Jami says. "Compared to these new video games, laser-bowling is way too boring!"

GO ON →

Name: ______________________________ Date: ________

Now answer Numbers 11 through 20. Base your answers on "A Saturday Morning Adventure."

11 What is the main problem in the passage?

Ⓐ The players do not have enough tokens.

Ⓑ The robot does not do what it should.

Ⓒ The players' joystick does not work.

Ⓓ The players' spaceship is lost.

12 Read this sentence from the passage.

Without a doubt, their true favorites are the ones that take place in outer space.

What does the idiom *without a doubt* mean?

Ⓕ to be likely

Ⓖ to be certain

Ⓗ to be unsure

Ⓘ to be unknown

13 Read this sentence from the passage.

"They're so much better than the outdated ones of the last century."

What does *outdated* mean in the sentence above?

Ⓐ old-fashioned

Ⓑ much more useful

Ⓒ far more advanced

Ⓓ what one is used to

GO ON →

Name: ______________________________ Date: __________

14 What happens right before Jami's joystick breaks?

Ⓕ An attack ship heads toward them.

Ⓖ An attack ship thuds into their ship.

Ⓗ Jami's grandpa imitates older robots.

Ⓘ Jami finds herself thrown forward from her seat.

15 Read these sentences from the passage.

But Jami doesn't get bent out of shape. She carefully checks to make sure that her spacesuit hasn't been damaged.

What does the idiom *get bent out of shape* mean?

Ⓐ to start over

Ⓑ to begin to laugh

Ⓒ to become upset

Ⓓ to start screaming

16 What text evidence shows how Rasheed feels about the experience of having played this particular game?

Ⓕ "We'd better do something quick!"

Ⓖ "These new video games are really cool!"

Ⓗ "The attack ship just rotated and turned around."

Ⓘ "Maybe next week we can go laser-bowling instead of playing video games."

17 Read this sentence from the passage.

Realizing that the ball is in her court, Jami calmly pulls up on her joystick.

What does the idiom *the ball is in her court* mean?

Ⓐ She needs to catch a ball.

Ⓑ It is her turn to take action.

Ⓒ She has to try harder to win.

Ⓓ It is time to let Rasheed take over.

GO ON →

Name: ______________________________ Date: ________

18 Read these sentences from the passage.

> **"Maybe next week we can go laser-bowling instead of playing video games. After all, variety is the spice of life!"**

What does the idiom *variety is the spice of life* mean?

Ⓕ Trying new things in life is difficult.

Ⓖ Only strange people try new things.

Ⓗ Doing different things makes life interesting.

Ⓘ You're better off if you always do the same thing.

19 Which statement best compares how Jami and Rasheed each react to the problem?

Ⓐ Jami stays calm, and Rasheed panics.

Ⓑ Jami panics, and Rasheed stays calm.

Ⓒ Both children react with excitement; then Jami reacts practically.

Ⓓ Both children react with excitement; then Rasheed reacts practically.

20 How is the children's problem solved?

Ⓕ They run out of tokens and the game ends.

Ⓖ Rasheed adjusts the speed so they get away.

Ⓗ A robot picks them up while they float in space.

Ⓘ Jami fixes the joystick and lands the ship safely.

STOP

Name: ______________________ Date: __________

21 Explain how Luis and Jami are similar in their approach to problem solving. Provide text evidence in your explanation.

Answer Key Name: ______________________

Question	Correct Answer	Content Focus	CCSS	Complexity
1	A	Character, Setting, Plot: Problem and Solution	RL.4.3	DOK 2
2	I	Idioms	L.5.5b	DOK 2
3	C	Idioms	L.5.5b	DOK 2
4	G	Character, Setting, Plot: Problem and Solution	RL.4.3	DOK 2
5	D	Character, Setting, Plot: Problem and Solution	RL.4.3	DOK 2
6	H	Character, Setting, Plot: Problem and Solution	RL.4.3	DOK 2
7	B	Idioms	L.5.5b	DOK 2
8	G	Character, Setting, Plot: Sequence	RL.3.3	DOK 1
9	D	Idioms	L.5.5b	DOK 2
10	F	Context Clues: Sentence Clues	L.5.4a	DOK 2
11	C	Character, Setting, Plot: Problem and Solution	RL.4.3	DOK 2
12	G	Idioms	L.5.5b	DOK 2
13	A	Context Clues: Sentence Clues	L.5.4a	DOK 2
14	F	Character, Setting, Plot: Sequence	RL.3.3	DOK 1
15	C	Idioms	L.5.5b	DOK 2
16	I	Character, Setting, Plot: Problem and Solution	RL.4.3	DOK 2
17	B	Idioms	L.5.5b	DOK 2
18	H	Idioms	L.5.5b	DOK 2
19	C	Character, Setting, Plot: Problem and Solution	RL.4.3	DOK 2
20	I	Character, Setting, Plot: Problem and Solution	RL.4.3	DOK 2
21	see below	Comparing Across Texts	RL.5.9	DOK 4

Comprehension 1, 4, 5, 6, 8, 11, 14, 16, 19, 20	/10	%
Vocabulary 2, 3, 7, 9, 10, 12, 13, 15, 17, 18	/10	%
Total Weekly Assessment Score	/20	%

21 To receive full credit for the response, the following information should be included: Both Luis and Jami remain calm. Luis patiently follows clues in an orderly way to find the owner of a wallet. Jami follows steps in an orderly way to bring the ship safely into dock.

Read the article "The Burrowing Owl" before answering Numbers 1 through 10.

The Burrowing Owl

Have you ever been lucky enough to see an owl in the wild? If it was small and brown with white spots, it could have been a burrowing owl. These owls are found across North America. People often see them at nature preserves or in conservation areas. That is because these are safe places for the owls to live.

Burrowing owls make an interesting sound. This is a good way to identify them. The sound is similar to someone saying "coo-whooh." It is a quavering, chattering sound that is unlike any other. If a ranger were to conduct a nature walk, he or she might tell you to listen for this sound.

If you were looking for the owl, you would search for a bird with brown feathers that is dappled with white marks. It also has long legs. The owl has bright yellow eyes above curved bills. It has white markings over its eyes. Unlike some other owls, the burrowing owl does not have tufted ears, or ears that have long hair.

Among the smallest of owls, the burrowing owl is eight to ten inches tall and weighs only about eight ounces. Most owls are night creatures, but burrowing owls are active during the day. People might spot one on the ground or perched in a tree along a nature trail.

GO ON →

The burrowing owl got its name because of how it makes its home. This owl does not build a nest in a tree. Instead, it nests in holes under the ground, called burrows, that are no longer used by prairie dogs and ground squirrels. The owl takes over the burrows once the other animals abandon them. For this reason, burrowing owls are found in grasslands and prairies from southwestern Canada all the way to Mexico. People in the western United States and in Florida often see them. In the western states, the owl moves from place to place, but in Florida the birds do not.

If you are lucky enough to see a burrowing owl, remember to stay away from it. If a human comes near, then the owl may become upset or excited. It will make loud noises and bob its head. The burrowing owl has even been known to dive at people. Some people have heard a frightened owl hissing at them like a snake.

It is important to protect the burrowing owl so that it does not become endangered. In several states, the burrowing owl is listed as a "species of special concern." That does not mean it is endangered yet. If it continues to decrease in numbers though, it will be at risk of becoming extinct in the future. There are fewer burrowing owls today than there were in the past. This is because of a few different reasons. Cities have spread across land once used for farming. As a result, the owls lose their habitats, or natural homes. In areas used for farming, large machines can destroy owl nests in the ground.

People can help save the burrowing owl in a few different ways. They can talk to their family members and friends and tell them not to destroy any burrows they find on their property. The owls may return to their nesting area. People can put up a sign to warn of a nest. They can also encourage others not to use pesticides in gardens because burrowing owls eat insects and may be affected by the chemicals. People can spread the word about burrowing owls if they post flyers that inform others about this special bird. We can all do our part to make sure the burrowing owl is here to stay for many years to come.

GO ON →

Name: ______________________________ Date: ________

Now answer Numbers 1 through 10. Base your answers on "The Burrowing Owl."

1 In the first paragraph of the article, what reason does the author give for seeing a burrowing owl in a nature preserve?

Ⓐ It is a safe place for the owl to live.

Ⓑ Some people are lucky to see the owl.

Ⓒ The owl is found across North America.

Ⓓ The owl is small and brown with white spots.

2 Read this sentence from the article.

> **If a ranger were to conduct a nature walk, he or she might tell you to listen for this sound.**

Which definition fits the homograph *conduct* in the sentence above?

Ⓕ to move through

Ⓖ to lead as a guide

Ⓗ to act in a certain way

Ⓘ to direct an orchestra or choir

3 What word from the article means "a bird's beak" but can also be a word that means "a piece of paper money"?

Ⓐ bill

Ⓑ flyer

Ⓒ listed

Ⓓ post

GO ON →

Name: ______________________________ Date: __________

4 In the last paragraph of the article, what reason does the author provide for not using pesticides in gardens?

Ⓕ The pesticides destroy burrows.

Ⓖ The pesticides kill all insects.

Ⓗ The pesticides affect insects that owls eat.

Ⓘ The pesticides create new nesting areas for owls.

5 How did burrowing owls get their name?

Ⓐ by where they nest

Ⓑ by their appearance

Ⓒ by the way they behave

Ⓓ by the sound they make

6 Which word from the article that means "to display a message for others to see" is a homograph for the word defined below?

a pole used for support

Ⓕ ground

Ⓖ nest

Ⓗ post

Ⓘ sign

7 How does the author help the reader understand why burrowing owls are a "species of special concern"?

Ⓐ by describing their appearance

Ⓑ by comparing them to other owls

Ⓒ by explaining how they got their name

Ⓓ by giving reasons why there are fewer now

GO ON →

Name: ______________________________ Date: ________

8. Read this sentence from the article.

It will make loud noises and bob its head.

Which definition fits *bob* in the sentence above?

Ⓕ to cut hair short

Ⓖ to move up and down

Ⓗ to fish with a float or cork

Ⓘ to grab at objects with the teeth

9. How does the author organize the second paragraph from the end of page 26?

Ⓐ by telling what an endangered species is

Ⓑ by showing how to protect the burrowing owl

Ⓒ by defending why burrowing owls need protection

Ⓓ by explaining why burrowing owls will keep decreasing

10. Read this sentence from the article.

If you were looking for the owl, you would search for a bird with brown feathers that is dappled with white marks.

What does *dappled* mean in the sentence above?

Ⓕ added

Ⓖ broken

Ⓗ dotted

Ⓘ hidden

GO ON →

Read the article "Wild in the City" before answering Numbers 11 through 20.

Wild in the City

As cities grow, people expand into areas where wild animals live. When this happens, some animals move away from the lights and noise of city life, but many of them adapt, or change to fit their new situation. For this reason the number of wild animals living in cities is growing.

Wild animals live in parks, on golf courses, and even in backyards. They find food in trash. They drink the water in ponds. They often make homes in hollow logs, trees, or shrubs because they need a safe place to sleep and to raise their young.

Rats

Throughout history, rats have been city dwellers. Black and brown rats traveled from Asia to Europe. They came to North America on ships. Brown rats live throughout the United States, but most black rats live near the Gulf Coast. They can gnaw through wood and metal. For this reason, they make homes in basements and sewers. They are not picky about food and will eat both plants and animals. Rats live in big groups. Sometimes they band together to attack their prey.

Birds

Many birds live in cities too. One is the nighthawk. These birds nest on flat roofs. They eat insects and dive to catch them. Another is the pigeon. Many pigeons were brought to America as pets. Others were used to carry messages. Later they were freed, and the numbers grew rapidly. In cities, they pick through trash for food. They nest on

GO ON →

windowsills, the ledges of tall buildings, or under eaves. They are often seen in large flocks in the heart of a big city like Chicago or New York.

Coyotes

Once coyotes lived in grasslands, mountains, and open prairies. As cities grew and took over open land, coyotes learned to live near people. Since they are intelligent, they adapted well to city life. In some cities, the numbers of coyotes are growing at an alarming rate because they are good at finding food in trash. Like rats, they will eat almost anything. People should be alert when coyotes are reported in a neighborhood since they have attacked small animals. Coyotes may attack a human to protect their pups. People can hear them whine at night. They also growl and bark when threatened.

Bears

Surprisingly, black bears now wander in built-up neighborhoods. In an area of New Jersey only forty miles from New York City, they are seen regularly. Like other city animals that adapt well, black bears eat almost anything. They are found in the United States, Canada, and Mexico. While many people fear them because of their large size, they usually do not attack unless threatened. In most areas, the number of them is either growing or remaining steady. However, the status of the Louisiana black bear and the Florida black bear is "threatened species."

Cougars

At one time, cougars lived across North America. Also called *mountain lion, puma,* and *panther,* the cougar is a large cat. Cities spread into the foothills of mountains in the West. As a result, cougars adapted and now live in neighborhoods near wooded areas and canyons. Many live in Colorado and California. Their numbers are growing rapidly in the western states.

Although people enjoy watching wildlife, they often feel threatened by it. In order to protect themselves, people should be careful not to leave out food. They should put garbage in a covered can. They should also keep dogs and cats indoors most of the time.

GO ON →

Name: ______________________________ Date: ________

Now answer Numbers 11 through 20. Base your answers on "Wild in the City."

11 How does the author organize the information in the article?

Ⓐ by explaining the effect of cities on wildlife

Ⓑ by telling the solution to the problem of wildlife

Ⓒ by telling the order of events in the growth of cities

Ⓓ by comparing and contrasting the sizes of animals

12 Read this sentence from the article.

However, the status of the Louisiana black bear and the Florida black bear is "threatened species."

What does *status* mean in the sentence above?

Ⓕ current condition

Ⓖ signs of danger

Ⓗ full name

Ⓘ location

13 Read this sentence from the article.

In cities, they pick through trash for food.

Which definition fits *pick* in the sentence above?

Ⓐ to rush

Ⓑ to break up

Ⓒ to proceed slowly

Ⓓ to choose and pull from

GO ON →

Name: ______________________________ Date: ________

14 How does the author explain what causes wild animals to live in cities?

Ⓕ by identifying where they live in cities

Ⓖ by telling that cities were built on their land

Ⓗ by showing how easily they adapt to city life

Ⓘ by contrasting life in the wild to life in the city

15 Cougars now live in city neighborhoods in the West because

Ⓐ cougars are large cats and need large cities.

Ⓑ cougars are welcomed by the people in cities.

Ⓒ cities have downtown areas to attract cougars.

Ⓓ cities have grown into the areas cougars lived in.

16 Read this sentence from the article.

Since they are intelligent, they adapted well to city life.

Which definition fits *well* in the sentence above?

Ⓕ in a safe way

Ⓖ in a familiar way

Ⓗ in a satisfactory way

Ⓘ an underground source of water

17 How does the author explain why black bears adapt well to living in cities?

Ⓐ by describing their intelligence

Ⓑ by showing how they solve problems

Ⓒ by saying they eat a wide variety of food

Ⓓ by comparing them to other wild animals

GO ON →

Name: ______________________________ Date: __________

18 How does the author help the reader understand why birds survive in cities?

Ⓕ by comparing nighthawks and pigeons

Ⓖ by telling how many pigeons live in cities

Ⓗ by describing the appearance of different birds

Ⓘ by explaining where birds find food and make nests

19 Which word from the article that means "a short, sharp sound" is a homograph for the word defined below?

the tough, outer covering of a tree

Ⓐ bark

Ⓑ gnaw

Ⓒ growl

Ⓓ whine

20 Read this sentence from the article.

They should put garbage in a covered can.

Which definition fits *can* in the sentence above?

Ⓕ be able to

Ⓖ a container

Ⓗ to fire from a job

Ⓘ to know how to do

STOP

Name: ______________________________ Date: ________

21 How does the way people use land affect the wildlife in "The Burrowing Owl" and "Wild in the City"? Use text evidence in your response.

Answer Key

Name: ____________________

Question	Correct Answer	Content Focus	CCSS	Complexity
1	A	Text Structure: Cause and Effect	RI.5.3	DOK 2
2	G	Homographs	L.5.5c	DOK 1
3	A	Homographs	L.5.5c	DOK 1
4	H	Text Structure: Cause and Effect	RI.5.3	DOK 1
5	A	Cause and Effect	RI.5.3	DOK 2
6	H	Homographs	L.5.5c	DOK 1
7	D	Cause and Effect	RI.5.3	DOK 2
8	G	Homographs	L.5.5c	DOK 1
9	C	Text Structure: Cause and Effect	RI.5.3	DOK 2
10	H	Context Clues: Sentence Clues	L.5.4a	DOK 2
11	A	Text Structure: Cause and Effect	RI.5.3	DOK 2
12	F	Context Clues: Sentence Clues	L.5.4a	DOK 2
13	D	Homographs	L.5.5c	DOK 1
14	G	Text Structure: Cause and Effect	RI.5.3	DOK 2
15	D	Text Structure: Cause and Effect	RI.5.3	DOK 2
16	H	Homographs	L.5.5c	DOK 1
17	C	Text Structure: Cause and Effect	RI.5.3	DOK 2
18	I	Text Structure: Cause and Effect	RI.5.3	DOK 2
19	A	Homographs	L.5.5c	DOK 1
20	G	Homographs	L.5.5c	DOK 1
21	see below	Text Structure: Cause and Effect	RI.5.3	DOK 4

Comprehension 1, 4, 5, 7, 9, 11, 14, 15, 17, 18	/10	%
Vocabulary 2, 3, 6, 8, 10, 12, 13, 16, 19, 20	/10	%
Total Weekly Assessment Score	/20	%

21 To receive full credit for the response, the following information should be included: In "The Burrowing Owl," burrowing owls lost their habitats and their numbers decreased because people developed the land. Birds, coyotes, black bears, and cougars in "Wild in the City" adapted when they lost their habitats, and the effect is that now both people and wild animals live in cities across America.

Read the article "Bicycles, Then and Now" before answering Numbers 1 through 10.

Bicycles, Then and Now

Today's balance bikes for children look remarkably like an early model by Baron Karl von Drais Sauerbrun. Bicycles began with this German inventor. A biography of him reveals that he also worked on an early version of the typewriter. The bicycle-like contraption he made in 1817 had two wheels and was made of wood. It had a seat but no pedals. To move, the rider had to use his legs to push the machine forward. It weighed about 50 pounds! It must have been like riding a very heavy scooter.

Drais exhibited his running machine in 1818 and was given a patent for it the same year. In Germany, it was called the *Draisine*. In France, it became the *Draisienne*, and in England, it was called a hobby horse. For a number of reasons, this early bicycle was popular only a short time. Riders' boots wore out too quickly. It was hard to steer. The roads were often rutted at this time in history, and it was difficult to balance on the machine. Riders who decided to use sidewalks instead were crashing into pedestrians and causing injuries.

The history of bicycles shows the chronological order of events as inventors kept improving the design. A Scottish blacksmith named Kirkpatrick Macmillan is believed to have invented the pedal for a bike in 1840. In the 1860s, the velocipede, which means "fast feet," came along. It had pedals, wooden wheels, and an iron frame. In England, it had two wheels and was known as the "Boneshaker"

GO ON →

because of the rough rides people experienced. Nevertheless, two-wheel bikes became popular. One was designed with a large front wheel and a small back wheel. It was also lighter than earlier bicycles.

A British bicycle maker named James Starley made improvements in both the bicycle and the tricycle, a three-wheeled bicycle. His nephew John Kemp Starley worked for him, and the younger man, who had mechanical skills, built the Rover in 1885. It is often described as the first modern bicycle. It had two 26-inch wheels, ball bearings, tires, and a chain drive. The chain drive had been used before but not on bicycles. It is a chain that moves power from one place to another. On bicycles, it distributes power between the two wheels.

In the United States, bicycles were produced at record rates in the late 1800s. The spectacular growth led to more inventions. During the 1900s, rubber wheels filled with air replaced the wooden wheels. Other improvements followed, including the invention of two-speed and three-speed bicycles.

Then the market for bicycles decreased. Cars and motorcycles became a more important way to get around. As a result, in the 1920s through the 1950s, children were the primary market for bicycle manufacturers. Then in the 1960s and 1970s, people were interested in fitness and the environment. The industry began growing again. Some bikes were made especially for racing, and others for rough, mountainous land.

The most recent bicycle development is balance bikes. These are amazingly similar to Baron Karl von Draise Sauerbrun's *Draisine*. Sometimes balance bikes are called push bikes or run bikes. Like the *Draisine*, they have no pedals. Children start by walking the bike and pushing it along. Then they can start gliding. As young children gain confidence, they can move on to bikes with pedals.

GO ON →

Name: ______________________________ Date: __________

Now answer Numbers 1 through 10. Base your answers on "Bicycles, Then and Now."

1 How does the author help the reader understand the history of bicycles from the *Draisine* to the balance bike?

Ⓐ by explaining the problems with the *Draisine*

Ⓑ by comparing the *Draisine* and the Boneshaker

Ⓒ by telling why fewer people rode bikes in the 1920s

Ⓓ by explaining in time order the different improvements made

2 Read the following sentence from the article.

> **A biography of him reveals that he also worked on an early version of the typewriter.**

The word *biography* comes from two Greek roots, *bio* and *graph*. *Bio* means "life." *Graph* can mean "write." What does *biography* mean?

Ⓕ an old story

Ⓖ a story with photographs

Ⓗ a story about a person's life

Ⓘ a story told in two sections or parts

3 How does the author explain why one bicycle was called the "Boneshaker"?

Ⓐ by describing its parts

Ⓑ by saying people got rough rides

Ⓒ by explaining why it became popular

Ⓓ by naming the country where it was popular

GO ON →

Name: ______________________________ Date: ________

4 How does the author help the reader understand that bicycles improved through the years?

Ⓕ by comparing different bicycles

Ⓖ by telling the sequence of improvements

Ⓗ by contrasting the *Draisine* and balance bikes

Ⓘ by explaining what caused people to start using cars

5 At the beginning of the article, why does the author describe Baron Karl von Drais Sauerbrun's invention?

Ⓐ to describe an unusual invention

Ⓑ to tell about the life of the inventor

Ⓒ to show that the first bikes were the best

Ⓓ to introduce the sequence of bicycles from then to now

6 Read this sentence from the article.

The history of bicycles shows the chronological order of events as inventors kept improving the design.

The root of *chronological* is *chron*, meaning "time." So *chronological order* is in order of

Ⓕ importance.

Ⓖ interest.

Ⓗ when things happen.

Ⓘ why things happen.

7 Read this sentence from the article.

For a number of reasons, this early bicycle was popular only a short time.

The origin of the word *cycle* is the Greek root *cycl*, meaning "circle." This tells you that a *bicycle* has two

Ⓐ frames.

Ⓑ pedals.

Ⓒ wheels.

Ⓓ chain drives.

GO ON →

Name: ______________________________ Date: ________

8 Read this sentence from the article.

His nephew John Kemp Starley worked for him, and the younger man, who had mechanical skills, built the Rover in 1885.

The origin of *mechanical* is the Greek word *mekhane*, meaning "having to do with tools." Which of the following words is most likely to also come from that Greek word?

Ⓕ chain

Ⓖ echo

Ⓗ machine

Ⓘ use

9 How does the author organize the second paragraph from the end of page 38?

Ⓐ by comparing bicycles to motorcycles

Ⓑ by explaining why the market for bicycles changed

Ⓒ by comparing modern bicycles to those in the past

Ⓓ by explaining why cars and motorcycles became popular

10 What word from the article means "to guide" and is also a word that means "a male cow"?

Ⓕ frame

Ⓖ model

Ⓗ pedal

Ⓘ steer

GO ON →

Read the article "Living Better, Thanks to Inventions!" before answering Numbers 11 through 20.

Living Better, Thanks to Inventions!

Inventions improve people's lives in many ways. Most people use inventions every day. They never pause to consider who made them or how they were made. But life would be quite different without the many inventions we have come to rely on.

Automobiles

One of the most important inventions was the automobile. This invention forced people to improve roads and turn them from muddy gravel paths into paved highways. It led to the development of suburbs as more people moved out of large cities. The automobile helped people interact with each other by making it easier for them to get together. People could drive to their jobs or to their friends' and relatives' homes. The distance between places seemed to contract with the arrival of the automobile.

Wheelchairs

Other inventions help fewer people, but they are no less important. The wheelchair, for example, assists people who cannot walk because of physical problems. A wheelchair is just that—a chair with wheels. Many of them also have motors. All wheelchairs are the same in one way: they all help physically challenged people get around. You may think this invention will never be of use to you, but you can't be sure. Anyone could fall and break a leg, or another kind of injury or illness could make walking difficult.

GO ON →

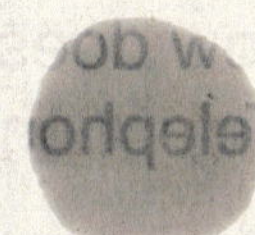

Telephones

The next time your telephone rings, express your gratitude to Alexander Graham Bell. He was the man who invented this device. Bell first tested his machine on March 10, 1876. It quickly became popular. His initial invention opened up a whole new way of communicating. It made communicating over a distance almost immediate. If you can imagine such a thing, contemplate what life would be like without telephones.

Computers

Today much of the work of transmitting phone calls, and thousands of other tasks, is done by computers. Computers are everywhere in the United States, and the country could not function without them. If computers were taken away, traffic would come to a halt. Businesses would close their doors. Lights would go out, and things would get out of control.

Photography

Another invention that has changed our way of living is photography. Early photographs tell the story of important events in history. People used to paint pictures to record that history. But photographs allow us to see what really happened, not an artist's interpretation. Today we take photographs to record the events of our daily lives as well as world events.

Taking It Forward

Many inventions have been combined in order to make life easier. Many cell phones have built-in cameras so people can take photographs on the go. Using a computer and the Internet, people can share those photographs with friends and family right away. People can use their computers to have video telephone calls. They can talk with friends, family, and coworkers around the world as if they were sitting across the table from each other. Without the invention of the photograph, telephone, or computer, these tasks would not be possible.

Because these inventions are so familiar to us and we use them every day, they may seem simple. Actually, they are not simple at all, but they have simplified and improved our lives.

GO ON →

Name: ______________________________ Date: ________

Now answer Numbers 11 through 20. Base your answers on "Living Better, Thanks to Inventions!"

11 How does the author organize the section labeled "Telephones"?

Ⓐ by comparing the invention of the telephone with other similar inventions

Ⓑ by asking questions about the telephone and then answering those questions

Ⓒ by describing the invention of the telephone and then telling what happened afterward

Ⓓ by explaining the idea that Alexander Graham Bell had and then telling how he acted on it

12 Read this sentence from the article.

The distance between places seemed to contract with the arrival of the automobile.

Which definition fits *contract* in the sentence above?

Ⓕ to establish

Ⓖ to become shorter

Ⓗ to reduce by forcing together

Ⓘ a document describing terms

13 How does the author highlight the effects of the invention of the telephone?

Ⓐ by explaining who invented it

Ⓑ by describing how people communicate

Ⓒ by sequencing the dates of its development

Ⓓ by considering what life would be like without it

GO ON →

Name: ______________________ Date: ________

14 The author writes about the telephone before the computer to show that

Ⓕ computers are better.

Ⓖ telephones are no longer used.

Ⓗ telephones are more important.

Ⓘ computers were invented after the telephone.

15 The origin of the word *automobile* comes from the Greek words *autos* meaning "self" and *mobile* meaning "capable of moving." This name suggests that the automobile

Ⓐ can have only one owner.

Ⓑ is available to any independent person.

Ⓒ is large enough to move smoothly on bad roads.

Ⓓ can move by itself without being pulled by an animal.

16 The author suggests that one effect of having only painted pictures of world events is that the viewer has to depend on the painter's

Ⓕ ideas about what happened.

Ⓖ ability to be in many places.

Ⓗ technique.

Ⓘ skill.

17 Read this sentence from the article.

> **If you can imagine such a thing, contemplate what life would be like without telephones.**

What does *contemplate* mean in the sentence above?

Ⓐ ignore

Ⓑ think about

Ⓒ laugh about

Ⓓ attempt to copy

GO ON →

Name: ______________________________ Date: ________

18 Read this sentence from the article.

The next time your telephone rings, express your gratitude to Alexander Graham Bell.

The Greek word *tele* means "far off" and *phon* means "sound." What is the meaning of *telephone*?

Ⓕ a sound that is close by

Ⓖ a sound that is very loud

Ⓗ a sound that travels quietly

Ⓘ a sound that travels a long way

19 The author tells about the invention of the photograph, telephone, and computer first and then describes how computers can be used to have video telephone calls so that the reader can

Ⓐ learn about the older inventions that led to newer inventions.

Ⓑ understand how the inventions work together.

Ⓒ be interested in the combined inventions.

Ⓓ see how important new inventions are.

20 Read this sentence from the article.

Another invention that has changed our way of living is photography.

The word *photography* comes from the Greek roots *phos* meaning "light," and *graph* meaning "draw" or "write." The meaning of *photography* is

Ⓕ making a picture using light.

Ⓖ making a picture using paints.

Ⓗ making a picture using a laser.

Ⓘ making a picture drawing with pencils.

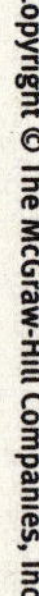

STOP

Name: ______________________ **Date:** __________

21 Use text evidence from "Bicycles, Then and Now" and "Living Better, Thanks to Inventions!" to show how the sequence of the text in each passage helps to explain the authors' ideas.

Answer Key Name: ______________________

Question	Correct Answer	Content Focus	CCSS	Complexity
1	D	Text Structure: Sequence	RI.5.5	DOK 2
2	H	Greek Roots	L.5.4b	DOK 1
3	B	Text Structure: Cause and Effect	RI.5.3	DOK 2
4	G	Text Structure: Sequence	RI.5.5	DOK 2
5	D	Text Structure: Sequence	RI.5.5	DOK 2
6	H	Greek Roots	L.5.4b	DOK 1
7	C	Greek Roots	L.5.4b	DOK 1
8	H	Greek Roots	L.5.4b	DOK 1
9	B	Text Structure: Cause and Effect	RI.5.3	DOK 2
10	I	Homographs	L.5.5c	DOK 1
11	C	Text Structure: Sequence	RI.5.5	DOK 2
12	G	Homographs	L.5.5c	DOK 1
13	D	Text Structure: Cause and Effect	RI.5.3	DOK 2
14	I	Text Structure: Sequence	RI.5.5	DOK 2
15	D	Greek Roots	L.5.4b	DOK 1
16	F	Text Structure: Cause and Effect	RI.5.3	DOK 2
17	B	Context Clues: Sentence Clues	L.5.4a	DOK 2
18	I	Greek Roots	L.5.4b	DOK 1
19	A	Text Structure: Sequence	RI.5.5	DOK 2
20	F	Greek Roots	L.5.4b	DOK 1
21	see below	Comparing Across Texts	RI.5.9	DOK 4

Comprehension 1, 3, 4, 5, 9, 11, 13, 14, 16, 19	/10	%
Vocabulary 2, 6, 7, 8, 10, 12, 15, 17, 18, 20	/10	%
Total Weekly Assessment Score	/20	%

21 In "Bicycles, Then and Now," the author tells about the history of bicycles in chronological order. This helps the reader understand how bicycles slowly changed over a period of time. In "Living Better, Thanks to Inventions!" the author presents earlier inventions first and more modern inventions later to show how inventions progressed over time and were eventually combined to create our newest inventions today.

Read the article "Smart Cars for Clean Air" before answering Numbers 1 through 10.

Smart Cars for Clean Air

Cars take us to school, work, and anywhere else we want to go. We rely on cars to get us to a wide variety of places…and fast! There is no doubt that the automobile has made our lives easier in a number of ways. But there is also no doubt that cars are slowly killing our planet. It is clearly time to rethink how we use cars in our daily lives.

While cars have given us the convenience of easy travel, the pollution they cause is a serious consequence. The Environmental Protection Agency, or EPA, says that gas-powered vehicles such as cars, trucks, and bulldozers are the main cause of air pollution in large cities in the United States. In fact, they cause air pollution throughout the entire world. Environmentalists have talked about the dangerous effects of air pollution for decades. One way to stop this pollution is to buy hybrids, or cars that run on both gasoline and electricity.

Vehicles are responsible for air pollution because they run on gasoline, a fossil fuel. When this fuel is burned in the process of running a car, pollutants are released into the air. As long ago as the 1900s, some experts said that burning gasoline in automobiles could damage the environment. Studies show that we are now paying the price with our quality of air today. Those experts were right!

GO ON →

Hybrid vehicles currently coexist with gas-powered cars. Hybrids could significantly reduce the pollution we release into the air. It is true that these cars still use gasoline, but they certainly use a lot less of it. Hybrid cars utilize a combination of gasoline and electricity. One specific type of hybrid is a particularly good choice. This is because this type relies mostly on electric power. An electric motor turns the car's wheels, and gasoline is used to generate the electricity. The car is recharged by plugging it into an electrical outlet.

If everyone were required to drive a hybrid car such as this one, the amount of pollution from the use of gas would be hugely reduced. The government could make it a precondition that all new car owners buy hybrids. We would also be conserving our fossil fuels for other machines or necessary uses.

Hybrid cars have other advantages, too. Since they use gasoline, they can be refueled at any gas station so that the driver is not left stranded if there is nowhere to charge the battery. They are a great choice because they do not require a huge lifestyle change for drivers. They are very similar to the gas-powered cars that we are so familiar with. They just have one major difference: they greatly improve the environment in which we live.

Hybrid cars are the best choice to reduce air pollution around the world. Transcontinental car manufacturers should be required to stop selling the gas-guzzling cars of yesterday. Instead, they should sell hybrids at reasonable prices so that all people will be able to buy them. The future of our planet is at stake!

GO ON →

Name: ______________________ Date: ________

Now answer Numbers 1 through 10. Base your answers on "Smart Cars for Clean Air."

1 With which of the following statements would the author most likely agree?

Ⓐ We should look for new sources of gasoline.

Ⓑ The automobile was the best invention ever.

Ⓒ We need to make cars that do not pollute the air.

Ⓓ The government should stop production of all cars.

2 Read this sentence from the article.

> **It is clearly time to rethink how we use cars in our daily lives.**

The prefix *re*- can mean either "again" or "back." Which answer choice uses *re*- in the same way as *rethink*?

Ⓕ read

Ⓖ reheat

Ⓗ resource

Ⓘ reward

3 What reason from the text best supports the author's point of view that cars make life better for people?

Ⓐ Hybrid cars can run on gasoline.

Ⓑ Burning gasoline damages the environment.

Ⓒ Hybrid cars do not require a lifestyle change.

Ⓓ We rely on cars to take us anywhere we want to go.

GO ON →

Name: ______________________________ Date: __________

4 Which statement best states the author's point of view about gas-powered cars?

Ⓕ They are best used in city environments.

Ⓖ They are the best form of transportation.

Ⓗ They should be replaced with better cars for the environment.

Ⓘ They should be donated to the Environmental Protection Agency.

5 Read this sentence from the article.

Hybrid vehicles currently coexist with gas-powered cars.

What does *coexist* mean?

Ⓐ exit

Ⓑ are born

Ⓒ learn from each other

Ⓓ are used at the same time

6 What is one effect of using a hybrid car?

Ⓕ spending less time charging a car battery

Ⓖ reducing traffic problems on the roads

Ⓗ saving fossil fuels for other uses

Ⓘ promoting safe driving habits

7 Read this sentence from the article.

Environmentalists have talked about the dangerous effects of air pollution for decades.

The word *decades* includes the Greek root *dekas*, meaning "group of ten." What does *decades* mean?

Ⓐ ten-year periods

Ⓑ profitable years

Ⓒ times in history

Ⓓ ten dollars

GO ON →

Name: _______________________________ Date: _______

8 Which statement supports the author's point of view on transportation?

Ⓕ It is not necessary to change driving habits.

Ⓖ Cars are a convenient way to travel.

Ⓗ People rarely use their cars.

Ⓘ Cars are more important than the problems of pollution.

9 Read this sentence from the article.

The government could make it a precondition that all new car owners buy hybrids.

Based on this sentence, you can tell the prefix *pre-* means

Ⓐ after.

Ⓑ against.

Ⓒ before.

Ⓓ without.

10 Read this sentence from the article.

Transcontinental car manufacturers should be required to stop selling the gas-guzzling cars of yesterday.

The prefix *trans-* means "beyond" or "through." What does the word *transcontinental* mean?

Ⓕ near the continent

Ⓖ under the continent

Ⓗ above the continent

Ⓘ across the continent

GO ON →

Read the article "Fewer Cars for Clean Air" before answering Numbers 11 through 20.

Fewer Cars for Clean Air

Cars are a major part of most of our lives. In many areas, people count on their cars to do the things they need to do every day. But there is a downside to having so many cars on the road. As gasoline is burned, it releases dangerous pollution and harmful greenhouse gases into the air. These gases get trapped in our atmosphere and increase the overall temperature of Earth. As the planet's temperature goes up, ice melts and ocean levels rise. This can create dangerous international problems for many people who live on coastlines. Rising temperatures also affect people, animals, and plants around the world.

The intake of polluted air can be harmful to people. If people were to burn less gasoline, there would be fewer carbon emissions from our cars. This in turn would create less air pollution. Public transportation is the solution to our air pollution problem. People need to stop using their cars and find other ways to get places.

Public transportation is the use of buses, trains, subways, ferries, and other vehicles meant to carry a group of passengers. The benefit of using public transportation is that there is only one vehicle releasing air pollutants, as opposed to many cars. Consider if 50 people rode a bus instead of driving their cars. That would eliminate a lot of gasoline and emissions!

Public transportation has other benefits, too. If this mode of travel were put into effect everywhere in the United States, it could greatly improve traffic problems on the streets. It would also save people money that they would be spending at the gas pump. Having fewer cars on the road also reduces the use of fossil fuels that are slowly being used up. These fossil fuels are not renewable resources, meaning we cannot create more fuel once it is all gone.

GO ON →

Some people have supported the use of electric or hybrid cars as an alternative to gas-powered cars, but I disagree. These vehicles still involve the use of gas in some cases. They are also expensive and are still being perfected. Public transportation has already been proven to work and improve the quality of our environment.

Public transportation may require a slight change in lifestyle, but do not misjudge the amount of help it can do. Isn't it worth it to ride a train or bus when you consider that you are helping to keep the air you breathe as clean as possible? We owe it to the planet to try to protect and respect it. After all, Earth is the only home we have. Let's do our part to improve the world in which we live.

GO ON →

Name: ______________________________ Date: ________

Now answer Numbers 11 through 20. Base your answers on "Fewer Cars for Clean Air."

11 Which sentence from the article supports the author's point that public transportation is the best way to reduce air pollution?

Ⓐ People need to stop using their cars and find other ways to get places.

Ⓑ Public transportation is the use of buses, trains, subways, ferries, and other vehicles meant to carry a group of passengers.

Ⓒ These fossil fuels are not renewable resources, meaning we cannot create more fuel once it is all gone.

Ⓓ Public transportation has already been proven to work and improve the quality of our environment.

12 Read this sentence from the article.

Public transportation may require a slight change in lifestyle, but do not misjudge the amount of help it can do.

The prefix *mis-* is a negative prefix that can mean "incorrectly." So when you *misjudge* something, you

Ⓕ decide quickly.

Ⓖ refuse to decide.

Ⓗ make the right decision.

Ⓘ make the wrong decision.

13 Which of the following sentences best expresses the author's point of view about air pollution?

Ⓐ It is a growing problem that must be addressed.

Ⓑ It is the result of poor planning by our government.

Ⓒ It is not as important as the shortage of fossil fuels.

Ⓓ It is not as dangerous as scientists want us to believe.

GO ON →

Name: ______________________________ Date: ________

14 How does the author show direct support for the use of buses and trains?

Ⓕ by explaining their positive effects

Ⓖ by explaining where they are used

Ⓗ by discussing why air pollution is dangerous

Ⓘ by discussing the need for a change in lifestyle

15 Read this sentence from the article.

This can create dangerous international problems for many people who live on coastlines.

Inter- means "between." *International* problems are

Ⓐ in one town.

Ⓑ in one country.

Ⓒ in at least two countries.

Ⓓ in one very large city.

16 What evidence does the author provide to show that hybrid cars are poor solutions?

Ⓕ who buys the cars

Ⓖ how the cars still use gas

Ⓗ why the cars are used

Ⓘ where the cars are available

17 Read this sentence from the article.

The intake of polluted air can be harmful to people.

The prefix *in-* can mean "in, within, or toward" or it can mean "not." Which answer choice uses *in-* in the same way as *intake*?

Ⓐ incorrect

Ⓑ indoors

Ⓒ insecure

Ⓓ invisible

GO ON →

Name: ______________________________ Date: __________

18 Read this sentence from the article.

Some people have supported the use of electric or hybrid cars as an alternative to gas-powered cars, but I disagree.

The prefix *dis-* means "the opposite of." To *disagree* means to

Ⓕ not respond.

Ⓖ not understand.

Ⓗ argue with someone.

Ⓘ believe in something.

19 According to the article, what is one effect of using public transportation?

Ⓐ People would be happier.

Ⓑ People would save money.

Ⓒ People would have more time.

Ⓓ People would get places faster.

20 Read these sentences from the article.

Consider if 50 people rode a bus instead of driving their cars. That would eliminate a lot of gasoline and emissions!

What does the word *eliminate* mean in the sentence above?

Ⓕ ignore

Ⓖ get rid of

Ⓗ help to make

Ⓘ give an answer to

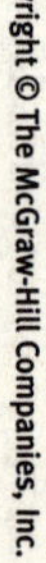

STOP

Name: ______________________ Date: ________

21 Compare and contrast the points of view of the authors of "Smart Cars for Clean Air" and "Fewer Cars for Clean Air." Use text evidence from both articles to explain how the viewpoints are similar and different.

Answer Key

Name: ______________________

Question	Correct Answer	Content Focus	CCSS	Complexity
1	C	Author's Point of View	RI.6.6	DOK 3
2	G	Greek and Latin Prefixes	L.5.4b	DOK 1
3	D	Author's Point of View	RI.6.6	DOK 3
4	H	Author's Point of View	RI.6.6	DOK 3
5	D	Greek and Latin Prefixes	L.5.4b	DOK 1
6	H	Cause and Effect	RI.5.3	DOK 2
7	A	Greek Roots	L.5.4b	DOK 1
8	G	Author's Point of View	RI.6.6	DOK 3
9	C	Greek and Latin Prefixes	L.5.4b	DOK 1
10	I	Greek and Latin Prefixes	L.5.4b	DOK 1
11	D	Author's Point of View	RI.6.6	DOK 3
12	I	Greek and Latin Prefixes	L.5.4b	DOK 1
13	A	Author's Point of View	RI.6.6	DOK 3
14	F	Author's Point of View	RI.6.6	DOK 3
15	C	Greek and Latin Prefixes	L.5.4b	DOK 1
16	G	Author's Point of View	RI.6.6	DOK 3
17	B	Greek and Latin Prefixes	L.5.4b	DOK 1
18	H	Greek and Latin Prefixes	L.5.4b	DOK 1
19	B	Cause and Effect	RI.5.3	DOK 2
20	G	Context Clues: Sentence Clues	L.5.4a	DOK 2
21	see below	Author's Point of View	RI.6.6	DOK 4

Comprehension 1, 3, 4, 6, 8, 11, 13, 14, 16, 19	/10	%
Vocabulary 1, 5, 7, 9, 10, 12, 15, 17, 18, 20	/10	%
Total Weekly Assessment Score	/20	%

21 To receive full credit for the response, the following information should be included: Both authors believe that air pollution is a major problem that is due primarily to the use of gas-powered cars. Both authors believe that these cars should be replaced, but they disagree on how to reduce air pollution. The author of "Smart Cars for Clean Air" thinks that hybrids are the best way to cut back on polluting the air. The author of "Fewer Cars for Clean Air" thinks that cars should be replaced with public transportation to reduce emissions and the pollutants that enter the air.

Read the article "Compromise" before answering Numbers 1 through 10.

Compromise

In the year 1850, disagreement between the North and the South about slavery was growing. An earlier settlement called the Missouri Compromise had helped to solve the problem for some thirty years. As in any compromise, neither side was completely satisfied, but each got part of what it wanted. Then in 1849, California asked to join the Union as a free state. There were 15 slave states and 15 free states. Adding another free state would upset the balance.

Henry Clay was known as the "Great Compromiser." He worked to keep the states united. In 1849, Clay was elected to the U.S. Senate from Kentucky. As a senator, he wanted to find a way to solve the controversy (serious arguments) between the North and South. A number of issues needed to be resolved.

- The first was statehood for California. Congress was not likely to approve admission for another free state.
- The United States had been at war with Mexico. As a result, the federal government got new territory. Should the territory allow slavery or not?
- Texas claimed that its territory extended to Santa Fe. The government disagreed; that is, it disputed Texas's right to expand into what is now New Mexico.
- Slaves were traded in Washington, D.C. Many believed that was wrong in the capital of the nation.

Clay presented his ideas in the Senate. He hoped these ideas would keep the country united. Not everyone agreed with Clay's ideas. The debate that followed lasted months.

GO ON →

Clay asked that California become a state, but Congress could not decide whether it would be free or slave. He proposed that the people living in a territory set up on land gained in the war with Mexico could decide the question of slavery for themselves. Also, the borders of Texas would not include any part of New Mexico. In return, Texas would be paid for the land in dispute. Slavery in the District of Columbia could not be ended without the people's consent. However, slaves could no longer be traded in the nation's capital. Laws would provide for the return of runaway slaves. Finally, the Congress would have no power over the trading of slaves between slave states.

Months of debate in the Senate followed Clay's proposals. John C. Calhoun, Senator from South Carolina, was leader of the opposition. He wrote a response but was too ill to deliver it. Instead, another senator read it for him. Clay's legislation was voted down. Then Daniel Webster, a senator from Massachusetts, and Stephen A. Douglas, a senator from Illinois, helped win approval for a compromise. Douglas later became famous for his debates with Abraham Lincoln.

The Compromise of 1850 included five acts of Congress. The laws covered the main issues that had come up because of California's request to become a free state. They were based on Clay's resolutions. California could join the Union as a free state. The settlers in the territories of New Mexico and Utah would be able to vote on whether they would allow slavery or not. Texas received ten million dollars. In return, Texas had to give up claims to disputed territories. The Fugitive Slave Law went into effect. Runaway slaves were to be returned if they were caught. However, the slave trade ended in the District of Columbia.

The Compromise of 1850 solved the problem for a time, but conflicts soon grew again. A major point of contention, that is, a point that caused a great deal of argument, was the Fugitive Slave Act. Northerners believed it was too unfair to slaves. Many still helped slaves escape to Canada through the Underground Railroad. Because of the Fugitive Slave Law, another compromise was not possible. Eventually the Civil War broke out in 1861. North and South fought in battle after battle until the war ended in 1865.

GO ON →

Name: ______________________________ Date: __________

Now answer Numbers 1 through 10. Base your answers on "Compromise."

1 The author examines the issue of slavery in order to show

Ⓐ the rise of California as a major state.

Ⓑ the conflict between states and territories.

Ⓒ the effects of a labor shortage on farming.

Ⓓ the growing division between the North and the South.

2 Read this sentence from the article.

As in any compromise, neither side was completely satisfied, but each got part of what it wanted.

What does *compromise* mean in the sentence above?

Ⓕ a promise to stand behind your word

Ⓖ both sides refuse to reach an agreement

Ⓗ something that gives hope of success in the future

Ⓘ both sides agree to give up something to solve a conflict

3 Read this sentence from the article.

As a senator, he wanted to find a way to solve the controversy (serious arguments) between the North and South.

What does the word *controversy* mean in the sentence above?

Ⓐ conflict

Ⓑ agreement

Ⓒ a way to transfer property

Ⓓ something that carries something

GO ON →

Name: ______________________________ Date: ________

4 The author helps the reader understand Clay's difficulty in reaching a lasting compromise by discussing

Ⓕ the angry debate about California's borders.

Ⓖ the dispute over the Missouri Compromise.

Ⓗ the argument about the Fugitive Slave Law.

Ⓘ the admission of New Mexico to the Union.

5 The author uses a bulleted list in the article in order to

Ⓐ point out basic ideas of the U.S. Constitution.

Ⓑ briefly explain the articles of the Fugitive Slave Law.

Ⓒ clearly present issues leading to the 1850 Compromise.

Ⓓ briefly describe steps in a state's joining the Union.

6 Read this sentence from the article.

The government disagreed; that is, it disputed Texas's right to expand into what is now New Mexico.

What does *disputed* mean in the sentence above?

Ⓕ argued against

Ⓖ agreed with

Ⓗ confirmed

Ⓘ supported

7 Which happened before Clay was elected to the Senate?

Ⓐ Slave trading was forbidden in Washington, D.C.

Ⓑ War broke out between the U.S. and Mexico.

Ⓒ California became a state in the Union.

Ⓓ The Fugitive Slave Law was passed.

GO ON →

Name: ______________________________ Date: ________

8 Read this sentence from the article.

In the year 1850, disagreement between the North and the South about slavery was growing.

The prefix *dis-* tells you that *disagreement* means to

Ⓕ agree again.

Ⓖ fail to agree.

Ⓗ want to agree.

Ⓘ completely agree.

9 Why does the author mention Stephen Douglas's later debate with Abraham Lincoln?

Ⓐ to focus on Douglas's dislike of slavery

Ⓑ to show that Douglas and Lincoln were political rivals

Ⓒ to reveal that Douglas would make a popular president if he were elected

Ⓓ to show that Douglas's debating skills helped him work out compromises in Congress

10 Read this sentence from the article.

A major point of contention, that is, a point that caused a great deal of argument, was the Fugitive Slave Act.

What does *contention* mean in the sentence above?

Ⓕ approval

Ⓖ disagreement

Ⓗ mistake

Ⓘ unhappiness

GO ON →

Read the article "Democracy in the United States" before answering Numbers 11 through 20.

Democracy in the United States

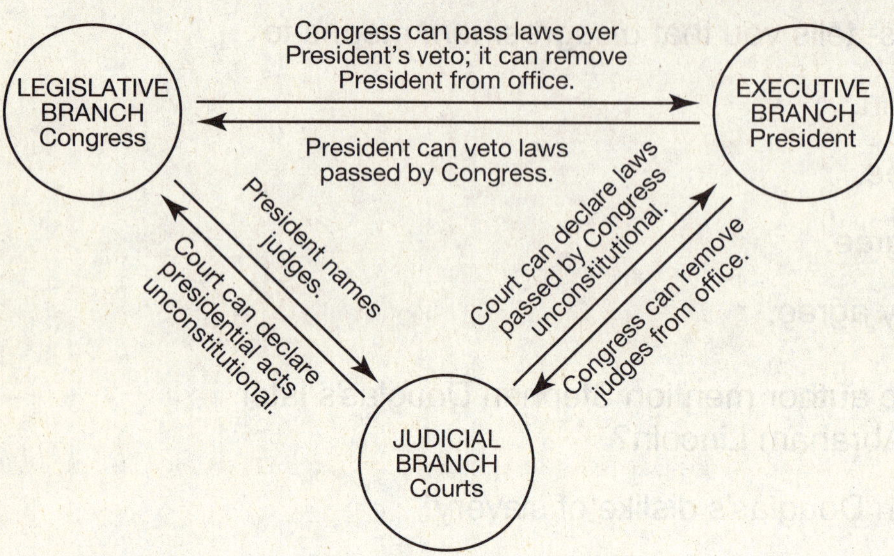

Before the United States became its own country, it was made up of 13 British colonies. These colonies were ruled by the king of England. Many colonists demanded a say in making the laws they had to follow. They didn't like the fact that a king had so much control over their lives. So the colonists decided to break away from England and form a new nation called the United States of America.

The United States is a democracy. Democracy is a form of government. It is a government for the people. In a democracy, the people choose their leaders by voting. The leaders then share the responsibility of running the country. This prevents one person or group of people from having all of the power. Not all countries are democracies. In some, a king or queen has the lion's share of the power. Because others have little power, he or she can do almost anything. The people who wrote the Constitution of the United States set up a democracy because they wanted their government to be different. The Constitution is a written statement of the rules that the U.S. government must follow. Those who created it wanted every voter to have an equal voice in the decisions made by the government because it takes many people working together to make a government work well.

GO ON →

The U.S. government has three parts, or "branches." One is the executive branch, which includes the president and the cabinet. The president's cabinet is made up of people who advise the president. They help the president deal with problems in the country and in the world. The president and the cabinet members work together as a team to make important decisions and carry out the laws.

The legislative branch of government creates the laws. The main part of this branch is the Congress. Congress is made up of two groups of people that form the Senate and the House of Representatives. These people represent, or act for, the people in the states that elected them. Members of each group create ideas for laws. When an idea is written down to be presented, it is called a bill. The bill is discussed and may be changed in several or many ways. Finally, it is voted on. If it passes in one group, then it goes to the other and must also pass there. If it passes in the House of Representatives and the Senate, it goes to the president to be signed and become a law. Not all bills become laws.

The third branch of government is the judicial branch. It includes the Supreme Court, which has nine justices. These judges explain the laws if there are disagreements about them. They also may agree to hear arguments about a case decided in a lower court. To do their jobs, the judges must understand the Constitution. They decide how the laws of the Constitution apply to certain situations.

Though each branch of the government has its own leaders, these branches must work together to make a democracy work. Each branch of government must check the actions of the other two branches. This prevents one branch from having too much power.

The U.S. government has survived for more than 200 years. But it takes more than good leaders for a democracy to last. Citizens must get involved in the government too. In the United States, citizens may vote when they reach 18 years of age. Then they can help elect the country's leaders. They can vote for the president of the United States. They can also vote for leaders who represent them in Congress. People who take part affect the whole country. They have an impact on what happens in the United States.

GO ON →

Name: ______________________________ Date: ________

Now answer Numbers 11 through 20. Base your answers on "Democracy in the United States."

11 Why does the author begin this article by referring to the American colonists' break with England?

Ⓐ to show that Americans would fight for their rights

Ⓑ to present the ideals of the American political system

Ⓒ to explain democracy's deep roots in American history

Ⓓ to present a history of democracy in the Western world

12 Read these sentences from the article.

> **In a democracy, the people choose their leaders by voting. The leaders then share the responsibility of running the country.**

What does *democracy* mean in the sentences above?

Ⓕ a government that makes laws

Ⓖ a government that is permanent

Ⓗ a government with a single leader

Ⓘ a government created by the people

13 Why does the author refer to the Constitution when discussing the Supreme Court?

Ⓐ The Supreme Court wrote the Constitution.

Ⓑ The Court's justices are above the Constitution's influence.

Ⓒ The Supreme Court amends the Constitution every other year.

Ⓓ The Court's justices decide how the Constitution applies to certain situations.

GO ON →

Name: ______________________ Date: ________

14 The author states that each branch of government checks the other branches in order to

Ⓕ allow American citizens to have a say in government.

Ⓖ keep the president from taking control of government.

Ⓗ prevent any single branch from having too much power.

Ⓘ divide powers between the federal government and the states.

15 Read this sentence from the article.

The U.S. government has three parts, or "branches."

What does *branches* mean in the sentence above?

Ⓐ ancestors

Ⓑ leaders

Ⓒ sections

Ⓓ tree limbs

16 What text evidence supports the author's view that citizens should participate in government?

Ⓕ Citizens are urged to vote.

Ⓖ Citizens are asked to protest.

Ⓗ Citizens are encouraged to write bills.

Ⓘ Citizens are requested to present ideas for bills.

17 Read these sentences from the article.

Members of each group create ideas for laws. When an idea is written down to be presented, it is called a bill.

What does *bill* mean in the sentence above?

Ⓐ any composition

Ⓑ a common custom

Ⓒ written idea for a law

Ⓓ statement of money owed

GO ON →

Name: ______________________________ Date: ________

18 Read these sentences from the article.

One is the executive branch, which includes the president and the cabinet. The president's cabinet is made up of people who advise the president.

What does *cabinet* mean in the sentences above?

Ⓕ Congress

Ⓖ a storage case

Ⓗ a group of citizens

Ⓘ a group of advisors

19 Why does the author end the article by discussing voting?

Ⓐ to list voting qualifications

Ⓑ to compare voting today with voting in the past

Ⓒ to analyze how people voted in recent elections

Ⓓ to stress the importance of citizens' involvement

20 Read these sentences from the article.

In some, a king or queen has the lion's share of the power. Because others have little power, he or she can do almost anything.

What does the idiom "the lion's share" mean in the sentences above?

Ⓕ all

Ⓖ the biggest part

Ⓗ an equal share in

Ⓘ something to be fought for

STOP

Name: ______________________ Date: __________

21. How do the authors of "Compromise" and "Democracy in the United States" use the ideas of democracy to help readers understand how they can help solve national problems? Use clear text evidence to support your answer.

Answer Key

Name: ______________________

Question	Correct Answer	Content Focus	CCSS	Complexity
1	D	Text Structure: Problem and Solution	RI.5.3	DOK 3
2	I	Context Clues: Definitions and Restatements	L.5.4a	DOK 2
3	A	Context Clues: Definitions and Restatements	L.5.4a	DOK 2
4	H	Text Structure: Problem and Solution	RI.5.3	DOK 3
5	C	Text Structure: Problem and Solution	RI.5.3	DOK 3
6	F	Context Clues: Definitions and Restatements	L.5.4a	DOK 2
7	B	Sequence	RI.5.3	DOK 2
8	G	Greek and Latin Prefixes	L.5.4b	DOK 1
9	D	Text Structure: Problem and Solution	RI.5.3	DOK 3
10	G	Context Clues: Definitions and Restatements	L.5.4a	DOK 2
11	C	Text Structure: Problem and Solution	RI.5.3	DOK 3
12	I	Context Clues: Definitions and Restatements	L.5.4a	DOK 2
13	D	Text Structure: Problem and Solution	RI.5.3	DOK 3
14	H	Text Structure: Problem and Solution	RI.5.3	DOK 3
15	C	Context Clues: Definitions and Restatements	L.5.4a	DOK 3
16	F	Author's Point of View	RI.6.6	DOK 3
17	C	Context Clues: Definitions and Restatements	L.5.4a	DOK 2
18	I	Context Clues: Definitions and Restatements	L.5.4a	DOK 2
19	D	Text Structure: Problem and Solution	RI.5.3	DOK 2
20	G	Idioms	L.5.5b	DOK 2
21	see below	Text Structure: Problem and Solution	RI.5.3	DOK 3

Comprehension 1, 4, 5, 7, 9, 11, 13, 14, 16, 19	/10	%
Vocabulary 2, 3, 6, 8, 10, 12, 15, 17, 18, 20	/10	%
Total Weekly Assessment Score	/20	%

21 To receive full credit for the response, the following information should be included: In "Compromise," conflict between states was temporarily solved in the Compromise of 1850 when each side gave up things to keep one nation. In "Democracy in the United States," the problem of creating a new nation was solved when a government of three power-sharing branches was formed.

Read the article "Yellowstone Adventure" before answering Numbers 1 through 10.

Yellowstone Adventure

"Hey, Olivia," says Jayden, "I overheard Mom and Dad planning a trip to Boise to see our grandparents."

"We have never been to Boise. Do you know where it is?" asks Olivia.

"It is in Idaho," says Jayden, "and I do not want to go because all my friends will be here this summer."

"It could be fun," Olivia disagrees.

That night Mom talks about the car trip and asks Jayden and Olivia to do some research to learn about a national park they can visit along the way.

"Great!" Olivia says. She looks at maps, but Jayden is too busy. Olivia discovers they will go through South Dakota and Wyoming to get to Boise. Next, she looks up national parks on the Internet and finds four good possibilities. Two are in South Dakota, Wind Cave National Park and Badlands National Park. Grand Teton National Park is in Wyoming, and Yellowstone National Park is in Wyoming, with parts in Montana and Idaho.

Olivia does some more research. If they want to see an unusual cave, they should stop at Wind Cave. For cliffs and wildflowers, Badlands National Park is the best choice, but to see forests and mountains with high peaks, they should stop at Grand Teton. Yellowstone has animals and waterfalls, and it is enormous.

She tells Jayden what she has found. He says, "You are a walking encyclopedia! You choose because I really do not want to go anyway." Olivia chooses Yellowstone and her parents agree.

Nothing much happens the first day on the road. Jayden says to Olivia, "Just as I predicted, this is going to be one boring trip."

On the second day of driving, Dad says, "We will make a stop at Wind Cave National Park. It is not out of the way."

GO ON →

They find a camping area for the night and the next day take a tour of the cave. Olivia is fascinated by the formations of crystals on the walls and ceiling. The patterns are like the honeycombs where bees store honey. Mom says, "Outside, the wind is roaring like a lion. But inside here, it sounds like a purring kitten."

After two more days, they get to Yellowstone. It is a huge park, with parts in three states. Dad suggests that Jayden and Olivia try the Junior Ranger Program. They hike a trail and find a waterfall as loud as thunder. Jayden and Olivia test their skills in the Yellowstone Wildlife Olympics by moving like different animals that live in the park. Afterwards, they meet with a ranger who gives them badges. They are having a good time, but Jayden is not yet convinced about this trip.

The following day the family is off to see Old Faithful. It is a geyser, a spout of hot spring water heated to boiling under the ground and forced into the air. It usually erupts about once every hour and a quarter. When he sees it, Jayden says, "Cool!"

They are exhausted from the hiking. After a picnic dinner, they only want to sleep. First, however, they hang their leftover food in a bag high up in a tree. That's what the ranger has told them to do. During the night, Olivia awakes to a terrible, crashing sound. Suddenly everyone is awake and frightened that a bear may be searching for food. Dad whispers, "We have to frighten that animal away. Let's sing as loud as we can." As they sing, Dad peeks out of the tent and says, "There are two raccoons running away."

Jayden stops singing and starts to guffaw. In between his howls of laughter, he says, "Our singing must have hurt their ears!" In the morning, they see that their empty cooler has been overturned. Jayden starts laughing again. "We could make a CD of ourselves singing," he says. "We could sell it to scare away animals. I can't wait to tell my friends. This is the greatest vacation ever!"

GO ON →

Name: ______________________________ Date: __________

Now answer Numbers 1 through 10. Base your answers on "Yellowstone Adventure."

1 How is Jayden's attitude toward the trip different at the end of the passage than it was at the beginning?

Ⓐ He changes from being excited to being bored.

Ⓑ He changes from being surprised to being scared.

Ⓒ He changes from being bored to being disappointed.

Ⓓ He changes from not liking the idea to being enthusiastic.

2 Read this sentence from the passage.

The patterns are like the honeycombs where bees store honey.

Why is the author comparing patterns and honeycombs?

Ⓕ to show how the patterns look

Ⓖ to explain where bees store honey

Ⓗ to describe the color of the patterns

Ⓘ to show that the patterns are much larger than honeycombs

3 Read these sentences from the passage.

Mom says, "Outside, the wind is roaring like a lion. But inside here, it sounds like a purring kitten."

Mom uses this comparison to emphasize that, inside, the wind sounds

Ⓐ cute.

Ⓑ mild.

Ⓒ sleepy.

Ⓓ dangerous.

GO ON →

Name: ______________________________ Date: ________

4. Why does the family think the crashing sound is a problem?

Ⓕ They are afraid they are in danger from a bear.

Ⓖ They did not want to be awakened from sleep.

Ⓗ They do not want to lose their food supplies.

Ⓘ They are worried about a thunderstorm.

5. How are Badlands National Park and Wind Cave different?

Ⓐ They are in different states.

Ⓑ Wind Cave does not allow camping.

Ⓒ Badlands has more cliffs and wildflowers.

Ⓓ Only Badlands is one of the national parks.

6. Read this sentence from the passage.

He says, "You are a walking encyclopedia!"

When Jayden calls Olivia a "walking encyclopedia," he means that she

Ⓕ spends a lot of time at the library.

Ⓖ has a great deal of knowledge.

Ⓗ likes to read books.

Ⓘ is a dull person.

7. Which sentence from the passage tells you that the setting has changed?

Ⓐ Yellowstone has animals and waterfalls, and it is enormous.

Ⓑ Nothing much happens the first day on the road.

Ⓒ "We have to frighten that animal away."

Ⓓ "We have never been to Boise."

GO ON →

Name: ______________________________ Date: __________

8 Read this sentence from the passage.

They hike a trail and find a waterfall as loud as thunder.

Why is the author comparing a waterfall with thunder?

Ⓕ to describe how noisy it is

Ⓖ to describe how much water is falling

Ⓗ to describe how wet it makes the family

Ⓘ to suggest that there may soon be a storm

9 How is the inside of the cave at Wind Cave National Park different from the outside?

Ⓐ There are bears inside the cave.

Ⓑ There are beehives inside the cave.

Ⓒ The wind is not very loud from inside the cave.

Ⓓ There is a spout of hot spring water inside the cave.

10 Read these sentences from the passage.

Jayden stops singing and starts to guffaw. In between his howls of laughter, he says, "Our singing must have hurt their ears!"

What does *guffaw* mean in the sentence above?

Ⓕ talk

Ⓖ take a break

Ⓗ laugh loudly

Ⓘ giggle secretly

GO ON →

Read the article "A Good Defense" before answering Numbers 11 through 20.

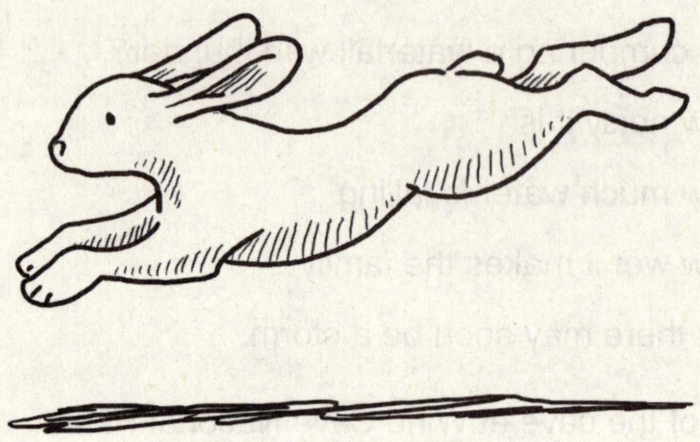

A Good Defense

One cool Saturday morning, Will slipped into his favorite jacket with worn, frayed edges and hiked to one of the deep arroyos around Albuquerque. Will had lived in New Mexico his whole life. Yet, he never got tired of the beauty of the arroyo, a gully carved from the ground by flowing water. In the summer, the season of sudden storms, the arroyos were full. But now, in early November, the arroyo was as dry as a bone.

Outdoors provided a soothing place to reflect, but Will's thoughts were not calm or happy. He was thinking about the bully who had chased him from the schoolyard on Friday afternoon. And worse, he was thinking about how he had fled from the older boy. His face was on fire at the memory. Why had he run away? Sure, Sam was obviously much stronger than Will. Still, Will should have stayed and defended himself. He did not want to be a coward.

Will had told his grandfather about what happened. "Every moment in life presents a choice," his grandfather said. "Every choice creates a new moment."

Will considered that. "But I chose to run away," he replied. "How do I know if that was the right choice to make?"

GO ON →

"Think about the moments that came as a result of your choice," said his grandfather. "If you had made the choice to stay and fight, would those moments have been better or worse?"

Will had thought about it, but he was not sure. All he knew for certain was that he felt bad about what had happened.

Will sat down at the edge of the arroyo, where weeds and flowers grew freely. The breeze blew softly, and the air was clean and cool. The banks of the arroyo offered a protected home for the small animals that hid from larger animals. Snakes, ground squirrels, and rabbits lived in the soft soil bed of the arroyo. Will sat silently while the life of the arroyo went on around him. He gazed at a jackrabbit nibbling the tall grasses and smiled at the creature's long ears, twitching nervously as it listened for enemies. A jackrabbit was prey for a lot of different animals. Then Will fought down a sinking feeling: he was just like a jackrabbit himself. It was an upsetting thought.

Suddenly, a shadow crossed over him, and Will glanced up to see a large hawk wheeling overhead. It hung in the sky for an instant like a threatening cloud. Will realized the bird had gotten a glimpse of the jackrabbit. The jackrabbit froze like a statue to avoid arousing the hawk's attention. Some animals defended themselves this way, while others turned to fight.

The hawk hovered lower in the sky. Will knew that if that rabbit did not want to be the hawk's meal, it had better move fast, but the little brown fellow seemed stunned by the nearness of the hawk and remained motionless. So the two creatures had recognized one another: hunter and hunted.

As the bird swooped lower, Will could hesitate no longer. As quick as a flash, he grabbed a small stone and flung it right at the jackrabbit. Stunned into movement, the desperate rabbit leaped away for denser cover in the underbrush.

"Good for you," Will thought. "You're not a coward; you just needed to escape." Sometimes, he realized, it was the wiser choice to run from trouble.

GO ON →

Name: ______________________________ Date: ________

Now answer Numbers 11 through 20. Base your answers on "A Good Defense."

11 What detail from the passage tells you that Will and the jackrabbit are alike?

Ⓐ They are both animals.

Ⓑ They both have big ears.

Ⓒ They are both very fast runners.

Ⓓ They are both afraid of enemies.

12 Read this sentence from the passage.

His face was on fire at the memory.

What does *His face was on fire* mean?

Ⓕ He is blushing.

Ⓖ He is really hot.

Ⓗ He is sunburned.

Ⓘ He is too near a fire.

13 What word best describes the jackrabbit and Will?

Ⓐ anxious

Ⓑ cowardly

Ⓒ hungry

Ⓓ small

GO ON →

Name: ______________________________ Date: __________

14 Read this sentence from the passage.

Yet, he never got tired of the beauty of the arroyo, a gully carved from the ground by flowing water.

What does the word *arroyo* mean in the sentence above?

Ⓕ desert
Ⓗ landscape
Ⓖ ditch
Ⓘ river

15 Read this sentence from the passage.

It hung in the sky for an instant like a threatening cloud.

What mood does the author create by using this simile?

Ⓐ boredom
Ⓒ joy
Ⓑ danger
Ⓓ sadness

16 How are the hawk and Sam, the bully, alike?

Ⓕ They both can fly.
Ⓖ They are both hungry.
Ⓗ They both threaten weaker creatures.
Ⓘ They are both taller than other creatures.

17 Read this sentence from the passage.

The jackrabbit froze like a statue to avoid arousing the hawk's attention.

Why is the author comparing the jackrabbit to a statue?

Ⓐ to show how still it is
Ⓑ to show how beautiful it is
Ⓒ to show that Will is an artist
Ⓓ to show that it is the color of stone

GO ON →

Name: ______________________________ Date: ________

18 How is the arroyo in summer different from the arroyo in fall?

Ⓕ In summer, it is full of water. In fall, it is dry.

Ⓖ In summer, snakes live there. In fall, snakes hibernate.

Ⓗ In summer, flowers grow freely. In fall, the flowers dry up.

Ⓘ In summer, a big river flows through it. In fall, the river is a small stream.

19 Read this sentence from the passage.

As quick as a flash, he grabbed a small stone and flung it right at the jackrabbit.

What does *as quick as a flash* mean?

Ⓐ brightly

Ⓑ really fast

Ⓒ faster than light

Ⓓ going on and off

20 How does Will solve the problem he has been thinking about?

Ⓕ by deciding to help the jackrabbit

Ⓖ by realizing that his choice was a smart one

Ⓗ by making up his mind not to be like the jackrabbit

Ⓘ by figuring out that the bully was not really a danger

STOP

Name: ______________________________ **Date:** __________

21 Compare how Jayden in "Yellowstone Adventure" and Will in "A Good Defense" change from the beginning to the end of the passages. Give clear evidence stated in the text and examples from inferences you make.

Answer Key

Name: ______________________

Question	Correct Answer	Content Focus	CCSS	Complexity
1	D	Character, Setting, Plot: Compare and Contrast	RL.5.3	DOK 3
2	F	Simile	L.5.5a	DOK 2
3	B	Simile	L.5.5a	DOK 2
4	F	Character, Setting, Plot: Problem and Solution	RL.4.3	DOK 2
5	C	Character, Setting, Plot: Compare and Contrast	RL.5.3	DOK 2
6	G	Metaphor	L.5.5a	DOK 2
7	B	Character, Setting, Plot: Compare and Contrast	RL.5.3	DOK 2
8	F	Simile	L.5.5a	DOK 2
9	C	Character, Setting, Plot: Compare and Contrast	RL.5.3	DOK 2
10	H	Context Clues: Definitions and Restatements	L.5.4a	DOK 1
11	D	Character, Setting, Plot: Compare and Contrast	RL.5.3	DOK 2
12	F	Metaphor	L.5.5a	DOK 2
13	A	Character, Setting, Plot: Compare and Contrast	RL.5.3	DOK 1
14	G	Context Clues: Definitions and Restatements	L.5.4a	DOK 1
15	B	Simile	L.5.5a	DOK 2
16	H	Character, Setting, Plot: Compare and Contrast	RL.5.3	DOK 2
17	A	Simile	L.5.5a	DOK 2
18	F	Character, Setting, Plot: Compare and Contrast	RL.5.3	DOK 2
19	B	Simile	L.5.5a	DOK 2
20	G	Character, Setting, Plot: Problem and Solution	RL.4.3	DOK 2
21	see below	Character, Setting, Plot: Compare and Contrast	RL.5.3	DOK 3

Comprehension 1, 4, 5, 7, 9, 11, 13, 16, 18, 20	/10	%
Vocabulary 2, 3, 6, 8, 10, 12, 14, 15, 17, 19	/10	%
Total Weekly Assessment Score	/20	%

21 To receive full credit for the response, the following information should be included: The reader can infer that both boys feel different about their situations in the end. Jayden is no longer sorry he had to go on the trip, and Will feels better about his decision to run from Sam when he sees how the jackrabbit avoids danger.

Read the article "Watching Earth from Space" before answering Numbers 1 through 10.

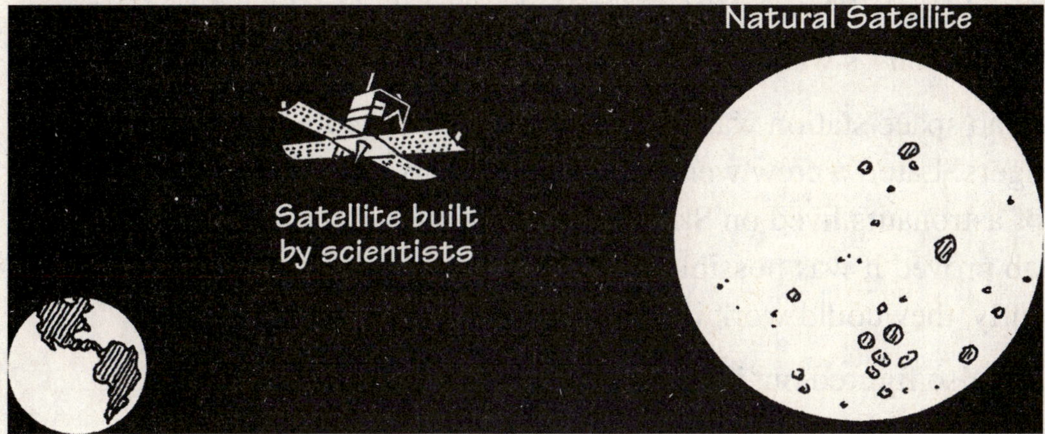

Watching Earth from Space

We are learning about life on Earth from a large satellite in space. Scientists built the satellite and used a rocket to launch it into space in 1998. It is the International Space Station, or ISS. Fifteen countries cooperated to build and operate it. The space station is about 250 miles above Earth and orbits, or circles, Earth sixteen times a day. It is a little longer than a United States football field and weighs almost a million pounds.

Since 2000, people have lived and been active on the space station. One purpose of the ISS is to learn about living in space. Another is to conduct experiments. The findings should make life better for people on Earth. Crews live on the ISS to gather information about space and Earth. A part that is like a big sunroom was attached to the space station in 2010. From here astronauts can view Earth from space. They can observe lights of cities on Earth. They can watch other astronauts walking in space and study objects like asteroids in space. It is like having an eye on the universe.

In 2011, a new camera was placed on the space station. It records happenings on Earth. The camera gives scientists a better tool to research natural events on Earth, such as lightning. It also gives information about the effects of human activities on our planet.

GO ON →

Space exploration began over fifty years ago when Russia sent the first human-made satellite into orbit. In 1962, John Glenn, an American, orbited Earth. Then in 1969, people around the world watched Neil Armstrong's walk on the surface of the moon.

The Skylab space station was launched in 1973. It had no human passengers. Later, a crew went to live on Skylab for a month. Three crews of astronauts lived on Skylab over the following nine months. Skylab proved it was possible for people to survive in space. More importantly, they could work in orbit.

Scientists also figured out how to make a vehicle that could go back and forth between Earth and space. The next step was building such a space shuttle. Having such a vehicle would greatly simplify space exploration. *Columbia,* launched in 1981, was the first shuttle that carried astronauts. The space shuttles were larger than the earlier spaceships. They carried both pilots and scientists. *Challenger*, *Discovery*, *Atlantis*, and *Endeavour* later joined the fleet of shuttles.

The shuttle was important in building the International Space Station. At first, shuttle flights brought construction parts into space. Later, flights brought crews to live on the space station. Shuttles continue to serve as transportation for crews and supplies.

For more than ten years, the ISS's space laboratory has given new information that will improve our future on Earth. Studies about infectious diseases have opened new ways to prevent those diseases. The benefits of ultrasound have increased due to its use on the space station. Ultrasound has deepened understanding about gravity's effects on the human body. It also has helped to discover the health problems of people living on the space station.

We have learned new ways to treat heart disease, cancer, and bone disease as a result of research on the ISS. Experiments with plants have shown they can grow and be used as food on space expeditions. Moreover, they are a way to make air and water clean. We have already seen many good things come from experiments on the ISS. Scientists believe we will continue to benefit from work done in space.

GO ON →

Name: ______________________________ Date: __________

Now answer Numbers 1 through 10. Base your answers on "Watching Earth from Space."

1 Based on text evidence, how does the author organize the article?

Ⓐ by showing cause and effect in space

Ⓑ by sequence of events in exploring space

Ⓒ by comparing and contrasting Earth and space

Ⓓ by problem and solution in using a camera in space

2 Read this sentence from the article.

> **Since 2000, people have lived and been active on the space station.**

The suffix *-ive*, as in *active*, means "tending to or being likely to." So someone who is *communicative* probably enjoys

Ⓕ eating.

Ⓖ playing.

Ⓗ reading.

Ⓘ talking.

3 Read these sentences from the article.

> **Scientists also figured out how to make a vehicle that could go back and forth between Earth and space. The next step was building such a space shuttle.**

What does the word *shuttle* mean in the sentences above?

Ⓐ something that goes into space

Ⓑ something that lasts a long time

Ⓒ something that goes back and forth

Ⓓ something that can remain in orbit around the Earth

GO ON →

Name: ______________________________ Date: ________

4 In which sequence does the author place the events related to the International Space Station (ISS)?

Ⓕ The ISS was launched into space; a part was added; a camera was placed on the space station; people started living on the space station.

Ⓖ A camera was placed on the space station; people started living on the space station; the ISS was launched into space; a part was added.

Ⓗ The ISS was launched into space; people started living on the space station; a part was added; a camera was placed on the space station.

Ⓘ A camera was placed on the space station; a part was added; people started living on the space station; the ISS was launched into space.

5 Read this sentence from the article.

Having such a vehicle would greatly simplify space exploration.

When you *simplify*, you make something

Ⓐ twice as simple.

Ⓑ not simple.

Ⓒ less simple.

Ⓓ more simple.

6 Where in sequence does the author place the flight of *Columbia* in 1981?

Ⓕ as the last space shuttle flight

Ⓖ as the first space shuttle flight

Ⓗ after *Discovery* in the fleet of shuttles

Ⓘ before *Discovery* and after *Endeavor*

GO ON →

Name: ______________________________ Date: _______

7 Why does the author mention Glenn's orbit of Earth?

Ⓐ It was the first solo flight into space.

Ⓑ It was the first flight of the space shuttle.

Ⓒ It came before Russia launched a satellite into space.

Ⓓ It was the first flight of an American around the planet.

8 Read this sentence from the article.

The shuttle was important in building the International Space Station.

The suffix *-al*, as in *international*, means "having to do with." So if you were looking into a dog's *behavioral* characteristics, you would want to know

Ⓕ how it acted.

Ⓖ how it looked.

Ⓗ how fast it could run.

Ⓘ how long it could live.

9 Read this sentence from the article.

Scientists believe we will continue to benefit from work done in space.

The suffix *-ist*, as in *scientist*, means "one who deals with." So a writer who is a *humorist* writes things that are

Ⓐ easy.

Ⓑ funny.

Ⓒ true.

Ⓓ wrong.

10 Which is an effect of experiments done on the International Space Station?

Ⓕ We have learned how to keep a satellite in orbit.

Ⓖ We have learned new ways to treat some diseases.

Ⓗ Astronauts have been able to walk on Earth's moon.

Ⓘ People from many countries learned how to cooperate.

GO ON →

Read the article "The Life of a Hurricane" before answering Numbers 11 through 20.

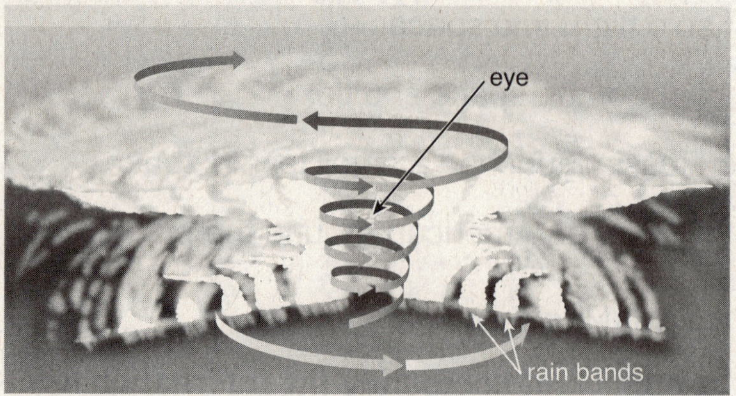

The Life of a Hurricane

What do hurricanes, cyclones, and typhoons have in common? They are all different names for the same severe tropical storm that is known as a tropical cyclone. In this article, the word *hurricane* will be used to discuss this type of storm.

What creates the possibility for a hurricane to develop over ocean water? At least three elements must be present. First, the water must be warm enough to give off heat and moisture into the atmosphere. Second, water already in the air must mix with the heat and moisture from the ocean. Finally, easterly winds must be blowing. Conditions are usually best for hurricanes in the late summer or early fall.

The warm, wet air rises because warm air is lighter than cold air. The wind moves the heat and water high into the atmosphere. Then Earth's turning begins to work against the easterly winds. This twists the growing storm into a tube shape. The center of this tube is called the eye. The heat and moisture from the ocean's surface come into contact with the cooler air higher up. This creates thunderstorms. Then the cooler air travels back toward the ocean's surface. It pulls more moisture from the ocean. Once that moisture rises into the thunderclouds, it is released as heavy rain. This type of rain usually accompanies hurricanes.

The winds increase in speed. They begin to move the enormous storm across the ocean. As long as hurricanes remain over water, they have the ability to keep increasing in size and strength.

GO ON →

Usually the weather is calm in the eye of the hurricane. The eye may range from 2 miles to 200 miles across. The hurricane itself might be as big as 400 to 500 miles across. Rain bands spin toward the center of the hurricane. They often bring high winds and heavy rainfall. Calmer weather is found between the rain bands.

A tropical storm qualifies as a hurricane when its winds reach 74 miles an hour. Scientists have measured winds in hurricanes that move at more than twice that speed. Hurricanes have been given names since 1950. The names of the worst storms are retired—that is, they are not used again.

Hurricanes are given a number from 1 to 5. Hurricanes with the number 1 are the least dangerous. Those given a 5 are the most dangerous. The strongest hurricane ever to hit the United States struck Florida in 1935. The second strongest was Hurricane Katrina, which struck Louisiana in 2005.

What causes the storm to end? Sometimes the power of a hurricane diminishes, or fades, when it travels into the path of strong westerly winds. This disturbs its course. It may cause the storm to move over cooler northern waters. It no longer gets power from the warm ocean water. The storm finally dies out.

At other times, a hurricane travels until it hits land. Once it is over land, it causes almost unbelievable damage. Tornadoes may form in the rain bands. High winds knock over structures. The ocean can flood towns. These floods are responsible for a great deal of damage. Cars, houses, and businesses are often destroyed. But a hurricane over land doesn't have the warm ocean water to help it grow. It will quickly lose power. At last, it ends up as nothing more than rain showers.

Scientists study hurricanes to understand them and predict them better. They use weather satellites to find out more about the storms. Sometimes, they fly planes right into the eye of the hurricane to get information! What they learn will help people when these terrible storms threaten.

GO ON →

Name: ______________________________ Date: ________

Now answer Numbers 11 through 20. Base your answers on "The Life of a Hurricane."

11 Why does the author consider the blowing of easterly winds an important occurrence?

Ⓐ It contributes to flooding.

Ⓑ It causes hurricanes to end.

Ⓒ It creates the eye of the hurricane.

Ⓓ It contributes to hurricane formation.

12 Read this sentence from the passage.

Hurricanes with the number 1 are the least dangerous.

The suffix *-ous* tells you that *dangerous* means

Ⓕ after danger.

Ⓖ before danger.

Ⓗ marked by danger.

Ⓘ without any danger.

13 Before the growing storm twists into a tube shape,

Ⓐ the storm gets a number.

Ⓑ the storm is named.

Ⓒ the warm air rises.

Ⓓ heavy rain falls.

GO ON →

Name: ______________________________ Date: ________

14 Read the following sentence from the passage.

What creates the possibility for a hurricane to develop over ocean water?

The suffix *-ity*, as in *possibility*, means "state or quality of." So, if you are told to show *civility*, you are being told to be

Ⓕ amusing.

Ⓖ brave.

Ⓗ polite.

Ⓘ unkind.

15 Read this sentence from the passage.

Sometimes, they fly planes right into the eye of the hurricane to get information!

The suffix *-ation*, as in *information*, means "the act of" or "that which is." So, a statement of *accusation* is one that

Ⓐ blames someone.

Ⓑ takes responsibility.

Ⓒ brags about an action.

Ⓓ makes another person jealous.

16 At what stage in the life of a hurricane does the author discuss the effects of a hurricane's move over cooler northern waters?

Ⓕ when the hurricane ends

Ⓖ when the eye of the hurricane forms

Ⓗ when the hurricane becomes stronger

Ⓘ when a tropical storm becomes a hurricane

GO ON →

Name: ____________________ Date: ________

17 Read this sentence from the passage.

Sometimes the power of a hurricane diminishes, or fades, when it travels into the path of strong westerly winds.

What does *diminishes* mean in the sentence above?

Ⓐ gets weaker
Ⓑ gets stronger
Ⓒ lasts much longer
Ⓓ goes away completely

18 What happens after the warm air and moisture rise and meet cooler air higher up in the atmosphere?

Ⓕ The storm dies out.
Ⓖ Easterly winds blow.
Ⓗ Strong thunderstorms form.
Ⓘ The eye of a hurricane becomes wider.

19 Read this sentence from the passage.

Once it is over land, it causes almost unbelievable damage.

The suffix *-able*, as in *unbelievable*, means "able to or capable of." So, which of the following is *expandable*?

Ⓐ a crib
Ⓑ a rock
Ⓒ a balloon
Ⓓ a pair of eyeglasses

20 After reaching land, the hurricane

Ⓕ grows stronger.
Ⓖ begins to lose power.
Ⓗ blends with easterly winds.
Ⓘ releases moisture into the atmosphere.

STOP

Name: ______________________ Date: ________

21 Compare and contrast how the authors of "Watching Earth from Space" and "The Life of a Hurricane" use sequence in the articles. Use clear evidence from both articles to support your answer.

Answer Key

Name: ______________________

Question	Correct Answer	Content Focus	CCSS	Complexity
1	B	Text Structure: Sequence	RI.5.5	DOK 3
2	I	Greek and Latin Suffixes	L.5.4b	DOK 1
3	C	Context Clues: Definitions and Restatements	L.5.4a	DOK 2
4	H	Text Structure: Sequence	RI.5.5	DOK 2
5	D	Greek and Latin Suffixes	L.5.4b	DOK 1
6	G	Text Structure: Sequence	RI.5.5	DOK 3
7	D	Text Structure: Sequence	RI.5.5	DOK 3
8	F	Greek and Latin Suffixes	L.5.4b	DOK 1
9	B	Greek and Latin Suffixes	L.5.4b	DOK 1
10	G	Cause and Effect	RI.5.3	DOK 2
11	D	Text Structure: Sequence	RI.5.5	DOK 3
12	H	Greek and Latin Suffixes	L.5.4b	DOK 1
13	C	Sequence	RI.5.3	DOK 2
14	H	Greek and Latin Suffixes	L.5.4b	DOK 1
15	A	Greek and Latin Suffixes	L.5.4b	DOK 1
16	F	Text Structure: Cause and Effect	RI.5.3	DOK 3
17	A	Context Clues: Definitions and Restatements	L.5.4a	DOK 2
18	H	Sequence	RI.5.3	DOK 2
19	C	Greek and Latin Suffixes	L.5.4b	DOK 1
20	G	Sequence	RI.5.3	DOK 2
21	see below	Text Structure: Sequence	RI.5.5	DOK 3

Comprehension 1, 4, 6, 7, 10, 11, 13, 16, 18, 20	10/10	%
Vocabulary 2, 3, 5, 8, 9, 12, 14, 15, 17, 19	/10	%
Total Weekly Assessment Score	/20	%

21 To receive full credit for the response, the following information should be included: Both authors organize the texts by showing the sequence in which things happen. In "Watching Earth from Space," the author shows developments from early space flights to recent experiments on the ISS. In "The Life of a Hurricane," the author shows the stages in the development of a hurricane.

Read the passage "The Spider Monkey and the Marmoset" before answering Numbers 1 through 10.

The Spider Monkey and the Marmoset

Based on Aesop's Fable "The Ant and the Grasshopper"

In the rainforests of Brazil lived two friends, Spider Monkey and Marmoset. Spider Monkey loved to spend his days swinging through the trees, eating as much fruit as his belly could hold. The generous trees provided Spider Monkey with lots of delicious fruit.

Marmoset loved to eat fruit, but knew he had to plan for the future. The elder marmosets spoke of times when finding fruit was difficult. Sometimes, the fruit would get a terrible disease, or cruel, vicious winds would whip through the branches and knock the fruit to the ground. So, Marmoset saved two bites of fruit for every bite he ate.

Spider Monkey laughed at Marmoset as he saw him carrying fruit. "Silly Marmoset!" Spider Monkey shrieked. "We will never be out of fruit. The fruit leaps off the tree, glad to be your snack."

Marmoset ignored Spider Monkey and still collected fruit. "Someday," Marmoset would say, "Spider Monkey will regret making fun of me." Soon, Marmoset's storage place was full and Marmoset smiled with contentment.

GO ON →

Not long after this, Marmoset and Spider Monkey noticed the fruit drooping on the branches. One day, great numbers of fruit plummeted to the ground. That is, it fell off the branches fast and hard. Soon after this, it began to become difficult to find fruit to eat.

At first, Spider Monkey was amused. "It makes for a great game!" he chortled. "The fruit is playing hide and seek with me." But in a short time, Spider Monkey realized that it would not be easy to find enough fruit to fill his belly.

Then he remembered the storage place of his friend, Marmoset. "I know!" Spider Monkey said excitedly. "I'll just ask Marmoset to share with me. He is such a great friend that I know he will be generous."

Spider Monkey swung through the trees to find Marmoset. He was resting near his storage place. When Spider Monkey approached, Marmoset opened one eye and looked at him warily. "How can I help you, Spider Monkey?" Marmoset asked.

"I have come to share your fruit," Spider Monkey announced triumphantly. "You were so smart to plan ahead, and I am forever grateful for your planning."

Marmoset slowly shook his head before responding. "Spider Monkey," he began. "This fruit is for my family. We don't know how long it will be difficult to find fruit, so I can't share what I've gathered. I'm sorry, but you will have to find food elsewhere. You should have been planning for a day like this yourself." Marmoset turned from Spider Monkey and took his place in front of the entrance to the storage place. He set up his position as guard in front of the food.

Spider Monkey's mouth hung open. He was not expecting this from his friend. Slowly, he turned to walk away from Marmoset. As he swung through the trees, in search of food, he thought of Marmoset's words. "Maybe," he thought. "Maybe I should plan ahead."

GO ON →

Name: ______________________________ Date: ________

Now answer Numbers 1 through 10. Base your answers on "The Spider Monkey and the Marmoset."

1 What is the theme of this passage?

Ⓐ Friends don't always share.

Ⓑ Needs can be hard to fulfill.

Ⓒ One must plan ahead.

Ⓓ Eat one bite, save two.

2 Read this sentence from the passage.

The generous trees provided Spider Monkey with lots of delicious fruit.

Why does the author make the tree seem human?

Ⓕ to show that the tree grew lots of fruit

Ⓖ to show that the tree handed fruit to Spider Monkey

Ⓗ to show that Spider Monkey took a lot of fruit from the tree

Ⓘ to show that Spider Monkey hurt the tree when picking

3 Spider Monkey realizes he has behaved foolishly when

Ⓐ the fruit becomes hard to find.

Ⓑ he sees Marmoset storing up fruit.

Ⓒ he remembers Marmoset's storage place.

Ⓓ Marmoset refuses to share his family's food with him.

4 Read the following sentence from the passage.

Sometimes, the fruit would get a terrible disease, or cruel, vicious winds would whip through the branches and knock the fruit to the ground.

What mood does the author create by saying that the winds were cruel and vicious?

Ⓕ cheerful

Ⓖ harsh

Ⓗ thoughtful

Ⓘ welcoming

GO ON →

Name: ______________________________ Date: ________

5 Read this sentence from the passage.

"The fruit leaps off the tree, glad to be your snack."

What does "fruit leaps off the tree" mean?

Ⓐ The fruit tastes delicious.

Ⓑ The fruit has legs and jumps.

Ⓒ The fruit is hard to remove from the branches.

Ⓓ The fruit seems to come off the tree of its own power.

6 Which sentence best supports the passage's theme?

Ⓕ "I'll just ask Marmoset to share with me."

Ⓖ He was not expecting this from his friend.

Ⓗ Spider Monkey swung through the trees to find Marmoset.

Ⓘ "You should have been planning for a day like this yourself."

7 Read these sentences from the passage.

Marmoset loved to eat fruit, but knew he had to plan for the future. The elder marmosets spoke of times when finding fruit was difficult.

How do these sentences support the theme?

Ⓐ They show that Marmoset loved to eat fruit.

Ⓑ They show that Marmoset listened to his elders.

Ⓒ They show that Marmoset knew he must plan ahead.

Ⓓ They show that Marmoset did not want to work hard to find fruit.

GO ON →

Name: ______________________________ Date: ________

8 Read these sentences from the passage.

One day, great numbers of fruit plummeted to the ground. That is, it fell off the branches fast and hard.

What word is most similar in meaning to *plummeted*?

Ⓕ drifted

Ⓖ floated

Ⓗ plunged

Ⓘ sank

9 Read this sentence from the passage.

"The fruit is playing hide and seek with me."

What is the purpose of comparing what the fruit is doing to a game?

Ⓐ to show that the fruit is having fun

Ⓑ to show that Spider Monkey is not worried

Ⓒ to show that Spider Monkey has a good attitude

Ⓓ to show that games can sometimes be misunderstood

10 Which is the main way in which Spider Monkey and Marmoset are different?

Ⓕ Marmoset is selfish; Spider Monkey shares.

Ⓖ Marmoset is practical; Spider Monkey is not.

Ⓗ Spider Monkey doesn't need much to eat; Marmoset does.

Ⓘ Spider Monkey knows how to have fun; Marmoset doesn't.

GO ON →

Read the passage "Raven the Trickster and Fish Hawk" before answering Numbers 11 through 20.

Raven the Trickster and Fish Hawk

A Retelling of a Native American Tale

Tricksters have ways of getting what they want. However, trouble is a close companion of tricksters. One day, a bird named Fish Hawk was unfortunate enough to meet Raven on the riverbank. Raven acted very kindly toward Fish Hawk, hoping the bird would do him a favor.

"Ah, my dearest friend," Raven greeted Fish Hawk. "The wind is howling along the shore of the river. The weather has turned cold and bitter. The warmth of your house is calling to me. Let us go there."

Fish Hawk was too polite to refuse, but it was without enthusiasm that he led Raven to his home. Once inside, Raven glanced about slyly and noticed that the hawk had laid in a large supply of food. Fish Hawk also had a very inviting home. He had made his home quite comfortable with soft blankets of leaves and grasses.

"What a lot of things you have here," sneaky Raven said. "You could open your own store and sell what you have!"

GO ON →

When Fish Hawk said nothing in response, Raven continued. “All the birds that have wasted the summer singing and flitting about, instead of storing food for the winter, would be eager to buy some of this. You will need a treasurer to help you with sales and to help you collect profits on these goods. That requires a lot of time and effort! Why don’t I visit with you during the winter months? We can share some of the burdens of keeping shop and housekeeping.”

Fish Hawk doubted the wisdom of this plan, but he let Raven stay with him. It soon became clear that Raven would not lift a feather to help his kind host. In time, Fish Hawk grew tired of his lazy guest. But Raven talked to him sweetly, saying, “Don’t worry, dear friend. This beach will wear a thick cloak of fish, and you will not have to catch them. I’ll get our dinner for us while you rest.” However, he never did, and Fish Hawk's life just got harder and harder.

Weeks passed by and Raven did nothing to help. He made his host gather food for both of them while he slept and ate up the meals. Thanking Fish Hawk many times after each large dinner, he would say, “What a rich, wise friend you are! I have so much appreciation for your kindness. Words can hardly express my feelings.” Raven’s flattery was ceaseless. He would always end his speeches by again assuring Fish Hawk that he would catch fish. But, of course, nothing came of this empty promise.

Fish Hawk finally grew disgusted by Raven’s laziness and greed. He flew away from his own house, towards a sun that was peeking around clouds. “That will teach you, Raven!” he called out. “Now you will have to fend for yourself!” He hoped to educate Raven by teaching him a lesson. Yet deep in his heart, he knew that the old trickster would never change.

Fish Hawk soon built himself a cozy new home. And Raven had to find his own dinner from then on.

GO ON →

Name: ______________________________ Date: ________

Now answer Numbers 11 through 20. Base your answers on "Raven the Trickster and Fish Hawk."

11 What is the theme of this passage?

Ⓐ Tricksters often change their ways.

Ⓑ Visitors always help with the chores.

Ⓒ Tricksters always keep their promises.

Ⓓ Tricksters often cause problems for others.

12 Read this sentence from the passage.

However, trouble is a close companion of tricksters.

What does the sentence mean?

Ⓕ Trouble can find anyone.

Ⓖ Tricksters know all about trouble.

Ⓗ Trouble often goes where tricksters go.

Ⓘ Tricksters enjoy causing trouble for themselves.

13 The main way that Raven is a problem for Fish Hawk is that Raven

Ⓐ takes up room.

Ⓑ eats the food supplies.

Ⓒ tries to flatter Fish Hawk.

Ⓓ uses all the soft blankets.

14 Read this sentence from the passage.

"The warmth of your house is calling to me."

By saying that the house is "calling to me," Raven means that

Ⓕ he wants to go to it.

Ⓖ he can hear the furnace working.

Ⓗ the house is making some kind of noise.

Ⓘ the house is very close to where they are.

GO ON →

Name: ______________________________ Date: ________

15 Read this sentence from the passage.

Raven's flattery was ceaseless.

The suffix *-less* means "without." So, the author is saying that Raven's flattery was

Ⓐ unending.

Ⓑ without cause.

Ⓒ not to be believed.

Ⓓ always spoken for Raven's own good.

16 Read these sentences from the passage.

Weeks passed by and Raven did nothing to help. He made his host gather food for both of them while he slept and ate up the meals.

How do these sentences support the theme?

Ⓕ They show that Raven is helpful.

Ⓖ They show that Raven is unable to help.

Ⓗ They show that Fish Hawk enjoys having a guest.

Ⓘ They show that Raven is causing trouble for Fish Hawk.

17 Which sentence from the passage best supports the theme?

Ⓐ Fish Hawk was too polite to refuse.

Ⓑ Fish Hawk soon built himself a cozy new home.

Ⓒ Fish Hawk finally grew disgusted by Raven's laziness and greed.

Ⓓ Fish Hawk doubted the wisdom of this plan, but he let Raven stay with him.

GO ON →

Name: ______________________________ Date: __________

18 Read this sentence from the passage.

This beach will wear a thick cloak of fish, and you will not have to catch them.

What does "wear a thick cloak of fish" mean?

Ⓕ There will be a few fish.

Ⓖ Fish will be hard to find.

Ⓗ Fish will cover the beach.

Ⓘ There will be a cloak made of fish.

19 Read this sentence from the passage.

He flew away from his own house, towards a sun that was peeking around clouds.

What does "a sun that was peeking around clouds" mean?

Ⓐ Clouds were covering part of the sun.

Ⓑ Clouds completely covered the sun.

Ⓒ There were a few clouds in the sky.

Ⓓ There were no clouds in the sky.

20 What is the main way in which Raven and Fish Hawk are different?

Ⓕ Fish Hawk is more patient than Raven.

Ⓖ Fish Hawk does much more work than Raven.

Ⓗ Fish Hawk has more possessions than Raven has.

Ⓘ Fish Hawk eats fish, but Raven eats whatever he can find.

STOP

Name: ______________________ Date: ________

21 Using clear text evidence, compare the themes of "The Spider Monkey and the Marmoset" and "Raven the Trickster and Fish Hawk." How do Marmoset and Fish Hawk respond when their plans are challenged by Spider Monkey and Raven?

Answer Key

Name: ______________________

Question	Correct Answer	Content Focus	CCSS	Complexity
1	C	Theme	RL.5.2	DOK 3
2	F	Personification	L.5.5a	DOK 2
3	D	Theme	RL.5.2	DOK 3
4	G	Personification	L.5.5a	DOK 2
5	D	Personification	L.5.5a	DOK 2
6	I	Theme	RL.5.2	DOK 3
7	C	Theme	RL.5.2	DOK 3
8	H	Context Clues: Definitions and Restatements	L.5.4a	DOK 2
9	B	Personification	L.5.5a	DOK 2
10	G	Character, Setting, Plot: Compare and Contrast	RL.5.3	DOK 3
11	D	Theme	RL.5.2	DOK 3
12	H	Personification	L.5.5a	DOK 2
13	B	Theme	RL.5.2	DOK 3
14	F	Personification	L.5.5a	DOK 2
15	A	Greek and Latin Suffixes	L.5.4b	DOK 1
16	I	Theme	RL.5.2	DOK 3
17	C	Theme	RL.5.2	DOK 3
18	H	Personification	L.5.5a	DOK 2
19	A	Personification	L.5.5a	DOK 2
20	G	Character, Setting, Plot: Compare and Contrast	RL.5.3	DOK 3
21	see below	Theme	RL.5.2	DOK 3

Comprehension 1, 3, 6, 7, 10, 11, 13, 16, 17, 20	/10	%
Vocabulary 2, 4, 5, 8, 9, 12, 14, 15, 18, 19	/10	%
Total Weekly Assessment Score	/20	%

21 To receive full credit for the response, the following information should be included: Marmoset planned ahead. He did not share with Spider Monkey because Spider Monkey did not plan. Fish Hawk prepared for winter and as a result, Raven tricked Fish Hawk into letting him stay with him. Fish Hawk realized he was being tricked and so he left his own home and made Raven fend for himself.

Read the passage "Four Short Weeks" before answering Numbers 1 through 10.

Four Short Weeks

Audra scanned the directions for her social studies assignment as her teacher read. They were supposed to research and report on one of the fifty states. The project was due in one month and included a five-page report, a poster, and an oral report. Audra feared she would never complete this in four short weeks.

"Mrs. Peterson, do you have advice for starting this project?" Audra asked. She tried to console herself a little, though she couldn't soothe herself much.

Mrs. Peterson smiled. "Plan how you will complete each part of the project, and write your plan down. Break the assignment into smaller pieces, and do not wait until the last minute to start!"

Later that afternoon Audra walked through her front door and almost ran into her older brother, Gus.

"Sorry," Audra muttered. She dug the directions for the project out of her backpack and put them on the dining room table. Then she plopped on a chair and began to contract, or become smaller, into a little ball. She wished she had someone to commiserate with about the project so that they could each express sorrow for the other.

"Is something wrong?" Gus asked, sitting down beside her.

"Why do teachers subject us to difficult assignments?" Audra wailed. "This assignment is due in a month, and I will never finish it on time!"

Gus smiled and said, "Let me see if I can help you." Audra slid the directions towards him and Gus skimmed the top sheet.

GO ON →

"Audra, this is not so bad," Gus began. When Audra started to protest, he put up his hand to stop her. "I am not trying to bluff you, because it is a big project and you will have to work hard. But you can break the project down into little ones with shorter due dates."

Gus pulled a blue notebook from a desk drawer. He said, "Today is October 1 and the entire project is due on October 30. If you spend one week on each of the four parts, you will finish the project on time."

Audra watched as Gus opened the notebook. He drew a two-column chart. In the left column, he wrote a requirement for the project. In the right column, he wrote a date that was a few weeks before the final due date for the project.

Requirement	Due Date for Each Part
Five page research report, typed	October 15
Oral Presentation, 2–3 minutes in length	October 29

As Audra looked at Gus's schedule, she began to feel as though this project might be possible after all.

For the next four weeks, Audra followed Gus's schedule. Whenever she started to feel overwhelmed, she looked at her schedule and relaxed. It would all get done, she told herself. She was right!

The night before the project's due date, Audra thanked her brother with the following poem:

Racing thoughts, beating heart
What to do, how to start?
Wringing hands, the hour's late,
Four short weeks to my due date.

Gus arrives to save the day.
"Make a date each week away."
"Plan to do one thing a week."
Suddenly it's not so bleak.

Thanks to Gus there's time to spare.
I even wrote a rhyme to share.
If you plan you'll get things done.
And even have some time for fun!

GO ON →

Name: ______________________________ Date: __________

Now answer Numbers 1 through 10. Base your answers on "Four Short Weeks."

1 What is the theme of this passage?

Ⓐ Older brothers have all the answers.

Ⓑ Nothing is done well if left to the last minute.

Ⓒ When completing a large project, it is good to have a plan.

Ⓓ When feeling overwhelmed, it is good if others feel the same way.

2 Read this sentence from the passage.

Audra was able to console herself a little, though she couldn't soothe herself much.

Which definition fits the word *console* as it is used in the sentence above?

Ⓕ cabinet

Ⓖ case

Ⓗ comfort

Ⓘ help

3 What was most responsible for changing Audra's attitude from hopeless to cautiously hopeful?

Ⓐ her own determination

Ⓑ the interest her brother expressed

Ⓒ the chart her brother made for her

Ⓓ her conversation with Mrs. Peterson

GO ON →

Name: ______________________________ Date: ________

4 Read this sentence from the passage.

She wished she had someone to commiserate with about the project so that they could each express sorrow for the other.

What does *commiserate* mean in the sentence above?

Ⓕ criticize

Ⓖ laugh

Ⓗ sympathize

Ⓘ talk excitedly

5 Which word from the passage meaning "shrink" is a homograph for the word defined below?

written agreement

Ⓐ assignment

Ⓑ contract

Ⓒ plan

Ⓓ report

6 Read these sentences from the passage.

Mrs. Peterson smiled. "Plan how you will complete each part of the project, and write your plan down. Break the assignment into smaller pieces, and do not wait until the last minute to start!"

How do these sentences support the theme?

Ⓕ They tell Audra exactly how to finish her project.

Ⓖ They show that Mrs. Peterson thinks this project will be fun.

Ⓗ They explain how to plan out the steps for completing the project.

Ⓘ They warn Audra that she will not finish on time unless she gets help.

GO ON →

Name: ______________________________ Date: ________

7. Which sentence from the passage best supports the theme?

Ⓐ "But you can break the project down into little ones with shorter due dates."

Ⓑ "Today is October 1 and the entire project is due on October 30."

Ⓒ It would all get done, she told herself.

Ⓓ "Let me see if I can help you."

8. Read this sentence from the passage.

"Why do teachers subject us to difficult assignments?" Audra wailed.

Which definition fits *subject* as it is used in the sentence above?

Ⓕ topic

Ⓖ one who is ruled over

Ⓗ force to suffer through

Ⓘ something that is studied

9. Which word from the passage means "to fool or mislead" and is also the name for a steep bank or cliff?

Ⓐ bluff

Ⓑ break

Ⓒ overwhelmed

Ⓓ wrong

10. What happens right before Audra reads her poem?

Ⓕ She makes a plan.

Ⓖ She finishes her report.

Ⓗ She gets her assignment.

Ⓘ She gives her oral report.

GO ON →

Read the passage "The Big Contest" before answering Numbers 11 through 20.

The Big Contest

"We will win this contest," José bragged to Aisha at recess.

"I don't want to have a dispute with you because a quarrel won't get us anywhere, but I disagree," Aisha said. "How can we win? We're not experts. Why did the fifth grade pick us to represent everyone in the Big Bake-Off?"

"You should give us more credit," José said. "We are capable kids who can follow directions, so we should be able to use a recipe. The contest has many different categories, and I have a plan."

Aisha remembered the last time she listened to José's big plan. They had gotten into trouble because José made his own rules. They were thrown out of the contest altogether.

"Aisha, are you listening to me?" asked José.

Aisha shook herself back into the present and asked, "What is your plan?"

"We will bake a gigantic cake that will be larger than all the other cakes! It will be so huge that we will get the prize for the biggest cake," he said. "It won't matter what it tastes like!"

Aisha said, "That is an excellent plan, José, and I think you are on to something!"

GO ON →

The next day, Aisha and José went to the grocery store. They bought the ingredients for their gigantic cake. At Aisha's house, they set everything on the counter and started working.

"We will bake a few square cakes at a time. Then we will put them together and spruce them up with a lot of frosting," Aisha said.

Aisha measured flour, sugar, baking soda, and other ingredients while José cracked eggs into a bowl. They mixed the batter, poured it into pans, and placed two pans in the oven. While those cakes were in the oven, they started on the next batch. They worked until two rows of cakes stood on the table and a huge bowl of frosting was made. The kids slumped against the counter. They were very tired.

"My back hurts," moaned José as he put all the cakes on a large board. "I'll never be able to stand up straight again." Aisha brushed a strand of hair from her eyes before spreading the frosting on the cake.

The next day, with the help of Aisha's father and José's mother, the two kids took the huge cake to the school. They left it on one of the special tables set up in the cafeteria for the contest, surrounded by many smaller cakes.

That day felt like the longest school day ever. Finally it was the last period of the day and time for the contest to begin! All the students at the school went to the cafeteria, where they watched as the judges tasted each of the cakes. José and Aisha saw the judges, but they couldn't tell what the judges were thinking. Both kids waited with their hearts pounding.

"Well, now, the judging is over, and I am really nervous," Aisha said. "Maybe putting regular cakes together won't count as one cake," she fretted. José didn't reply because he was worried, too. One of the judges cleared his throat and announced, "The prize for the biggest cake goes to . . . Aisha Thomas and José Mora, representing the fifth grade!"

"I told you we were bound to win!" José said to Aisha with a smile. "I never doubted it for a minute!"

GO ON →

Name: ______________________________ Date: ________

Now answer Numbers 11 through 20. Base your answers on "The Big Contest."

11 What is the theme of this passage?

Ⓐ Always listen to your friends.

Ⓑ Big cakes always win contests.

Ⓒ Having a plan helps achieve goals.

Ⓓ Anyone can follow directions to win a contest.

12 Read this sentence from the passage.

"I don't want to have a dispute with you because a quarrel won't get us anywhere, but I disagree," Aisha said.

What does *dispute* mean in the sentence above?

Ⓕ agreement

Ⓖ argument

Ⓗ conversation

Ⓘ violent fight

13 Why does Aisha start to think that she and José might win the contest?

Ⓐ He always has good ideas.

Ⓑ His plan makes sense to her.

Ⓒ She thinks the judges are impressed.

Ⓓ She knows that she and José can bake well.

14 Which word from the passage means "to make neat" and is also the name of a type of evergreen tree?

Ⓕ brushed

Ⓖ present

Ⓗ spread

Ⓘ spruce

GO ON →

Name: ______________________________ Date: __________

15 Read this sentence from the passage.

They worked until two rows of cakes stood on the table and a huge bowl of frosting was made.

Which definition fits the word *rows* as it is used in the sentence above?

Ⓐ streets or ways

Ⓑ moves with oars

Ⓒ noisy quarrels or disturbances

Ⓓ objects arranged in straight lines

16 Read these sentences from the passage.

"We will bake a gigantic cake that will be larger than all the other cakes! It will be so huge that we will get the prize for the biggest cake," he said.

How do these sentences support the theme?

Ⓕ They describe José's plan to win the contest.

Ⓖ They explain why Aisha should listen to José.

Ⓗ They indicate how enthusiastic José is about his idea.

Ⓘ They explain how Aisha and José will follow directions.

17 Which sentence from the passage best supports the theme?

Ⓐ They were thrown out of the contest altogether.

Ⓑ "That is an excellent plan, José, and I think you are on to something!"

Ⓒ "Why did the fifth grade pick us to represent everyone in the Big Bake-Off?"

Ⓓ "Maybe putting regular cakes together won't count as one cake."

GO ON →

Name: ______________________________ Date: ________

18 Which word from the passage means “to abandon or leave helpless” and is also the name for a string?

Ⓕ contest

Ⓖ frosting

Ⓗ strand

Ⓘ thrown

19 Which word from the passage means “sure” and is also a homograph for the word defined below?

to leap or jump

Ⓐ bound

Ⓑ contest

Ⓒ count

Ⓓ trouble

20 What is the last thing that happens in the story?

Ⓕ The judges taste the cakes.

Ⓖ The announcement is made.

Ⓗ José pretends he was never nervous.

Ⓘ José and Aisha both think the same thing.

STOP

Name: ______________________ **Date:** __________

21 Using clear text evidence, compare the themes of "Four Short Weeks" and "The Big Contest." How does having a plan help Audra with her project and Aisha and José win a prize in the contest?

Answer Key

Name: ______________________________

Question	Correct Answer	Content Focus	CCSS	Complexity
1	C	Theme	RL.5.2	DOK 3
2	H	Homographs	L.5.5c	DOK 1
3	C	Theme	RL.5.2	DOK 3
4	H	Context Clues: Definitions and Restatements	L.5.4a	DOK 2
5	B	Homographs	L.5.5c	DOK 1
6	H	Theme	RL.5.2	DOK 3
7	A	Theme	RL.5.2	DOK 3
8	H	Homographs	L.5.5c	DOK 1
9	A	Homographs	L.5.5c	DOK 1
10	G	Character, Setting, Plot: Sequence	RL.3.3	DOK 2
11	C	Theme	RL.5.2	DOK 3
12	G	Context Clues: Definitions and Restatements	L.5.4a	DOK 2
13	B	Theme	RL.5.2	DOK 3
14	I	Homographs	L.5.5c	DOK 1
15	D	Homographs	L.5.5c	DOK 1
16	F	Theme	RL.5.2	DOK 3
17	B	Theme	RL.5.2	DOK 3
18	H	Homographs	L.5.5c	DOK 1
19	A	Homographs	L.5.5c	DOK 1
20	H	Character, Setting, Plot: Sequence	RL.3.3	DOK 2
21	see below	Theme	RL.5.2	DOK 3

Comprehension 1, 3, 6, 7, 10, 11, 13, 16, 17, 20	/10	%
Vocabulary 2, 4, 5, 8, 9, 12, 14, 15, 18, 19	/10	%
Total Weekly Assessment Score	/20	%

21 To receive full credit for the response, the following information should be included: Audra is able to finish her project because she breaks the large project into four smaller projects. Aisha and José are able to win the contest because they have a plan in mind to bake the biggest cake rather than the best-tasting one.

Read the passage "The Bake Sale" before answering Numbers 1 through 10.

The Bake Sale

Ms. Cross's fifth-grade class was planning a bake sale to make money for new equipment for the school grounds. Maia said, "Let's all bring some cookies to sell."

Jared put up his hand, "What if we sold bread? It is something almost everyone likes. We could make a variety of kinds."

Josie added, "Why don't we bring different breads that our families enjoy?"

Ms. Cross said, "What a great idea! You could each choose bread you would like to make. Some of you may want to work in pairs or teams along with an adult to help with the baking. Wash all the equipment you use so it will be sanitary."

Sophia said, "This is an important project, and our project has a better chance to succeed if we choose a good location."

Juan suggested setting up a table in front of the big grocery store near the school. The class started making plans. Because there would be customers, everyone could work a one-hour shift as a salesperson.

Ms. Cross reminded students that they would have to set a price for their breads and mark the prices on them. Maddie suggested that a committee go to grocery stores to take notes about the cost of bread. Another committee could find a long table. Other students were needed to get cards and markers to use for labeling.

Jake said, "Are we sure we want all this work?"

Tim said, "Of course we do! We need new soccer balls and other things too, and this is the only way we'll get them. The exertion will make us tired, but it will be worth it."

So they all agreed to help. Everyone got busy checking recipes for what they needed for ingredients. Since they would need advice on some things, they had to enlist parents to help them.

GO ON →

Liane loved the *mantou*, or steamed buns, that her grandmother learned to make in China before coming to America. Her grandmother offered to help her make a batch early Saturday morning so they would be fresh. When Liane got to her grandmother's house, the dough of water, a little sugar, yeast, and flour was mixed and rising. The yeast in the dough would make it rise. Grandmother told her to punch the dough down. Then they covered it and let it rise again. After about 20 minutes, Grandmother showed Liane how to knead the dough and shape it into rolls. They boiled water and placed the rolls in the steamer. In 10 minutes, the first batch of buns was cooked. They looked perfect, and Liane was proud of them.

When Liane got to the bake sale, several classmates were already there. Mauricio showed her the Cuban bread his grandfather had helped him make. He had started it with yeast, warm water, and flour like the steamed buns. The dough had to rest in the refrigerator for 24 hours. On Saturday morning, they added other ingredients to the "starter." They kneaded it, let it rise, and formed the dough into loaves. The loaves were baked, not steamed.

Carissa showed the Italian focaccia bread she made with her grandmother's help. It had similar ingredients to the other breads but more spices, including garlic and basil and some cheese. Erik brought crusty rye sourdough bread. His mother helped him make it the way her mother from Germany had taught her. Wendy made scones with her mother, whose family came from England in the seventeenth century. Scones are rich biscuits made without yeast.

Jay brought some chapati, a flatbread he learned about in India last summer. Patrick brought his mother's Irish soda bread with caraway seeds. David and Sarah brought challah, a bread traditionally served on Jewish holidays. With help from Sarah's mom, David and Sarah rolled the dough into "snakes" and braided them. Jake participated by bringing a loaf of whole wheat bread his father had helped him make and several dozen homemade rolls.

The bake sale was a huge success! The breads sold quickly, and the class made $370 for new equipment. Ms. Cross observed that bread is an important part of cultures around the world.

GO ON →

Name: ______________________________ Date: ________

Now answer Numbers 1 through 10. Base your answers on "The Bake Sale."

1 Which of the following is the major theme of this passage?

Ⓐ Most bread contains flour and water.

Ⓑ A successful project needs parents' help.

Ⓒ A bake sale featuring bread will always be a success.

Ⓓ People from different countries have things in common.

2 How are the characters in this passage alike?

Ⓕ They all participate in the project.

Ⓖ They all become experts in making bread.

Ⓗ They all recently came from different countries.

Ⓘ They all worry about the amount of work involved.

3 Read this sentence from the passage.

"The exertion will make us tired, but it will be worth it."

What does *exertion* mean in the sentence above?

Ⓐ bread

Ⓑ effort

Ⓒ game

Ⓓ viewpoint

4 Read this sentence from the passage.

Because there would be customers, everyone could work a one-hour shift as a salesperson.

What does *salesperson* mean in the sentence above?

Ⓕ someone whose work is selling

Ⓖ a person who hunts for bargains

Ⓗ anyone who takes pleasure in shopping

Ⓘ one who shops for different kinds of bread

GO ON →

Name: ________________________________ Date: ________

5 Which paragraph best supports the major theme in the passage?

Ⓐ Sophia said, "This is an important project, and our project has a better chance to succeed if we choose a good location."

Ⓑ Ms. Cross's fifth-grade class was planning a bake sale to make money for new equipment for the school grounds. Maia said, "Let's all bring some cookies to sell."

Ⓒ The bake sale was a huge success! The breads sold quickly, and the class made $370 for new equipment. Ms. Cross observed that bread is an important part of cultures around the world.

Ⓓ Juan suggested setting up a table in front of the big grocery store near the school. The class started making plans. Because there would be customers, everyone could work a one-hour shift as a salesperson.

6 Read this sentence from the passage.

"Wash all the equipment you use so it will be sanitary."

What does *sanitary* mean in the sentence above?

Ⓕ clean

Ⓖ fresh

Ⓗ tasty

Ⓘ useful

7 Read this sentence from the passage.

Since they would need advice on some things, they had to enlist parents to help them.

What does *enlist* mean in the sentence above?

Ⓐ inform

Ⓑ plead with

Ⓒ avoid telling

Ⓓ get assistance from

GO ON →

Name: ________________________________ Date: ________

8 Why does the passage refer to such things as focaccia, chapati, challah, and scones?

Ⓕ to show why the students needed help

Ⓖ to indicate why the project was successful

Ⓗ to point out the variety of breads the students brought

Ⓘ to show the different languages the students use at home

9 Which word from the passage means "a shaped mass of bread" and is also a word meaning "to do nothing"?

Ⓐ bun

Ⓑ loaf

Ⓒ roll

Ⓓ scone

10 Read this sentence from the passage.

Ms. Cross observed that bread is an important part of cultures around the world.

How does this sentence support the theme?

Ⓕ It explains how the students got help.

Ⓖ It tells why steamed buns are popular.

Ⓗ It shows why Ms. Cross helped the students.

Ⓘ It emphasizes that different cultures share a love of bread.

GO ON →

Read the passage "Fourteen Days in Tokyo" before answering Numbers 11 through 20.

Fourteen Days in Tokyo

It was July, and Todd wanted to hang out with his friends. Yet, on Friday, Todd and his family were flying to Tokyo, Japan. They would visit his grandmother, Obaasan. She liked being called by the Japanese word for *grandmother*. Obaasan promised to show them around Tokyo, but Todd really did not want to leave San Francisco.

First of all, they arrived early and had to sit in the airport for two hours before the flight. Finally they took off and were airborne, but it was still another eleven hours before they would land in Tokyo. Todd's mother was petite, so she didn't suffer from the small amount of space each passenger had. However, his father was soon complaining about leg cramps. This trip was even worse than Todd had expected.

After a taxi ride, they were at Obaasan's apartment in a modern building. She met them with a big hug. Inside her apartment, there were no doors. Screens separated the rooms. Instead of carpets, straw mats were on the floors. The furnishings with cushions for seating and a low dining table were different from the kind of furniture in Todd's home. Obaasan had flowers in every room.

GO ON →

Obaasan had prepared a special meal for them. Todd liked the rice and grilled tuna, but he didn't care for the cake of soybeans called tofu. He had never eaten pickled vegetables, but the taste was not bad.

Due to being awake during the protracted flight, Todd was exhausted and slept well. Obaasan served them breakfast and then took them to the Tokyo Metropolitan Government Building, the tallest building in the city. The observatory decks at the top are the best place to view all of Tokyo. It was a clear morning so they could see Mount Fuji, the tallest mountain in Japan and a kind of volcano. Todd had never seen such a view! Maybe this trip would not be boring after all.

Afterwards, they ate at a restaurant in the building. Everyone ordered sushi, a small, tasty food and a delicacy. Some pieces were rice rolled with fish and others were rice rolled with vegetables. The sushi in San Francisco was not nearly as good.

The next day, Obaasan took everyone to Sunshine City, a city within the city with shops, restaurants, and an indoor theme park with games and rides. It had a number of food theme areas like Ice Cream City where shops sell ice cream. While Obaasan and Mom went shopping, Dad and Todd visited the theme park where Todd played video games. Then they went to the aquarium to see sea animals. The stingrays were Todd's favorite.

Everything was turning out to be more interesting than Todd expected, but his best time was at a *bunraku*, or puppet theater. The puppets were as big as people and seemed to be alive. The people who worked the puppets were right on stage in front of the audience. Because the puppets were so large, everything they said and did seemed exaggerated. Todd loved the colorful costumes and sets.

When it was time to return to America, Todd did not want to leave. It had been the best two weeks of his life! He asked Obaasan if he could come back next summer, and she said, "I would love that."

GO ON →

Name: ______________________________ Date: ________

Now answer Numbers 11 through 20. Base your answers on "Fourteen Days in Tokyo."

11 What is the theme of this passage?

Ⓐ Tokyo is the best city in the world.

Ⓑ It is a long way from San Francisco to Tokyo.

Ⓒ Sometimes we have to try something new to enjoy it.

Ⓓ Many things in Japan are different from what an American is used to.

12 Read this sentence from the passage.

Finally they took off and were airborne, but it was still another eleven hours before they would land in Tokyo.

What does *airborne* mean in the sentence above?

Ⓕ off the ground

Ⓖ into orbit in space

Ⓗ thrown about by the wind

Ⓘ dizzy from the high altitude

13 Read this sentence from the passage.

Todd's mother was petite, so she didn't suffer from the small amount of space each passenger had.

What does *petite* mean in the sentence above?

Ⓐ cheerful

Ⓑ eager

Ⓒ patient

Ⓓ small

GO ON →

Name: ______________________________ Date: ________

14 Which text evidence best supports the theme of the passage?

Ⓕ Everyone ordered sushi, a small, tasty food and a delicacy.

Ⓖ When it was time to return to America, Todd did not want to leave.

Ⓗ First of all, they arrived early and had to sit in the airport for two hours before the flight.

Ⓘ Todd liked the rice and grilled tuna, but he didn't care for the cake of soybeans called tofu.

15 Read this sentence from the passage.

Due to being awake during the protracted flight, Todd was exhausted and slept well.

What does *protracted* mean in the sentence above?

Ⓐ boring

Ⓑ exciting

Ⓒ long

Ⓓ restful

16 Read this sentence from the passage.

Maybe this trip would not be boring after all.

How does this sentence support the theme?

Ⓕ It tells about the flight to Tokyo.

Ⓖ It explains that it was time to return home.

Ⓗ It shows that Todd enjoys having a good time.

Ⓘ It shows that Todd is changing his mind about the trip.

GO ON →

Name: ______________________ Date: ________

17 What word from the passage means "a type" and is also a word that means "good-hearted or caring"?

Ⓐ clear

Ⓑ kind

Ⓒ shop

Ⓓ well

18 What changes most about Todd during this passage?

Ⓕ his actions

Ⓖ his attitude

Ⓗ his affection for Obaasan

Ⓘ how American he seems

19 Read this sentence from the passage.

Because the puppets were so large, everything they said and did seemed exaggerated.

What does *exaggerated* mean in the sentence above?

Ⓐ magnified

Ⓑ played down

Ⓒ spoken loudly

Ⓓ decreased in size

20 Which of the following is most supportive of the theme of the passage?

Ⓕ how long the trip to Japan is

Ⓖ Todd's new, enjoyable experiences

Ⓗ Obaasan's efforts to show her affection

Ⓘ the differences between Japan and America

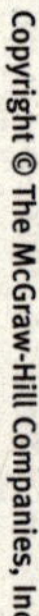

STOP

Name: ______________________ Date: ________

21 Compare and contrast the themes of "The Bake Sale" and "Fourteen Days in Tokyo." Include clear text evidence to show how characters in each respond to challenges.

Answer Key Name: ____________________

Question	Correct Answer	Content Focus	CCSS	Complexity
1	D	Theme	RL.5.2	DOK 3
2	F	Character, Setting Plot: Compare and Contrast	RL. 5.3	DOK 3
3	B	Context Clues: Cause and Effect	L.5.4a	DOK 2
4	F	Context Clues: Cause and Effect	L.5.4a	DOK 2
5	C	Theme	RL.5.2	DOK 3
6	F	Context Clues: Cause and Effect	L.5.4a	DOK 2
7	D	Context Clues: Cause and Effect	L.5.4a	DOK 2
8	H	Theme	RL.5.2	DOK 3
9	B	Homographs	L.5.5c	DOK 1
10	I	Theme	RL.5.2	DOK 3
11	C	Theme	RL.5.2	DOK 3
12	F	Context Clues: Cause and Effect	L.5.4a	DOK 2
13	D	Context Clues: Cause and Effect	L.5.4a	DOK 2
14	G	Theme	RL.5.2	DOK 3
15	C	Context Clues: Cause and Effect	L.5.4a	DOK 2
16	I	Theme	RL.5.2	DOK 3
17	B	Homographs	L.5.5c	DOK 1
18	G	Character, Setting, Plot: Compare and Contrast	RL.5.3	DOK 3
19	A	Context Clues: Cause and Effect	L.5.4a	DOK 2
20	G	Theme	RL.5.2	DOK 3
21	see below	Compare Across Texts	RL.5.9	DOK 3

Comprehension 1, 2, 5, 8, 10, 11, 14, 16, 18, 20	/10	%
Vocabulary 3, 4, 6, 7, 9, 12, 13, 15, 17, 19	/10	%
Total Weekly Assessment Score	/20	%

21 To receive full credit for the response, the following information should be included: The themes of "The Bake Sale" and "Fourteen Days in Tokyo" are similar in that characters in each story learn about other cultures and discover that people from different places have things in common. In "The Bake Sale," the students discover that people from many countries make and enjoy bread. In "Fourteen Days in Tokyo," Todd has a good time visiting new places and trying new foods in Japan.

Read the passage "The Stag at the Pool" before answering Numbers 1 through 10.

The Stag at the Pool

There was once a Stag who was tremendously proud of his beautiful horns. They were large and well-formed, with many points. He rubbed them often on the bark of trees, keeping them glossy and razor-sharp. The other animals of the forest bowed to him, and they often spoke of his antlers with admiration. "How beautiful your horns are!" the Fox and the Rabbit would say. "They are as glossy as satin or sunlight reflecting off water!" The Stag would bow his head, making sure his antlers caught the light of the sun so they would flash and glow. He knew the other animals were right, and he felt that their high regard was well deserved. No other Stag, and certainly none of the other animals, had such stunning horns.

Whenever the Stag passed a pool of water, he would stop to look in and admire his magnificent horns. One day, while passing through a meadow, he came to a clear pond. He bent to the water. There was his reflection, as glorious as ever. "No one in the world has such astonishing antlers as mine!" he said, preening as he turned this way and that.

For the first time, though, he noticed his legs reflected in the water. He frowned, and his reflection frowned back. "How lean my legs are!" he said. "I wish they were thicker and stronger. My wonderful antlers look ridiculous atop a body with such weak-looking legs!" For the first time he felt jealous of the Fox, with its short, thick limbs. He even envied the Rabbit, who could leap high into the air on its funny legs.

GO ON →

The Stag was so engrossed that he did not notice that a Lion had crept up alongside him. Suddenly, he saw the Lion reflected in the pond. For a moment the two animals stared at each other in the water. The Lion displayed his teeth, flaunting them as if he were bragging. The Stag leaped away, terrified. Immediately, the Lion gave chase.

Through the meadow the Stag raced, gasping in fear. The ground was flat and even, and the Stag moved with the velocity of an arrow shot from a bow. His legs kept him far ahead of the Lion, whose legs were much shorter and thicker than his own. From a distance, the other animals watched the chase.

"The Stag will surely outrun the Lion!" the Fox cried.

The Rabbit said, "Oh, he must, he must!" But then the Stag entered the forest, dense with trees.

Weaving among the trees, the Stag kept ahead of the Lion at first. He was not fatigued at all, for his long legs could carry him far and fast without tiring. But the branches of some of the trees hung low, and vines curled around them. The vines clutched at the Stag's antlers as he dodged among the trees. Before he knew it, the Stag had caught his antlers in the branches and vines. He struggled mightily, but the tangled vines held him tight. Closer and closer the Lion came, smiling with its sharp teeth showing. The Stag, knowing his end was near, closed his eyes and sighed deeply.

"Oh," he said, "how I have fooled myself! The long legs that I hated would have saved me, but the antlers that I loved have led to my destruction!"

GO ON →

Name: ______________________________ Date: ________

7 Read this sentence from the passage.

The ground was flat and even, and the Stag moved with the velocity of an arrow shot from a bow.

What does *velocity* mean in the sentence above?

Ⓐ curve
Ⓑ direction
Ⓒ sharpness
Ⓓ speed

8 What happens just before Fox and Rabbit discuss the chase?

Ⓕ They admire the Stag's horns.
Ⓖ They watch the Lion chasing the Stag.
Ⓗ The Stag complains about how his legs look.
Ⓘ The Stag sees the Lion's reflection in the pond.

9 Read this sentence from the passage.

The Stag was so engrossed that he did not notice that a Lion had crept up alongside him.

What does *engrossed* mean in the sentence above?

Ⓐ busy
Ⓑ irritated
Ⓒ sorrowful
Ⓓ uninterrupted

10 Read this sentence from the passage.

"Oh," he said, "how I have fooled myself!"

How does this sentence support the theme?

Ⓕ by stating that the Stag was not as smart as he was fast
Ⓖ by showing that the Stag was wrong about what was valuable
Ⓗ by showing that the Stag was not as fast as the Lion
Ⓘ by hinting that the Stag was not as fine-looking as he had thought

GO ON →

Read the passage "Hans in Luck" before answering Numbers 11 through 20.

Hans in Luck

Long ago, young men worked to learn a trade. When they were done, they were paid by their master and then went off to find work or open their own shops. After seven years of hard work, a young man named Hans asked for his wages. The master gave him a big piece of gold, which Hans thought must surely be the most valuable thing in the world. The young man left immediately to return to his village to see his mother. He yearned to see her like a homesick child.

On the road, Hans met a man on a fine horse. The youth said, "How easy it is for you to ride, compared to me, weary from the arduous effort of walking."

The rider got down from the animal and proposed a trade, saying, "I'll exchange my steed for that piece of gold in your hand."

When Hans agreed, the rider thrust the horse's bridle into the young man's hands. "Just utter 'C'ck! C'ck!' and the horse will gallop like lightning," the rider instructed and walked away.

Hans rode only for the briefest moment. The steed instantly threw him off, and he landed in a ditch beside the road.

Soon a woman happened to pass by, leading a cow. She was startled to see a young man in the ditch. Hans rubbed a sore arm and leg. Then he said, "You have a nice, quiet cow. No doubt it gives refreshing milk. I'd rather have your cow than this brute of a horse."

GO ON →

The peasant woman liked this idea and agreed to trade her cow for the horse. So Hans continued along the route to his village, driving the cow along and whistling merrily.

Hans grew thirsty and tried to milk the cow. But he went about it in a crude way, and the animal gave him a swift kick.

Sweating, thirsty, and bruised, Hans was in great despair by this point. Then along came a butcher driving a horse-drawn cart, and in the cart was a pig. It was gargantuan, seeming to be the size of a house. Hans told the butcher, "How I wish I had a pig. I'd have it butchered to make sausages and other delicacies."

"I'd be happy to trade you this prime pig for that worthless looking cow," offered the butcher. Of course, the cow was exactly what he wanted. The deal was quickly completed.

Before twilight fell, Hans met a man carrying a goose. "What an ancient pig!" the man exclaimed. "It would make a fine pet for my children." He smiled to himself as he offered his goose to Hans in exchange for the pig.

"My mother can use the goose's soft feathers to stuff a pillow," Hans told himself.

Finally he entered his village. The first person he saw was a scissors-grinder at his trade. "Where did you get that goose?" the man asked Hans.

"I exchanged it for my pig," Hans replied. Then he worked backward to relate all his adventures to the scissors-grinder. The man recommended that Hans trade the goose for his grinding stone. Then Hans would have a way to make money, sharpening scissors and knife blades. Hans agreed to the trade.

But with each step Hans took, the stone seemed to grow heavier. Soon he laid it by a stream that ran through the village. When he stooped to drink, the weighty stone tumbled into the water.

Free of any tiresome burdens now, Hans exclaimed, "I'm the luckiest man alive!" Then with the fleetness of a racer, he headed home to see his mother.

GO ON →

Name: ______________________________ Date: ________

Now answer Numbers 11 through 20. Base your answers on "Hans in Luck."

11 What happens right before Hans leaves for his village?

Ⓐ He works for seven years.

Ⓑ He complains about being weary.

Ⓒ He receives a large piece of gold.

Ⓓ He makes a trade in order to get a horse.

12 Read this sentence from the passage.

He yearned to see her like a homesick child.

What does *yearned* mean in the sentence above?

Ⓕ enjoyed greatly

Ⓖ deeply wanted

Ⓗ mildly wanted

Ⓘ fought bravely

13 What is the theme of this passage?

Ⓐ Fine possessions do not make a fine person.

Ⓑ You do not need possessions to be happy.

Ⓒ The best things come in small packages.

Ⓓ Beware of people who offer you gifts.

14 Read this sentence from the passage.

The youth said, "How easy it is for you to ride, compared to me, weary from the arduous effort of walking."

What does *arduous* mean in the sentence above?

Ⓕ basic

Ⓖ difficult

Ⓗ proper

Ⓘ unlucky

GO ON →

Name: ______________________________ Date: ________

15 Read these sentences from the passage.

Hans grew thirsty and tried to milk the cow. But he went about it in a crude way, and the animal gave him a swift kick.

What does *crude* mean in the sentences above?

Ⓐ brilliant

Ⓑ clumsy

Ⓒ painless

Ⓓ smooth

16 What text evidence best supports the theme of the passage?

Ⓕ Before twilight fell, Hans met a man carrying a goose.

Ⓖ The first person he saw was a scissors-grinder at his trade.

Ⓗ Then he worked backward to relate all his adventures to the scissors-grinder.

Ⓘ Free of any tiresome burdens now, Hans exclaimed, "I'm the luckiest man alive!"

17 Read this sentence from the passage.

It was gargantuan, seeming to be the size of a house.

What does *gargantuan* mean in the sentence above?

Ⓐ cute

Ⓑ expensive

Ⓒ huge

Ⓓ lively

GO ON →

Name: ________________________________ Date: __________

18 Read this sentence from the passage.

Sweating, thirsty, and bruised, Hans was in great despair by this point.

How does this sentence support the theme?

Ⓕ by describing how dangerous horses can be

Ⓖ by explaining how easy it was to cheat Hans

Ⓗ by telling how unhappy owning the animals had made Hans

Ⓘ by explaining how Hans was no longer eager to go to his home village

19 Read this sentence from the passage.

Then with the fleetness of a racer, he headed home to see his mother.

What does *fleetness* mean in the sentence above?

Ⓐ anxiety

Ⓑ cheerfulness

Ⓒ occupation

Ⓓ speed

20 Read this sentence from the passage.

But with each step Hans took, the stone seemed to grow heavier.

How does this sentence support the theme?

Ⓕ by hinting that Hans will never be a good scissors-grinder

Ⓖ by describing how owning the sharpening stone made Hans unhappy

Ⓗ by explaining that, no matter what he does, Hans is always miserable

Ⓘ by pointing out that Hans can never be happy until he has reached home

STOP

Name: ______________________ Date: __________

21 What lessons do Stag in "The Stag at the Pool" and Hans in "Hans in Luck" learn in the passages? Use text evidence from the stories to support your answer.

Answer Key

Name: ______________________________

Question	Correct Answer	Content Focus	CCSS	Complexity
1	D	Theme	RL.5.2	DOK 3
2	G	Context Clues: Comparison	L.5.4a	DOK 2
3	D	Theme	RL.5.2	DOK 3
4	I	Context Clues: Comparison	L.5.4a	DOK 2
5	B	Context Clues: Comparison	L.5.4a	DOK 2
6	I	Theme	RL.5.2	DOK 3
7	D	Context Clues: Comparison	L.5.4a	DOK 2
8	G	Character, Setting, Plot: Sequence	RL.3.3	DOK 1
9	A	Context Clues: Cause and Effect	L.5.4a	DOK 2
10	G	Theme	RL.5.2	DOK 3
11	C	Character, Setting, Plot: Sequence	RL.3.3	DOK 1
12	G	Context Clues: Comparison	L.5.4a	DOK 2
13	B	Theme	RL.5.2	DOK 3
14	G	Context Clues: Comparison	L.5.4a	DOK 2
15	B	Context Clues: Cause and Effect	L.5.4a	DOK 2
16	I	Theme	RL.5.2	DOK 3
17	C	Context Clues: Comparison	L.5.4a	DOK 2
18	H	Theme	RL.5.2	DOK 3
19	D	Context Clues: Comparison	L.5.4a	DOK 2
20	G	Theme	RL.5.2	DOK 3
21	see below	Theme	RL.5.2	DOK 3

Comprehension 1, 3, 6, 8, 10, 11, 13, 16, 18, 20	/10	%
Vocabulary 2, 4, 5, 7, 9, 12, 14, 15, 17, 19	/10	%
Total Weekly Assessment Score	/20	%

21 To receive full credit for the response, the following information should be included: Hans and the Stag both learn that the things they thought were of great value turned out to be not as valuable to them as they had once thought.

Read the article "The Fall of the Giants" before answering Numbers 1 through 10.

The Fall of the Giants

The Sequoia National Forest in California's Sierra Nevada Mountains is home to the most massive trees in the world. At its entrance is the Trail of 100 Giants. This is a short, easy, paved trail that people can walk. It gives visitors great views of more than a hundred sequoias. These trees grow only in the special geology of the slopes of the Sierra Nevadas. The largest of the trees is 20 feet around and 220 feet tall. You almost need a telescope to see the top of it!

The sequoia trees that line the Trail of 100 Giants have stood for generations. Many of these botanical wonders started growing in the Middle Ages. The trees watched the first Europeans settle in California. They grew while America fought its revolution and its civil war. They grew through the Gold Rush in the mid-1800s and two world wars. The trees were declared a national monument in 2000.

Then, in October 2011, two of the giants fell. There were only a few tourists nearby. One photographer from Germany used a video camera to record the trees crashing to the ground. Luckily, nobody was hurt. Watchers were astonished that these enormous trees could topple like babies trying to take their first steps. One explanation was that the summer had been very wet, and the ground was quite hydrated. The earth may have been too soggy to hold the shallow roots of the trees.

GO ON →

Some officials fear that the foot traffic from tourists might have weakened the trees. Even pollution from cars visiting the park could have damaged them. Three to four million people a year visit Yosemite National Park, where the Trail of 100 Giants is located. It might be, though, that the trees were simply old. It was the time in their life cycle to die.

The trees may have been as much as 1,500 years old. They were more than 200 feet tall. The two that fell were connected at their base, and most park scientists believe that when the first one fell, it brought the second one down with it.

The question now is, what should be done with the fallen trees? They fell across a popular path, crushing a bridge and blocking the walkway. The trunks are too big for most walkers to climb over, though some have tried. The path they block is designed for people in wheelchairs. There is no other path that these people can use. The Park Service asked the public what they thought.

People's ideas have been varied. Many biologists think the trees should be left just as they are, letting nature take its course. Some people feel that the Forest Service should drill a tunnel through the trunk so people can simply walk through. Some want to build a bridge over the trees, but the bridge would have to be one that wheelchairs could use. Some think the path should go around the trees. And some believe the trees should be cut up for firewood.

Park officials have decided to take their time deciding what to do. In the past, they have had to cut down dead trees to be sure that visitors to the park would be safe. Since the trees are national monuments now, though, any decision must be carefully considered. The sequoias are a rare treasure, and even in death, they should be treated with respect.

GO ON →

Name: ______________________________ Date: ________

Now answer Numbers 1 through 10. Base your answers on "The Fall of the Giants."

1 Read this sentence from the article.

> **These trees grow only in the special geology of the slopes of the Sierra Nevadas.**

The root of *geology* is *geo*, which means "earth." *Geology* is the study of

Ⓐ animals.

Ⓑ land.

Ⓒ peoples.

Ⓓ trees.

2 Read this sentence from the article.

> **The earth may have been too soggy to hold the shallow roots of the trees.**

How does this sentence support the central idea of the article?

Ⓕ It suggests a reason why two giant sequoias fell in the Sequoia National Forest.

Ⓖ It gives information about what the Sequoia National Forest looks like.

Ⓗ It shows how giant sequoias are able to grow as large as they do.

Ⓘ It provides details about what happened after the sequoias fell.

GO ON →

Name: ______________________________ Date: ______

3 Read this sentence from the article.

Many of these botanical wonders started growing in the Middle Ages.

The origin of *botanical* is the Greek word *botan*, meaning "plant." Which of the following would a botanist study?

Ⓐ grass

Ⓑ buildings

Ⓒ forest animals

Ⓓ ancient people

4 In which paragraph would the following key detail best belong?

The trees have seen much of our country's history.

Ⓕ paragraph 1, page 145

Ⓖ paragraph 2, page 145

Ⓗ paragraph 3, page 145

Ⓘ paragraph 1, page 146

5 Which key detail best supports the main idea of paragraph 3 on page 145?

Ⓐ People in wheelchairs should be given access to the trees.

Ⓑ The trees made a great noise as they fell to the ground.

Ⓒ Only California's redwood trees are taller than sequoias.

Ⓓ Some fallen sequoias have had tunnels cut through them.

6 Read this sentence from the article.

Watchers were astonished that these enormous trees could topple like babies trying to take their first steps.

What does *topple* mean in the sentence above?

Ⓕ fall over

Ⓖ stand up

Ⓗ move quickly

Ⓘ grow to be very tall

GO ON →

Name: ______________________________ Date: ________

7 How does the author present the event of the two trees falling at the same time?

Ⓐ as a humorous example

Ⓑ as part of a chronicle of daily events in the park

Ⓒ as a list of the benefits of creating national parks

Ⓓ as part of a review of explanations about the cause

8 Read this sentence from the article.

One explanation was that the summer had been very wet, and the ground was quite hydrated.

The root of *hydrated* is *hydr* meaning "water." *Hydrated* ground is probably

Ⓕ cracked.

Ⓖ dry.

Ⓗ flaky.

Ⓘ soaked.

9 What is the main idea of the article?

Ⓐ Not many people have the chance to see a sequoia fall.

Ⓑ The death of a sequoia is an important natural event.

Ⓒ It is lucky nobody was hurt when the sequoias fell.

Ⓓ People should do more to help save the sequoias.

10 Read this sentence from the article.

It was the time in their life cycle to die.

The origin of *cycle* is the Greek root *cycl*, which means "circle." This suggests that a cycle

Ⓕ moves very fast.

Ⓖ repeats itself.

Ⓗ is difficult to see.

Ⓘ can follow may paths.

GO ON →

Read the article "Super Snakes" before answering Numbers 11 through 20.

Super Snakes

Many people have a snake phobia because they know only the common myths about these reptiles. Few snakes are deadly. However, poisonous species have certainly given snakes a bad reputation! Here are some facts about snakes that will help you better understand these members of the animal kingdom that live in our biosphere.

Snakes can survive in many geographic areas. They are not found in the polar regions of the world, though. That is because snakes are cold-blooded. Their body thermostat changes their body temperature to match how hot or cold the air is. A snake would freeze and die in the Arctic or Antarctic.

Nature has given this creature many gifts. One of these gifts is the way its skin looks. Its patterns and coloring help the reptile hide from animals that will attack and eat it. Many snake species have skin the dull color of the ground. The kinds that slither up trees may be bright green, like leaves.

Snakes can go for weeks or even months between meals, and some snakes eat only once or twice a year. Because of this, they do not need to hunt constantly for food.

The snake's flickering tongue may look frightening as it vibrates. But it is part of an important sense organ for the snake.

GO ON →

This special organ is located on the roof of its mouth. The snake uses it to smell prey and to find a mate. Some snakes, like the python, have special cells on top of their heads. These microscopic cells help them locate warm-blooded animals.

Snakes use the muscles along the sides of their bodies to slither from place to place. They have four different ways to move. Some snakes bunch themselves up and then thrust themselves forward. Some push off and move in a wave-like motion. Some move the middle of their bodies up and down. This pushes their heads forward. And some grip the ground with their scales. They use the scales and their muscles to push themselves forward.

Most snakes feed on small mammals. Big snakes, like pythons, will attack much larger prey. Constrictor snakes wrap themselves around large prey and compress it like a belt that is much too tight. Snakes will often win what look like impossible battles. Because they can move so rapidly and quietly, snakes are very effective hunters. The same muscles that move the snake along help to move the snake's meal through its system.

Snakes have many enemies themselves. Raccoons, birds, foxes, coyotes, and even other snakes eat snakes. And humans can be their enemies too. Many humans are afraid of snakes and will hunt them to get rid of them. Humans also build communities in snake territory. With each generation, snakes have less and less room to live.

It is true that some snakes are poisonous. They use their poison to stun their prey before eating it. It is always best to be careful around snakes. Only an expert can tell which snakes are harmless and which are dangerous. However, a person can be careful around snakes without having a fear of them. The best advice is to find out if any poisonous snakes live in your area. In addition, if you are going camping or hiking, check to find out if the area has poisonous snakes.

If any poisonous snakes are found where you live or where you will be visiting, use photographs to learn to identify them. Also learn what steps to take when you come across a poisonous snake. With knowledge like this, you can replace your fear with caution.

GO ON →

Name: ______________________________ Date: ________

Now answer Numbers 11 through 20. Base your answers on "Super Snakes."

11 What is the best summary of the article?

Ⓐ Snakes have four ways to move. They can bunch up or push off. They can also move up and down or use their scales and muscles to pull them along.

Ⓑ Snakes have many enemies. Birds, mammals, and other snakes eat snakes. Humans can be enemies too, by hunting snakes or taking away their habitats.

Ⓒ You should find out what poisonous snakes are in your area or in an area you visit. You can learn how to identify those snakes. You can also find out what to do if you see one.

Ⓓ Many people fear snakes, but few snakes are dangerous. Snakes have amazing ways to survive. Learning about them will help people understand them more and fear them less.

12 Read this sentence from the article.

Many people have a snake phobia because they know only the common myths about these reptiles.

The root of *phobia* is *phob*, meaning "fear." Therefore, someone with a *phobia* is most likely to

Ⓕ laugh. Ⓗ sigh.

Ⓖ scream. Ⓘ yawn.

13 Which paragraph would best be supported by the following detail?

It is very hard for snakes to move on smooth surfaces.

Ⓐ paragraph 4, page 150 Ⓒ paragraph 1, page 151

Ⓑ paragraph 5, page 150 Ⓓ paragraph 4, page 151

GO ON →

Name: ______________________________ Date: __________

14 Read this sentence from the article.

> **Here are some facts about snakes that will help you better understand these members of the animal kingdom that live in our biosphere.**

The word *biosphere* comes in part from the Greek root *sphere*, from *sphaira*, meaning "globe or ball." This suggests that a *biosphere* is

Ⓕ flat.
Ⓖ round.
Ⓗ short.
Ⓘ thick.

15 Read this sentence from the article.

> **Their body thermostat changes their body temperature to match how hot or cold the air is.**

The root of *thermostat* is *therm*, meaning "heat." Therefore, a *thermostat* controls

Ⓐ anger.
Ⓑ emotions.
Ⓒ growth.
Ⓓ temperature.

16 Which key detail best supports the main idea of the second full paragraph on page 151 of the article?

Ⓕ Many other animals eat mice and rats too.
Ⓖ It can be very hard to see a snake because of its coloring.
Ⓗ Different poisonous snakes live in different parts of the world.
Ⓘ Some snakes have hinged jaws so they can open wide enough to swallow large prey.

GO ON →

Name: ______________________________ Date: ________

17 Read this sentence from the article.

These microscopic cells help them locate warm-blooded animals.

The word *microscopic* comes from the Greek roots *micro*, meaning "small," and *scop*, meaning "see." This suggests that *microscopic* cells are

Ⓐ easily found.
Ⓑ difficult to see.
Ⓒ enormous in size.
Ⓓ too many to count.

18 According to the author of this article, what results from learning more about snakes?

Ⓕ a love of them

Ⓖ a decrease in the fear of them

Ⓗ an increase in the fear of them

Ⓘ the ability to see them in spite of their patterned skin

19 Read this sentence from the article.

Constrictor snakes wrap themselves around large prey and compress it like a belt that is much too tight.

What does *compress* mean in the sentence above?

Ⓐ decorate
Ⓑ eat
Ⓒ kill
Ⓓ squeeze

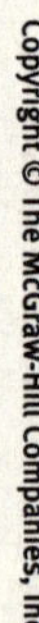

20 What is the main idea of the article?

Ⓕ Many people are very afraid of snakes.

Ⓖ Snakes can be both dangerous and very interesting.

Ⓗ Snakes have many gifts from nature, such as their skin.

Ⓘ If you are careless, you can be hurt or killed by snakes.

STOP

Name: ______________________ Date: __________

21 What is one thing you learned by reading each article that you find interesting? Use text evidence from each article to explain why you find that thing particularly interesting.

Answer Key

Name: ______________________

Question	Correct Answer	Content Focus	CCSS	Complexity
1	B	Greek Roots	L.5.4b	DOK 1
2	F	Main Idea and Key Details	RI.5.2	DOK 2
3	A	Greek Roots	L.5.4b	DOK 1
4	G	Main Idea and Key Details	RI.5.2	DOK 2
5	B	Main Idea and Key Details	RI.5.2	DOK 2
6	F	Context Clues: Comparison	L.5.4a	DOK 2
7	D	Text Structure: Cause and Effect	RI.5.3	DOK 2
8	I	Greek Roots	L.5.4b	DOK 1
9	B	Main Idea and Key Details	RI.5.2	DOK 2
10	G	Greek Roots	L.5.4b	DOK 1
11	D	Main Idea and Key Details	RI.5.2	DOK 2
12	G	Greek Roots	L.5.4b	DOK 1
13	C	Main Idea and Key Details	RI.5.2	DOK 2
14	G	Greek Roots	L.5.4b	DOK 1
15	D	Greek Roots	L.5.4b	DOK 1
16	I	Main Idea and Key Details	RI.5.2	DOK 2
17	B	Greek Roots	L.5.4b	DOK 1
18	G	Text Structure: Cause and Effect	RI.5.3	DOK 2
19	D	Context Clues: Comparison	L.5.4a	DOK 2
20	G	Main Idea and Key Details	RI.5.2	DOK 2
21	see below	Main Idea and Key Details	RI.5.2	DOK 3

Comprehension 2, 4, 5, 7, 9, 11, 13, 16, 18, 20	/10	%
Vocabulary 1, 3, 6, 8, 10, 12, 14, 15, 17, 19	/10	%
Total Weekly Assessment Score	/20	%

21 To receive full credit for the response, the following information should be included: (Answers may vary but text evidence must be included from each article as well as an explanation of why the student finds it interesting. Examples follow.) Sequoias can be so big that tunnels can be made in fallen ones that people can walk through. Some snakes eat only once or twice a year.

Read the article "Make a Model of the Water Cycle" before answering Numbers 1 through 10.

Make a Model of the Water Cycle

You can volunteer with three or four friends to do a team experiment. It will show you how heat evaporates water, changes it into droplets, and then turns it back to water. First, you need to know a little about the water cycle. Water moves from the oceans into the air. From the air, it falls as rain or snow back into the ocean or onto land. If it falls on land, it eventually works its way back into the ocean as an overflow of water called runoff. (See the diagram below.)

The water cycle starts when the sun heats ocean water. The sun converts the water into small, invisible particles of moisture called water vapor. The sun and wind cause the water vapor to rise into the air. Water vapor cools off in the atmosphere, or the air that surrounds Earth. Then it changes to drops of water. The drops then cluster, or hold together, forming a cloud.

The water in the cloud falls as rain or snow. It may fall back into the ocean, or it may fall on land. If it falls on land, it eventually works its way back to the ocean as a water overflow called runoff.

THE WATER CYCLE

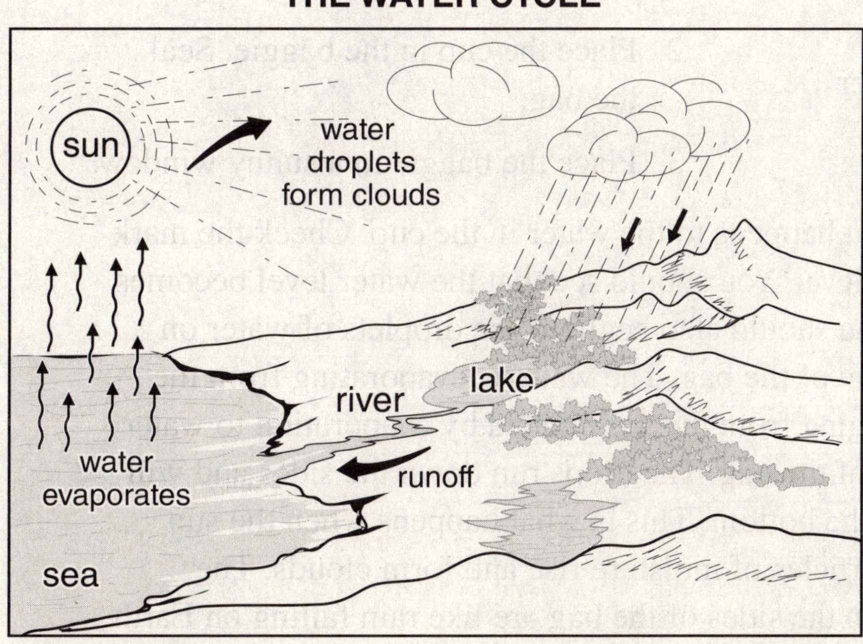

GO ON →

One way water does this is by falling into tributaries, which are rivers and streams that flow into larger bodies of water. The water may also collect in an underground layer of earth or rock. The rock must be porous enough to let the water flow through it. This water is called groundwater, and it, too, eventually finds its way to the ocean. Then the water cycle starts over again.

As you begin your experiment, remember this amazing fact. The amount of water on Earth now is the same as it was in the past and will be in the future. This means that the water you drank yesterday may once have been the water in the Delaware River when General Washington's troops crossed it during the Revolutionary War. About 71% of Earth's surface is water. This includes not only the water in oceans, rivers, and lakes. It also includes the water in clouds, rain, snow, and groundwater and in the icy regions at the North and South Poles.

Make a model of the water cycle with a partner or small group. Use the instructions below.

Water Cycle Baggie

Materials:
A plastic bag that seals
A small, clear plastic cup
Water
Red food color
A permanent marker

Steps:
1. Fill cup about halfway with water. Add red food color to the water. Stir. Use the marker to show water level.
2. Place the cup in the baggie. Seal the bag.
3. Place the baggie in a sunny window.

Observe what happens to the water in the cup. Check the mark showing the water level. You should see that the water level becomes gradually lower. You should also begin to see droplets of water on the sides and bottom of the bag. The water is evaporating from the heat and then changing from the gas created by evaporation to water drops on the sides of the bag. The drops run down the sides and will begin to collect at the bottom. This is what happens when the sun heats the ocean. Particles of moisture rise and form clouds. The drops running down the sides of the bag are like rain falling on Earth.

GO ON →

Name: ______________________________ Date: ________

Now answer Numbers 1 through 10. Base your answers on "Make a Model of the Water Cycle."

1 What is the main idea of the article?

Ⓐ In the water cycle, water evaporates, condenses, and falls as precipitation.

Ⓑ When the water in a cloud falls as precipitation, it may fall on land or water.

Ⓒ Water is about 71% of Earth's surface and needed by plants and animals.

Ⓓ You can do an experiment with a baggie, cup, water, food color, and a marker.

2 Read the following sentence from the article.

You can volunteer with three or four friends to do a team experiment.

The Latin root of *volunteer* is *vol*, meaning "will, wish." To *volunteer* means to

Ⓕ meet others.

Ⓖ do willingly.

Ⓗ learn lessons.

Ⓘ involves friends.

3 Read this sentence from the article.

(See the diagram below.)

Which word has the same root as *diagram*?

Ⓐ agree

Ⓑ diameter

Ⓒ grade

Ⓓ ramp

GO ON →

Name: ______________________________ Date: __________

4 What is the main idea of the section "Water Cycle Baggie"?

Ⓕ After you put the cup in the bag and seal it, drops will run down the sides and puddle in the bottom.

Ⓖ You need a plastic bag, clear cup, water, red food color, and a marker before setting up the experiment.

Ⓗ An important part of the experiment is adding the food color before putting the sealed plastic bag in a warm place.

Ⓘ An experiment with a plastic bag, cup, and water can show how water evaporates and then turns back to water.

5 Read this sentence from the article.

One way water does this is by falling into tributaries, which are rivers and streams that flow into larger bodies of water.

The Latin root of *tributary* is *trib*, meaning "pay." Which of the following words is most likely to come from that same root?

Ⓐ allowance

Ⓑ contribute

Ⓒ salary

Ⓓ tribe

6 Read this sentence from the article.

The rock must be porous enough to let the water flow through it.

The Latin root of *porous* means "passage." This tell you that *porous* rock

Ⓕ is old.

Ⓖ is flat.

Ⓗ has openings.

Ⓘ has many colors.

GO ON →

Name: ______________________________ Date: ________

7 Which key detail supports the main idea of the article?

Ⓐ The amount of water on Earth now is the same as it was in the past and will be in the future.

Ⓑ You can volunteer with three or four friends to do a team experiment.

Ⓒ The rock must be porous enough to let the water flow through it.

Ⓓ About 71% of Earth's surface is water.

8 Which key detail best supports the idea that water evaporates in sunlight?

Ⓕ Water moves from the ocean into air.

Ⓖ In the atmosphere water vapor changes to water drops.

Ⓗ The sun turns water into invisible particles of moisture.

Ⓘ Water vapor cools off in the atmosphere, or the air that surrounds Earth.

9 Read this sentence from the article.

The sun converts the water into small, invisible particles of moisture called water vapor.

The Latin root of *converts* is *vert*, meaning "to turn." Based on this information, what does *converts* mean?

Ⓐ allows

Ⓑ changes

Ⓒ helps

Ⓓ repeats

10 How did the author organize the steps to make the water cycle model?

Ⓕ by giving the steps in order

Ⓖ by showing the cause of water evaporation

Ⓗ by comparing and contrasting water and water vapor

Ⓘ by solving the problem of what causes condensation

GO ON →

Read the article "Be Prepared!" before answering Numbers 11 through 20.

Be Prepared!

Disasters happen all over the world. They include floods, tornadoes, hurricanes, earthquakes, landslides, and wildfires. Every family needs a plan in case an unexpected disaster strikes their home or community. Disaster plans will vary, and each family should consider the type of emergency most likely to occur.

Flooding is a common emergency. Some floods, called flash floods, develop quickly following heavy rainfall. They usually affect only a limited area. Other floods develop slowly and affect large areas. Although some floods occur in places never affected before, many places flood consistently. If you live in such an area, your family should be prepared at all times. Have an emergency kit, food and water, and a plan for evacuation, or leaving the affected area.

Hurricanes usually occur in coastal states. They are predicted several days to as much as a week ahead of time. When a hurricane strikes, high winds can cause serious destruction. Flooding is possible. Flooding results from a surge of water from the ocean or gulf. Authorities may mandate that you go to a different location. Thus, it is good to have an evacuation route planned. You may want to arrange to stay with friends or relatives. Many communities open centers that are safer than homes in a hurricane. If your center does not accept pets, you will need an alternate plan for the pet. Ahead of time, make sure your pet has had immunizations. An ID tag will help if you and your pet get separated. A carrier or cage will protect your pet.

GO ON →

Tornadoes are violent storms, and they can do serious damage. They may develop with little advance warning. Just before one touches down, you may notice one or more of the following:

- dark sky
- large-size hail
- air that is ominously still
- a low cloud that may be rotating, or turning in a circle
- a loud roar

If you are in a building during either a hurricane or tornado, go to a basement or to an inside room. Experts say that you should stay away from windows and outside walls. If you are outside, lie flat in the lowest place. Cover your head with your hands.

There are steps everyone should take no matter what the risks are in your particular area. First, hold a family meeting to make a plan. All family members need to know where the emergency supplies are kept. Decide a place for everyone to meet following a disaster. In an emergency, like a fire, plan to meet at a location right outside. Remember that family members may be in school and at work when a disaster strikes. Plan to go to a place where you can meet if you cannot return home. It is good to have a charged cell phone handy.

Below is a checklist you can use to be prepared for an emergency.

Gather Emergency Supplies

- ☐ For each person, 1 gallon of water a day for 3–7 days
- ☐ Packaged and canned meats and fish, fruits, and vegetables
- ☐ Manual can opener
- ☐ Special foods for family members, such as baby food
- ☐ Pet food if you have a pet
- ☐ First aid kit with bandages, gauze pads, antiseptic, and scissors
- ☐ Portable radio
- ☐ Flashlight/batteries

Other Items

- ☐ Paper cups, plates, and plastic utensils
- ☐ Paper towels and other paper products
- ☐ Trash bags
- ☐ Sturdy shoes and warm clothing
- ☐ Blankets/sleeping bags

Knowing what to expect and being prepared for the worst will help you and your family survive.

GO ON →

Name: ______________________________ Date: ________

Now answer Numbers 11 through 20. Base your answers on "Be Prepared!"

11 What is the main idea of the article?

Ⓐ Emergency supplies include canned food and water.

Ⓑ It is important for your family to have a plan in case of a disaster.

Ⓒ Flooding, tornadoes, and hurricanes can do serious damage to homes.

Ⓓ Be sure to have sturdy shoes, warm clothing, and blankets with your supplies.

12 Read this sentence from the article.

Although some floods occur in places never affected before, many places flood consistently.

What does *consistently* mean in the sentence above?

Ⓕ barely

Ⓗ heavily

Ⓖ clearly

Ⓘ regularly

13 Read this sentence from the article.

Authorities may mandate that you go to a different location.

The Latin root of *mandate* is *mand*, which means "to order." Something *mandatory* is

Ⓐ required.

Ⓑ suggested.

Ⓒ unclear.

Ⓓ unexpected.

GO ON →

Name: ______________________________ Date: __________

14 Before a tornado strikes, you might notice

Ⓕ flooding.
Ⓖ heavy rain.
Ⓗ destruction from wind.
Ⓘ a dark sky and low cloud.

15 Read this description of just before a tornado touches down.

air that is ominously still

The Latin root of *ominously* is *omen*, which means "a threatening sign." This suggests that an *ominous* event is one that causes

Ⓐ confusion.
Ⓑ curiosity.
Ⓒ fear.
Ⓓ sadness.

16 Read this phrase from the article.

Manual can opener

The word *manual* comes from the Latin root *man*, meaning "hand." This tells you that a *manual* can opener

Ⓕ cannot be bought.
Ⓖ must be plugged in.
Ⓗ cannot open small cans.
Ⓘ operates by a person turning a lever.

17 Which key detail best supports the main idea of the article?

Ⓐ Disasters happen all over the world.
Ⓑ Other floods develop slowly and affect large areas.
Ⓒ Many communities open centers that are safer than homes in a hurricane.
Ⓓ All family members need to know where the emergency supplies are kept.

GO ON →

Name: ______________________________ Date: ________

18 What sentence best summarizes the information given in the checklist?

Ⓕ A disaster may result in injuries that require first aid supplies.

Ⓖ A radio that works without electric power will provide news reports.

Ⓗ Everyone needs one gallon of water for each day water is not available.

Ⓘ Following a disaster, you will need to have certain supplies on hand.

19 Read this item from the checklist under "Gather Emergency Supplies."

Portable radio

The Latin root of *portable* is *port*, meaning "to carry." A *portable* radio would be

Ⓐ broken.

Ⓑ expensive.

Ⓒ heavy.

Ⓓ light.

20 What sentence best summarizes a plan to find family members after a disaster?

Ⓕ Someone needs to listen to a radio for news.

Ⓖ Members need to decide beforehand where to meet.

Ⓗ Someone needs to have a working flashlight and water.

Ⓘ Everyone should have sturdy shoes and warm clothing.

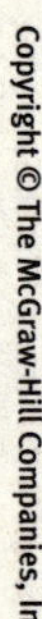

STOP

Name: ______________________ Date: __________

21 Identify the main ideas of "Make a Model of the Water Cycle" and "Be Prepared!" Then explain how both are related to weather. Give specific text evidence from the articles to support your response.

Answer Key

Name: ______________________________

Question	Correct Answer	Content Focus	CCSS	Complexity
1	A	Main Idea and Key Details	RI.5.2	DOK 2
2	G	Latin Roots	L.5.4b	DOK 1
3	B	Greek Roots	L.5.4b	DOK 1
4	I	Main Idea and Key Details	RI.5.2	DOK 2
5	B	Latin Roots	L.5.4b	DOK 1
6	H	Latin Roots	L.5.4b	DOK 1
7	A	Main Idea and Key Details	RI.5.2	DOK 2
8	H	Main Idea and Key Details	RI.5.2	DOK 2
9	B	Latin Roots	L.5.4b	DOK 1
10	F	Text Structure: Sequence	RI.5.5	DOK 2
11	B	Main Idea and Key Details	RI.5.2	DOK 2
12	I	Context Clues: Comparison	L.5.4a	DOK 2
13	A	Latin Roots	L.5.4b	DOK 1
14	I	Sequence	RI.5.3	DOK 1
15	C	Latin Roots	L.5.4b	DOK 1
16	I	Latin Roots	L.5.4b	DOK 1
17	D	Main Idea and Key Details	RI.5.2	DOK 2
18	I	Main Idea and Key Details	RI.5.2	DOK 2
19	D	Latin Roots	L.5.4b	DOK 1
20	G	Main Idea and Key Details	RI.5.2	DOK 1
21	see below	Main Idea and Key Details	RI.5.2	DOK 2

Comprehension 1, 4, 7, 8, 10, 11, 14, 17, 18, 20	/10	%
Vocabulary 2, 3, 5, 6, 9, 12, 13, 15, 16, 19	/10	%
Total Weekly Assessment Score	/20	%

21 To receive full credit for the response, the following information should be included: The main idea of "Make a Model of the Water Cycle" is that water in the ocean evaporates, condenses, and then falls as rain and snow to make its way back to the ocean. The main idea of "Be Prepared!" is that natural disasters can occur anywhere so families must make a plan. Both articles relate to weather, the first to details about precipitation and the second to steps in preparation for violent storms.

Read the article "The Terror of the Middle Ages" before answering Numbers 1 through 10.

The Terror of the Middle Ages

In 1347, a ship sailed into the port at Messina, Sicily. The sailors on board were very sick. They staggered through the streets and quickly died. The people of Messina were terrified. They had no idea what disease the sailors carried. It was the first hint of what was to come. The bubonic plague had arrived in Europe.

The bubonic plague was one of the most horrific events in world history. It started in Mongolia and was caused by tiny bacteria. The bacteria infected fleas, and the fleas that carried the germ jumped onto rats and then quickly spread. From the first landing in Sicily, the plague spread throughout Italy and then moved all across Europe. People bitten by fleas developed high fevers and terrible swellings on their bodies. The swellings were very painful. Sufferers died quickly and in huge numbers. An even worse form of the plague was airborne, passing from person to person through their breath. This form of the disease killed even more people and killed them faster.

It is hard to know how many people actually died in the epidemic. The numbers are between 33 percent and 50 percent of the total population of Europe. The plague also spread to the Middle East, through much of Asia, and to parts of North Africa.

GO ON →

Scientists have studied the plague to learn what caused it. Historians have studied it to find out how it affected people and the course of history itself. They looked at several sources. Some cities kept burial records that told how many people had been buried in the years of the plague. Other cities developed public health departments during the plague years, and these departments kept records of illnesses and deaths. Their numbers were not exact, but they gave researchers a good idea of the impact of the disease.

Some small towns and villages were completely destroyed by the disease. Everyone died, leaving cottages and other abodes empty. Historians could look at these ghost villages to see the impact of the plague.

Many writers in the 1300s described what happened in the plague years. Their writings tell of the fear and despair that people felt as the disease raced through their towns. At that time, people did not understand that germs caused disease. They had no idea why they were getting sick. There was no useful medicine to fight the plague. It took hundreds of years for scientists to discover the germ behind the plague, and even more time for them to find a way to treat it. In the Middle Ages, though, people thought that the plague was caused by bad air, bad water, or bad behavior. They tried a variety of things to prevent it. None of their efforts helped.

The plague continued in Europe until 1351. It had reached almost every inch of Europe at that point, and there were few people left to get sick. Gradually the disease ended, though it reappeared over and over again. It never again had such severe effects, so the earlier epidemic was the most devastating. Today, people still get bubonic plague. Even in the United States, a few people die from it each year. Now, though, we have medicine that can cure it. The research that scientists and historians have done on the plague has made sure that the disease will never again threaten the world as it did in 1347.

GO ON →

Name: ______________________________ Date: ________

Now answer Numbers 1 through 10. Base your answers on "The Terror of the Middle Ages."

1 Read these sentences from the article.

The sailors on board were very sick. They staggered through the streets and quickly died.

What does *staggered* mean in the sentences above?

Ⓐ hopped

Ⓑ marched

Ⓒ strolled

Ⓓ stumbled

2 What evidence from the text supports the author's view that people did not understand the plague?

Ⓕ The disease spread quickly over Europe, Asia, and parts of North Africa.

Ⓖ People thought the plague was caused by bad air, bad water, or bad behavior.

Ⓗ The plague was caused by bacteria that lived in fleas, and the fleas were carried by rats.

Ⓘ Some cities began to keep public health records that told how many people died and were buried.

3 Read this sentence from the article.

Everyone died, leaving cottages and other abodes empty.

What does *abodes* mean in the sentence above?

Ⓐ areas

Ⓑ homes

Ⓒ lawns

Ⓓ towns

GO ON →

Name: ______________________ Date: ________

4 Read this sentence from the article.

Some cities kept burial records that told how many people had been buried in the years of the plague.

What view of the author does this text evidence support?

Ⓕ The records kept in the Middle Ages were not very useful.

Ⓖ More people were buried than were born during the plague years.

Ⓗ Sources from the plague years helped historians find out what happened.

Ⓘ Fewer people died in the places where records were kept than in other places.

5 What supports the author's point that huge numbers of people died from the plague?

Ⓐ interviews from the time

Ⓑ films about the bubonic plague

Ⓒ sources from and about the time

Ⓓ the author's personal experience

6 Read this sentence from the article.

It is hard to know how many people actually died in the epidemic.

What word in the sentence helps the reader understand what *epidemic* means?

Ⓕ died

Ⓖ hard

Ⓗ know

Ⓘ people

GO ON →

Name: ______________________________ Date: ________

7 Read this sentence from the article.

The bubonic plague was one of the most horrific events in world history.

The Latin root of *horrific* is *horr*, meaning "to shudder at or to be frightened." This suggests that a *horrific* event is one that is

Ⓐ clear.
Ⓑ mysterious.
Ⓒ terrifying.
Ⓓ unexpected.

8 Read this sentence from the article.

It never again had such severe effects, so the earlier epidemic was the most devastating.

What does *devastating* mean in the sentence above?

Ⓕ destructive
Ⓖ limited
Ⓗ understood
Ⓘ well-defined

9 Which detail would best support the third paragraph on page 170?

Ⓐ Mongolia is located in Asia.
Ⓑ Writers vividly described widespread fear of the plague.
Ⓒ Scientists also looked at the bones of those who had died from the plague.
Ⓓ The death toll was higher in southern Europe and lower in northern Europe.

10 What evidence from the text supports the author's point that the bubonic plague was "The Terror of the Middle Ages"?

Ⓕ The disease caused a high fever.
Ⓖ People still get bubonic plague today.
Ⓗ Between 33 and 50 percent of the population died.
Ⓘ People did not understand how the sickness spread.

GO ON →

Read the article "The Cliff Palace" before answering Numbers 11 through 20.

The Cliff Palace

There was snow blowing across the Colorado mesa on December 18, 1888. Two cowboys were riding across the plains looking for stray cattle. The snow made it hard for the cowboys to be sure what they were seeing. As they described it, it looked like a magnificent city. The cowboys were probably the first people in six hundred years to set eyes on the Cliff Palace of Mesa Verde, deserted since its builders left.

The cowboys, Richard Wetherill and Charlie Mason, soon came back to look around some more. They found that the Cliff Palace was an enormous village. It included a series of rooms made of sandstone blocks, held together with a mixture of mud and water. The rooms were built into the side of a canyon. The Cliff Palace was similar to pueblos, or cliff dwellings, that had been discovered before. It was much larger than any of them, though. The cowboys began to bring tourists with them. People were amazed by the number of rooms. They camped out nearby and spent days walking through the village.

GO ON →

Archaeologists quickly came to study the ancient discovery. They knew it had been constructed by Native Americans, but they were not cognizant of when it was built. It wasn't until 1935 that they were able to learn that the village was built in the 1200s.

The Cliff Palace includes more than a hundred rooms. There are rooms called kivas that were used for religious events. There are walkways and towers. There are living rooms, storage rooms, and rooms for eating. Groups of rooms are organized around a central courtyard. Archaeologists assume that families lived in these rooms.

The Native Americans who lived in the Cliff Palace did not leave any written information. Archaeologists had to use the artifacts that had belonged to them to learn about them. These artifacts included pieces of jars, mugs, axes, pots, baskets, and sandals. The fragments, or pieces, of jars and pots tell them how food was stored. The remains of fireplaces tell them where the food was cooked and how people stayed warm. Archaeologists know that there was no source of water for the cliff dwellers. They had to go quite a distance to get water to bring to their village.

The Cliff Palace was unprotected for hundreds of years. A lot of valuable information about its people was lost. Most things made of wood and cloth were destroyed by weather. We do not know what clothing the people of the Cliff Palace wore. We cannot tell exactly what they ate. There is no furniture left in the Palace. Nobody knows how many artifacts were taken away by people who came to view the site. However, there is a slope in front of the village where the cliff dwellers threw their trash. Archaeologists look through this trash very carefully. They find many clues about the people who lived there.

In 1906, the area around the Cliff Palace was made into a national park. It is called Mesa Verde National Park. It includes many other cliff dwellings, too. The highlight of the park is the Cliff Palace because of its vast size and different kinds of rooms. Visitors must keep to the paths around the village now. This helps to preserve its structure. Thousands of people visit it each year. They are lucky to get a glimpse of a culture that has been gone for hundreds of years.

GO ON →

Name: ______________________________ Date: ________

Now answer Numbers 11 through 20. Base your answers on "The Cliff Palace."

11 Read this sentence from the article.

It included a series of rooms made of sandstone blocks, held together with a mixture of mud and water.

What words in the sentence help the reader understand what *mixture* means?

Ⓐ It included

Ⓑ mud and water

Ⓒ series of rooms

Ⓓ held together

12 Read this sentence from the article.

Most things made of wood and cloth were destroyed by weather.

What point of view does this text evidence support?

Ⓕ Much about the Cliff Palace people is unknown.

Ⓖ Archaeologists do not study things made of wood and cloth.

Ⓗ Archaeologists could not learn when the Cliff Palace was built.

Ⓘ The Cliff Palace people did not use things made of wood and cloth.

13 Read this sentence from the article.

Archaeologists quickly came to study the ancient discovery.

What word in the sentence helps the reader understand what *archaeologists* means?

Ⓐ ancient

Ⓑ came

Ⓒ discovery

Ⓓ quickly

GO ON →

Name: ______________________________ Date: ________

14 What evidence from the text supports the author's point that people were amazed by the Cliff Palace?

Ⓕ There were many different artifacts found at the Cliff Palace.

Ⓖ A lot of information about the Cliff Palace was lost.

Ⓗ The Cliff Palace was similar to other pueblos.

Ⓘ People spent days visiting the Cliff Palace.

15 With which sentence would the author most likely agree?

Ⓐ People in the Cliff Palace lived a very difficult life.

Ⓑ The Cliff Palace should have never been discovered.

Ⓒ The Cliff Palace should have been protected from visitors.

Ⓓ People in the Cliff Palace did not leave behind many things.

16 Read this sentence from the article.

These artifacts included pieces of jars, mugs, axes, pots, baskets, and sandals.

What does the word *artifacts* mean in the sentence above?

Ⓕ art

Ⓖ facts

Ⓗ objects

Ⓘ rooms

17 Which paragraph on page 175 would the following detail best support?

Their garbage included many artifacts that helped tell their story.

Ⓐ paragraph 1

Ⓑ paragraph 2

Ⓒ paragraph 3

Ⓓ paragraph 4

GO ON →

Name: ______________________________ Date: __________

18 Read this sentence from the article.

> **They knew it had been constructed by Native Americans, but they were not cognizant of when it was built.**

The origin of the word *cognizant* is the Latin root *cogn*, which means "to know." This suggests that *cognizant* means

Ⓕ aware.

Ⓖ disbelieving.

Ⓗ surprised to find out.

Ⓘ working to discover.

19 Read these sentences from the article.

> **It includes many other cliff dwellings, too. The highlight of the park is the Cliff Palace because of its vast size and different kinds of rooms.**

What does the word *vast* mean in the sentences above?

Ⓐ large

Ⓑ mountainous

Ⓒ pretty

Ⓓ small

20 What text evidence supports the author's point that people enjoy being able to see the Cliff Palace?

Ⓕ It is located on a mesa in Colorado.

Ⓖ It was unprotected for many years.

Ⓗ Thousands of people come to visit it every year.

Ⓘ The people who lived there left over six hundred years ago.

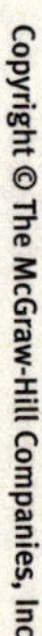

STOP

Name: ______________________ **Date:** __________

21 What text evidence in "The Terror of the Middle Ages" and "The Cliff Palace" supports the authors' view that historians and archaeologists use historical events to explain what happened in the past?

Answer Key

Name: ______________________

Question	Correct Answer	Content Focus	CCSS	Complexity
1	D	Context Clues: Sentence Clues	L.5.4a	DOK 2
2	G	Author's Point of View	RI.6.6	DOK 3
3	B	Context Clues: Sentence Clues	L.5.4a	DOK 2
4	H	Author's Point of View	RI.6.6	DOK 3
5	C	Author's Point of View	RI.6.6	DOK 3
6	F	Context Clues: Sentence Clues	L.5.4a	DOK 3
7	C	Latin Roots	L.5.4b	DOK 1
8	F	Context Clues: Sentence Clues	L.5.4a	DOK 2
9	B	Main Idea and Key Details	RI.5.2	DOK 2
10	H	Author's Point of View	RI.6.6	DOK 3
11	B	Context Clues: Sentence Clues	L.5.4a	DOK 2
12	F	Author's Point of View	RI.6.6	DOK 3
13	A	Context Clues: Sentence Clues	L.5.4a	DOK 2
14	I	Author's Point of View	RI.6.6	DOK 3
15	C	Author's Point of View	RI.6.6	DOK 3
16	H	Context Clues: Sentence Clues	L.5.4a	DOK 2
17	D	Main Idea and Key Details	RI.5.2	DOK 1
18	F	Latin Roots	L.5.4b	DOK 1
19	A	Context Clues: Sentence Clues	L.5.4a	DOK 2
20	H	Author's Point of View	RI.6.6	DOK 3
21	see below	Author's Point of View	RI.6.6	DOK 3

Comprehension 2, 4, 5, 9, 10, 12, 14, 15, 17, 20	/10	%
Vocabulary 1, 3, 6, 7, 8, 11, 13, 16, 18, 19	/10	%
Total Weekly Assessment Score	/20	%

21 To receive full credit for the response, the following information should be included: Each author explains that historians and archaeologists use sources from the historical time, such as artifacts and writings, to get information about the historical events.

Read the article "A Giant of a Man" before answering Numbers 1 through 10.

A Giant of a Man

Back in 1913, I worked on one of Paul Bunyan's famous crews. Let me tell you, there are many good tales about the legendary Paul Bunyan, but they don't tell half the story. He was a giant of a man who could pick up four horses with their load of logs and turn them around on the road. He led crews of us loggers to hew trees and chop them into logs during the days when this country was growing really fast. His helper was Babe, the big blue ox. Babe could pull any load, no matter how big. I saw Babe eat as much in one night as a crew could haul in a year.

Feeding Bunyan's crews of ravenous loggers was a big job. Paul had bad luck getting good cooks until he hired Big Joe. Big Joe wanted a griddle to cook pancakes. Big Ole, the blacksmith, made a griddle so immense a logger couldn't see across the steam made by a pancake that was cooking on it. The pancake batter was stirred in machines like concrete mixers. It was poured on the griddle with cranes. One day, a visitor at a camp saw a crew unloading sleds at the cook's shanty. It looked as if they were unloading logs. I set him straight. "Those aren't logs. They're sausages for the loggers' breakfast," I said.

GO ON →

Everything got buried in the Winter of the Deep Snow. It was a predicament. Paul dealt with the challenge by digging down to find the tops of the tall pine trees and lowering his loggers to chop logs. His blue ox, Babe, wore snowshoes to haul the wood to the surface of the snow. In another cold year, the year of the Two Winters, the Great Lakes that Paul had built froze all the way to the bottom. Paul had to chop the ice. He put it on the shore to melt in the sun.

Paul had a cow named Lucy. She had the appetite of a wolf. In the winter of the Deep Snow, the loggers gave Lucy a pair of Babe's old snowshoes and green goggles. They turned her out to graze in the snow. She learned to run in the snowshoes and ran all over North America. Finally, Paul put a big bell on her.

Chris Crosshaul was careless. He took a load of logs down the Mississippi River for Paul. When the logs were delivered, they were the wrong logs. Paul had to get them back upstream. Driving logs upstream is impossible, but an impossible job never stopped Paul. He fed Babe salt and took him to the upper Mississippi to drink. Babe drank the river dry and the logs traveled up the river faster than they had gone down.

Paul could solve problems like no one else I ever knew or you ever heard of. In the Winter of the Blue Snow, Shot Gunderson was in charge of the Big Tadpole River area. He chopped his logs so that they landed in a lake. He planned to move them in the spring. To his surprise, when he tried to move the logs, he discovered the lake had no outlet to the river. He thought the whole winter's work was lost until Paul, who was always clever, came up with an ingenious idea. He called in Sourdough Sam, a cook who made everything out of sourdough except the coffee. Paul ordered him to mix enough sourdough to fill the big water tank. Then he hitched Babe the Blue Ox to the tank and dumped the sourdough into the lake. Dough rises. As Sam said, it "riz" and pushed the logs over the hills that surrounded the lake, all the way to the river. Today a lake in Minnesota is named "Sourdough Lake."

GO ON →

Name: ______________________________ Date: __________

Now answer Numbers 1 through 10. Base your answers on "A Giant of a Man."

1 Who is the narrator of the passage?

Ⓐ Babe

Ⓑ a logger

Ⓒ Paul Bunyan

Ⓓ Big Joe the cook

2 Which pair of words from the passage have almost the same meaning?

Ⓕ *famous* and *legendary*

Ⓖ *good* and *legendary*

Ⓗ *logs* and *sausages*

Ⓘ *griddle* and *batter*

3 Read this sentence from the passage.

He led crews of us loggers to hew trees and chop them into logs during the days when this country was growing really fast.

What does *hew* mean in the sentence above?

Ⓐ plant

Ⓑ look at

Ⓒ cut down

Ⓓ push over

GO ON →

Name: ______________________________ Date: ________

4 What text evidence shows that the narrator is exaggerating?

Ⓕ Paul led crews of loggers.

Ⓖ Big Joe needed a griddle to cook pancakes.

Ⓗ A visitor at camp thought the sausages were logs.

Ⓘ Crosshaul took the wrong logs down the Mississippi.

5 Read this sentence from the passage.

> **Big Ole, the blacksmith, made a griddle so immense a logger couldn't see across the steam made by a pancake that was cooking on it.**

Which word means the OPPOSITE of *immense*?

Ⓐ hot

Ⓑ tiny

Ⓒ rough

Ⓓ round

6 Read the following sentence from the passage.

> **Paul could solve problems like no one else I ever knew or you ever heard of.**

How does this sentence support the theme?

Ⓕ It shows that Paul Bunyan loved Babe.

Ⓖ It explains Paul Bunyan's size and strength.

Ⓗ It supports the idea that lumberjacks were resourceful.

Ⓘ It strengthens the idea that legends are about larger-than-life characters.

7 Which word has almost the same meaning as *predicament*?

Ⓐ advantage

Ⓑ difficulty

Ⓒ prediction

Ⓓ solution

GO ON →

Name: ______________________________ Date: ________

8 If the passage were written from Paul Bunyan's point of view, the reader would know

Ⓕ how Old Joe got to be a cook.

Ⓖ what Paul Bunyan was thinking.

Ⓗ why the loggers liked Paul Bunyan.

Ⓘ what happened to Chris Crosshaul after he took the wrong logs down the river.

9 Read this sentence from the passage.

He thought the whole winter's work was lost until Paul, who was always clever, came up with an ingenious idea.

Which word means the OPPOSITE of *ingenious*?

Ⓐ difficult

Ⓑ impossible

Ⓒ unimaginative

Ⓓ useful

10 What text evidence supports the narrator's view of Paul as a giant of a man?

Ⓕ Feeding Bunyan's crews of ravenous loggers was a big job.

Ⓖ Driving logs upstream is impossible, but an impossible job never stopped Paul.

Ⓗ Paul dealt with the challenge by digging down to find the tops of the tall pine trees and lowering his loggers to chop logs.

Ⓘ He led crews of us loggers to hew trees and chop them into logs during the days when this country was growing really fast.

GO ON →

Read the story "The Magpie's Nest" before answering Numbers 11 through 20.

The Magpie's Nest

Once, long, long ago, all the birds came to see the magpie. Now the magpie is known to be a chatty, noisy bird, but she is the cleverest of birds when it comes to building a nest. That is why all the birds wanted her to teach them how.

Magpies are sleek and glossy with shiny black feathers. Their abdomens, or undersides, are white, and they have patches of white on their wings. Sometimes, depending on the way the light shines, a magpie looks blue, green, or purple. Magpies' relatives are the crows and jays. What distinguishes magpies, or sets them apart, from other birds is an unusually long tail.

So Madge, as she was named, called all the birds around her. First came the thrush with plump, soft feathers and one of the best singing voices of all the birds. Then came the blackbird. The female blackbird was actually dark brown in color, and all the birds knew she had a loud voice. The owl stood out from the others. What separates the owl from the other birds is her wide head, ruff of feathers, and hooked beak. The owl's sharp claws are called talons. Next, the small, brownish sparrow appeared. Although plain, the sparrow is popular because he sings pleasantly. Another songbird, the starling, came to learn about nest building. The starling's feathers are black with a greenish-purple shine. He has pointed wings, a short tail, and a sharp bill. Last of all, came the turtledove, a small, slender, graceful bird that makes soft, cooing sounds.

Once all the birds were assembled, Madge took some mud and formed it into a round cake. At that, the thrush said, "Oh, that's how it's done," and away she flew. Today that is how all thrushes build their nests.

GO ON →

Next Madge took some twigs and put them around in the cake of mud. With that, the blackbird exclaimed, “Now I know all about building a nest,” and off she flew. That is how the blackbirds make their nests to this very day.

Then Madge put another layer of mud over the twigs. “Oh, that’s quite apparent,” said the owl. “It’s obvious now.” Away she flew. Since then owls have never made better nests. In fact, they usually just use the old nests of other birds, such as hawks and crows, or even holes in trees and ledges in caves.

After this Madge began to gather some more twigs and wind them around the outside of the nest. “The very thing!” called out the sparrow, and off she went. So sparrows collect twigs and make messy nests to this day.

Now Madge took some feathers and other stuff and lined the nest to make it very comfortable. “That suits me,” cried the starling, and off he flew. You see, with starlings, the male starts the nest and decorates it with ornaments like flowers. Then the female comes along and helps finish it. Starlings have very comfortable nests even today.

So that is how the lesson went. Each bird learned a little bit about how to build a nest and left before Madge was finished.

Meanwhile, Madge worked and worked. The only bird left was the turtledove. The problem was that the turtledove had not paid any attention but instead kept repeating a silly cry, “Take two, Taffy, take two-o-o-o.”

Madge, the magpie, heard this just as she was putting a twig across the nest. She said, “One’s enough.”

The turtledove kept saying, “Take two, Taffy, take two-o-o-o.”

Madge became angry and said, “One’s enough I tell you,” but still she cried, “Take two, Taffy, take two-o-o-o.”

At last Madge looked up and saw nobody near but the silly turtledove. Then Madge became even angrier and flew away. She refused to tell the birds how to build nests again. And that is why different birds build their nests differently to this day.

GO ON →

Name: ______________________________ Date: ________

Now answer Numbers 11 through 20. Base your answers on "The Magpie's Nest."

11 If the passage were written from the turtledove's point of view, the reader would know

Ⓐ what Madge thought of the turtledove.

Ⓑ what different birds feed the babies in their nests.

Ⓒ how Madge learned to build a superior kind of nest.

Ⓓ why the turtledove was not paying attention during the lesson.

12 Read the following sentence from the passage.

Magpies are sleek and glossy with shiny black feathers.

What word has almost the same meaning as the word *sleek* in the sentence above?

Ⓕ dark

Ⓖ smooth

Ⓗ thin

Ⓘ well-known

13 Read this sentence from the passage.

Their abdomens, or undersides, are white, and they have patches of white on their wings.

What word has almost the same meaning as *abdomens*?

Ⓐ bellies

Ⓑ eyes

Ⓒ feathers

Ⓓ throats

GO ON →

Name: _______________________________ Date: __________

14 Madge thinks that the turtledove

Ⓕ is silly.

Ⓖ is frightening.

Ⓗ has a very loud song.

Ⓘ should use more twigs in her nest.

15 What is the theme of this passage?

Ⓐ Those who work the hardest are rewarded.

Ⓑ What we build in life does not have to be perfect.

Ⓒ Everyone must work together to get the job done right.

Ⓓ Those who do not listen to all the directions may miss important steps.

16 Which pair of words from the passage have almost the same meaning?

Ⓕ beak, ruff

Ⓖ gather, collect

Ⓗ pleasant, chatty

Ⓘ slender, plump

17 Read this sentence from the passage.

The owl's sharp claws are called talons.

What does the word *talons* mean in the sentence above?

Ⓐ wings

Ⓑ nails on feet

Ⓒ parts of door locks

Ⓓ hooked beaks on birds

GO ON →

Name: ______________________ Date: ______

18 What evidence from the text shows the thrush's idea about making a nest?

Ⓕ The thrush has one of the best singing voices of all the birds.

Ⓖ The female helps finish the nest after the male bird begins it.

Ⓗ Madge put twigs around the cake of mud to make it more comfortable.

Ⓘ The thrush said, "That's how it's done," after Madge formed mud into a cake.

19 Read the following sentences from the passage.

"Oh, that's quite apparent," said the owl. "It's obvious now."

Which word has the OPPOSITE meaning of the word *apparent?*

Ⓐ clever

Ⓑ plain

Ⓒ unclear

Ⓓ unique

20 Based on text evidence, with which of the following statements would the narrator most likely agree?

Ⓕ The magpie is the silliest of all the birds.

Ⓖ The sparrow sings too much and disrupts the lesson.

Ⓗ All the birds would build better nests if they had stayed for the lesson.

Ⓘ All birds could learn from the owl and save time by using other birds' old nests.

STOP

Name: ______________________ Date: __________

21 Compare and contrast how the two tales are told. How does the point of view affect what we learn in the stories? Give evidence from the text.

Answer Key

Name: ______________________

Question	Correct Answer	Content Focus	CCSS	Complexity
1	B	Point of View	RL.5.6	DOK 2
2	F	Synonyms and Antonyms	L.5.5c	DOK 1
3	C	Context Clues: Sentence Clues	L.5.4a	DOK 2
4	H	Point of View	RL.5.6	DOK 3
5	B	Synonyms and Antonyms	L.5.5c	DOK 2
6	I	Theme	RL.5.2	DOK 3
7	B	Synonyms and Antonyms	L.5.5c	DOK 1
8	G	Point of View	RL.5.6	DOK 3
9	C	Synonyms and Antonyms	L.5.5c	DOK 2
10	H	Point of View	RL.5.6	DOK 3
11	D	Point of View	RL.5.6	DOK 3
12	G	Synonyms and Antonyms	L.5.5c	DOK 3
13	A	Synonyms and Antonyms	L.5.5c	DOK 3
14	F	Point of View	RL.5.6	DOK 2
15	D	Theme	RL.5.2	DOK 3
16	G	Synonyms and Antonyms	L.5.5c	DOK 1
17	B	Context Clues: Definitions and Restatements	L.5.4a	DOK 2
18	I	Point of View	RL.5.6	DOK 3
19	C	Synonyms and Antonyms	L.5.5c	DOK 2
20	H	Point of View	RL.5.6	DOK 3
21	see below	Comparing Across Texts	RL.5.9	DOK 3

Comprehension 1, 4, 6, 8, 10, 11, 14, 15, 18, 20	/10	%
Vocabulary 2, 3, 5, 7, 9, 12, 13, 16, 17, 19	/10	%
Total Weekly Assessment Score	/20	%

21 To receive full credit, the following information should be included: "A Giant of a Man" is told in the first person, and "The Magpie's Nest" is in the third person. "A Giant of a Man" gives the personal point of view of a logger who worked on one of Bunyan's crews. In contrast, the point of view in "The Magpie's Nest" is that of a detached outside observer of the action.

Read "The Case of the Missing Sandwiches" before answering Numbers 1 through 10.

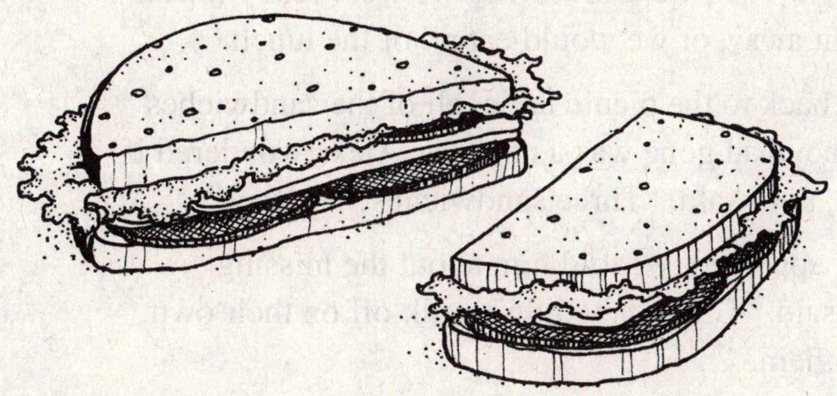

The Case of the Missing Sandwiches

Hi, I'm Mikayla, and my best friend is Alexa. When Mom describes us, she says, "Birds of a feather flock together." She means we are alike, and she's right. We are both eleven, and we both like movies, popcorn, and baseball. We have been friends for awhile, so we've had many adventures. Let me tell you about the latest one. It shows that we always should expect the unexpected.

Alexa and I went with our dogs, Sparky and Fetch, on a picnic, but my mom laid down one rule. Garrett, my brother, was going fishing, and we had to stay with him. I don't know if you have an older brother, but if you do, you know how bossy he can be. Garrett doesn't like for me to tag along with him either.

Alexa and I enjoy watching the ducks on the river, while Garrett fishes. As soon as we got to the picnic spot, Garrett told us not to leave there and went off with his tackle box and fishing pole.

Alexa and I played catch with the dogs. Then we watched some white ibis with orange, hooked beaks as they searched for insects in the grass. A blue heron flew over and landed not far away.

We were hungry, actually ravenous, so we opened the cooler and put the egg salad sandwiches on a plate. Before we could unwrap the ham and cheese sandwiches, we heard Garrett shout, "Mikayla! Alexa! Come quickly!"

GO ON →

We took off running, not knowing what to expect. At the riverbank, Garrett was trying to reel in a bass. We spent some time admiring the huge fish. Then we told Garrett we were ready to eat. He should come right away, or we would eat all of the lunch.

When we got back to the picnic table, all of the sandwiches were gone! Where they had gone was a mystery. Alexa wondered if a squirrel took them, but I said, "Three sandwiches? No way."

When Garrett appeared, we told him about the missing sandwiches, and he said, "Girls, they didn't walk off on their own. Maybe the dogs ate them."

Alexa said, "Sparky doesn't like eggs."

At the same time, I said, "Fetch hates eggs, and besides the dogs are asleep in the sun."

Garrett said, "Have you seen anyone?"

"No one," Alexa said.

Garrett asked, "Did you see anything else?"

Alexa said, "We saw some ibis, but they were eating insects."

"We saw a blue heron, but it wouldn't eat a sandwich," I said.

Garrett said, "If you had left out shrimp, a heron would have taken your lunch, but, no, a heron would not go for egg salad."

"So what did happen?" I asked.

Garrett pointed to the tree. "Those ravens perched there are like big crows. See how they watch the table? They are scavengers, so I think that they swooped down and took the sandwiches."

Alexa said, "The mystery is solved, but what about lunch?"

Garrett said, "I would divide up the ham and cheese sandwiches. If we're still hungry, I'll get us sandwiches at the stand."

"That's a good solution, Garrett," said Alexa. I had to agree that older brothers are sometimes helpful. As Mom always says, "Two heads are better than one," but this time, it took three heads to solve the mystery of the missing sandwiches.

GO ON →

Name: ______________________________ Date: ________

Now answer Numbers 1 through 10. Base your answers on "The Case of the Missing Sandwiches."

1 Who is the narrator of the passage?

Ⓐ Alexa

Ⓑ Garrett

Ⓒ Mikayla

Ⓓ A third-person observer of the action

2 Read this sentence from the passage.

When Mom describes us, she says, "Birds of a feather flock together."

What does "Birds of a feather flock together" mean?

Ⓕ Everyone should have as many friends as possible.

Ⓖ Birds from northern areas migrate south in the winter.

Ⓗ Birds live in flocks, unlike people who live in families.

Ⓘ People, like birds, associate with those who are like themselves.

3 Read this sentence from the passage.

We were hungry, actually ravenous, so we opened the cooler and put the egg salad sandwiches on a plate.

Which word is OPPOSITE in meaning to *ravenous* as used in the sentence above?

Ⓐ full

Ⓑ furious

Ⓒ glad

Ⓓ prepared

GO ON →

Name: ______________________________ Date: ________

4 Read this sentence from the passage.

It shows that we always should expect the unexpected.

What does "expect the unexpected" mean?

Ⓕ Life is full of surprises.

Ⓖ Imagination usually leads us astray.

Ⓗ What we think will happen never does.

Ⓘ It is unrealistic to expect all wishes to be fulfilled.

5 What is the main problem in the passage?

Ⓐ Mikayla wants to get along better with her brother.

Ⓑ Mikayla and Alexa are friends but have argued lately.

Ⓒ Alexa and Mikayla want to eat but must wait for Garrett.

Ⓓ Mikayla and Alexa want to solve the case of the missing sandwiches.

6 How does Mikayla's attitude change at the end of the passage?

Ⓕ She is sorry she went on the picnic.

Ⓖ She wishes she had left Fetch at home.

Ⓗ She is more upset than ever with Garrett.

Ⓘ She now thinks that Garrett can be helpful.

7 Read this sentence from the passage.

At the riverbank, Garrett was trying to reel in a bass.

Which definition fits *bass* as it is used in the sentence above?

Ⓐ the lowest part

Ⓑ a low-pitched sound

Ⓒ a musical instrument

Ⓓ a type of freshwater fish

GO ON →

Name: ______________________________ Date: ________

8 Why does Mikayla say, "We are both eleven, and we both like movies, popcorn, and baseball"?

Ⓕ It explains why they like picnics.

Ⓖ It shows that they are ordinary girls.

Ⓗ It shows that she and Alexa have many things in common.

Ⓘ It describes why the girls want to take their dogs on the picnic.

9 What is the theme of this passage?

Ⓐ Best friends stick together.

Ⓑ Brothers are a pain in the neck.

Ⓒ Dogs do not like egg sandwiches.

Ⓓ Sharing ideas can help solve mysteries.

10 Read this sentence from the passage.

As Mom always says, "Two heads are better than one," but this time, it took three heads to solve the mystery of the missing sandwiches.

What does "Two heads are better than one" mean?

Ⓕ A mom always knows best.

Ⓖ Sharing ideas can be helpful.

Ⓗ Every group needs a leader to make decisions.

Ⓘ One person cannot ever solve a problem without help.

GO ON →

Read "Who Were the Spiders?" before answering Numbers 11 through 20.

Who Were the Spiders?

The Cooper family was about to move because Dad had a new job in Colorado. He had been out of work for a year, and Natalie and Mason knew he had been unhappy. Now, a new job was making things look better. As Dad said, "Every cloud has a silver lining."

Dad was already in Colorado, but Mom stayed behind so that the twins Natalie and Mason could finish fifth grade at Oak School. Today, Natalie and Mason were helping pack boxes. They enjoyed looking at the old treasures, especially the photo albums.

Mason found many photos, and Natalie picked up one of a baseball team. The men's uniforms had CLEVELAND printed on them. Someone had written 1895 on the photo. Natalie asked, "Why is this photo here? The year is more than one hundred years ago."

Mason asked Mom, "Is there a famous baseball player in our family?"

"I don't know of anyone in my family, but maybe there was someone in your dad's family," she said. "Remind me to ask about the photo when I talk to your dad tonight."

GO ON →

That night Dad called, and Mason was eager to talk to him. "Dad, we found a photo today of a baseball team that played in 1895. Did one of your relatives play on a team a long time ago?"

Dad said, "It's familiar, but I don't know the story. Some of the photos are my father's. Why don't you call him and see if he knows."

Grandpa Ken recalled that a relative played for a Cleveland team. It was a cousin of his great-grandfather whose last name was Zimmer. Grandpa suggested they look up early Cleveland teams.

Mason and Natalie headed for the computer and found a baseball encyclopedia. They clicked on "Teams" and found links to "Active Franchises" and "Earlier Franchises." Mason knew that a franchise is a name for a professional sports team. Under "Earlier Franchises" they found three teams: Cleveland Blue, 1879–1884; Cleveland Infants, 1890–1890; and Cleveland Spiders, 1887–1899.

Mason shouted, "We found the answer! Our 1895 photo must show the Cleveland Spiders."

Natalie said, "You might be right. Let's find out about them."

They looked for Cleveland Spiders and found the headline, "Grand Opening. About Nine Thousand People See the First Game." A new Cleveland ballpark had opened on May 2, 1891. Cy Young was the starting pitcher, and Zimmer was listed as one of the players. "That's the cousin of our great-great-grandfather!" said Natalie.

Mom said, "That means he played on the same team as Cy Young, who won more games than any other pitcher in history. He was an exceptional pitcher."

Mason wanted to know more, so they searched a baseball almanac. Natalie saw a list of players, and Zimmer was a catcher in 1895. The team came in second that year. She also read that in 1899, the Spiders were baseball's worst team. Natalie checked the 1899 team. There was Zimmer again. "Oh, well, you can't win them all," she said.

Mom then said, "Early to bed and early to rise makes a man healthy, wealthy, and wise." They would have to find out more about the Cleveland Spiders tomorrow.

GO ON →

Name: ______________________________ Date: ________

Now answer Numbers 11 through 20. Base your answers on "Who Were the Spiders?"

11 If the passage were written from Mom's point of view, the reader might know

Ⓐ what Mom thought about the move to Colorado.

Ⓑ how Cy Young felt about playing for the Spiders.

Ⓒ Natalie's inner thoughts about moving from Cleveland.

Ⓓ what Mason thought the new school in Colorado would be like.

12 Read these sentences from the passage.

> **Now, a new job was making things look better. As Dad said, "Every cloud has a silver lining."**

What does "Every cloud has a silver lining" mean?

Ⓕ Winning is not everything.

Ⓖ There is never a right time.

Ⓗ Every problem has some good effect as well.

Ⓘ Clouds in the sky that produce rain may be silver underneath.

13 Who is the narrator of the passage?

Ⓐ Mason

Ⓑ Natalie

Ⓒ Grandpa Ken

Ⓓ an outside observer of the action

GO ON →

Name: ______________________________ Date: ________

14 Read this sentence from the passage.

The men's uniforms had CLEVELAND printed on them.

Which word has the same root as *uniform*?

Ⓕ forest
Ⓖ forget
Ⓗ transform
Ⓘ unicycle

15 Read this sentence from the passage.

Mason knew that a franchise is a name for a professional sports team.

What does the word *franchise* mean in the sentence above?

Ⓐ a sport
Ⓑ a baseball league
Ⓒ a professional baseball player
Ⓓ a sports team with professional players

16 What shows that Mason and Natalie were excited after finding information about the baseball photo?

Ⓕ They helped pack boxes.
Ⓖ They wanted to know more and searched an almanac.
Ⓗ They knew that a franchise describes a sports team.
Ⓘ They knew that their Dad had been unhappy.

17 Read these sentences from the passage.

Mom said, "That means he played on the same team as Cy Young, who won more games than any other pitcher in history. He was an exceptional pitcher."

Which word is most similar in meaning to *exceptional* as used in the sentence above?

Ⓐ average
Ⓑ curious
Ⓒ known
Ⓓ rare

GO ON →

Name: ______________________________ Date: ________

18 Read these sentences from the passage.

Mason wanted to know more, so they searched a baseball almanac. Natalie saw a list of players, and Zimmer was a catcher in 1895.

How does this sentence support the theme?

Ⓕ It explains the team's name.

Ⓖ It demonstrates Mason's interest in baseball.

Ⓗ It gives the sequence of events in Zimmer's career.

Ⓘ It shows that Mason and Natalie are discovering more about the photo.

19 Read these sentences from the passage.

Mom then said, "Early to bed and early to rise makes a man healthy, wealthy, and wise." They would have to find out more about the Cleveland Spiders tomorrow.

What does "Early to bed and early to rise makes a man healthy, wealthy, and wise" mean?

Ⓐ Good health requires hard work.

Ⓑ Rich people get up at dawn to start working.

Ⓒ It is good to both go to bed and get up early.

Ⓓ There is always another day to finish a task that is begun.

20 In the second to last paragraph of the passage, the narrator makes it clear that

Ⓕ Natalie is realistic.

Ⓖ Mason is very tired.

Ⓗ Mason is not realistic.

Ⓘ Mom has lost interest in the Spiders.

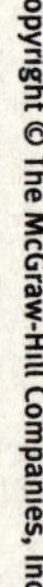

STOP

Name: ______________________ Date: __________

21 Both selections involve solving mysteries. How does point of view affect the telling of each story? Use text evidence to support your answer.

Answer Key Name: ____________________

Question	Correct Answer	Content Focus	CCSS	Complexity
1	C	Point of View	RL.5.6	DOK 2
2	I	Adages and Proverbs	L.5.5b	DOK 2
3	A	Synonyms and Antonyms	L.5.5c	DOK 1
4	F	Adages and Proverbs	L.5.5b	DOK 2
5	D	Character, Setting, Plot: Problem and Solution	RL.4.3	DOK 2
6	I	Point of View	RL.5.6	DOK 3
7	D	Homographs	L.5.5c	DOK 1
8	H	Point of View	RL.5.6	DOK 3
9	D	Theme	RL.5.2	DOK 3
10	G	Adages and Proverbs	L.5.5b	DOK 2
11	A	Point of View	RL.5.6	DOK 3
12	H	Adages and Proverbs	L.5.5b	DOK 2
13	D	Point of View	RL.5.6	DOK 3
14	H	Latin Roots	L.5.4b	DOK 1
15	D	Context Clues: Definitions and Restatements	L.5.4a	DOK 2
16	G	Point of View	RL.5.6	DOK 3
17	D	Synonyms and Antonyms	L.5.5c	DOK 2
18	I	Theme	RL.5.2	DOK 3
19	C	Adages and Proverbs	L.5.5b	DOK 2
20	F	Point of View	RL.5.6	DOK 3
21	see below	Point of View	RL.5.6	DOK 3

Comprehension 1, 5, 6, 8, 9, 11, 13, 16, 18, 20	/10	%
Vocabulary 2, 3, 4, 7, 10, 12, 14, 15, 17, 19	/10	%
Total Weekly Assessment Score	/20	%

21 To receive full credit for the response, the following information should be included: "The Case of the Missing Sandwiches" is told from the first-person point of view. In contrast, "Who Were the Spiders?" is told from the third-person point of view. This means that in "The Case of the Missing Sandwiches" the reader learns about the events as Mikayla sees them, but in "Who Were the Spiders?" the reader sees events through the eyes of an outside observer who knows the thoughts of all the characters.

Read the article "Small Loan, Big Effect" before answering Numbers 1 through 10.

Small Loan, Big Effect

In a small village in Nepal, a young woman wanted to start a tailor shop. She wanted to make clothes to sell. She did not have enough money, however, to get started. It was impossible for her to obtain a loan from a big bank; she knew she could never get the money from them. So she applied for a microloan.

What is a microloan? It is a loan of a small amount of money to a person or group. Some are made by banks or large organizations. Others are made by individuals. Microloans can go a long way in changing peoples' lives for the better. For example, a loan of as little as twenty-five dollars can allow the tailor in Nepal to buy the material needed to make several items of clothing. The tailor can then sell the clothes and make enough money to buy more material. If the tailor is careful, she can make enough to buy a sewing machine to make even more clothes. Then her business can really take off!

Microloans are made to people in developing countries in Africa, Asia, and South America. These people do not have access to banks. People in the United States can benefit from microloans too.

GO ON →

The loans are becoming increasingly popular. The World Bank believes that 160 million people around the world are now benefiting from microloans. Not all of these loans are used to start businesses. Some help families send their children to school or allow them to take classes to learn new skills. Some help farmers pay for seed, so their harvests will be bigger and earn the farmers more money.

For some people, the loans have a great effect. A carpenter in Afghanistan named Behnam received a $465 microloan. He used it to expand his carpentry business. With his larger business, he is able to provide more and better food and clothing for his four children. Lucas, who lives in Mozambique, used microloans to buy chickens and to irrigate his farmland. Now he is able to employ four people and to send his children to school. Beatrice, who lives in Kenya, started with a microloan of less than forty dollars. She used the money to buy vegetables, which she sold at local markets. Now she has a much larger business and sells to other businesses. Asaed, who lives in Jordan, used a microloan to buy some old machines, which he repaired and sold. Now he builds and sells machines that make hummus, a local food. An American woman named Liliana received a $500 loan and was able to open a day-care center where she cares for young children near Boston, Massachusetts.

Microloans often help other people in a community as well as the person who receives the loan. When the person's business does well, it brings money into a community. This makes a noticeable difference and helps other businesses sell or do more. Groups involved in microloans find that what is good for one person is also good for those around that person. Often, people who get microloans will repeatedly apply for loans to improve their businesses. This may, in turn, help the community even more.

What about paying these loans back? After all, a loan is not a gift. The people who receive microloans are often very poor. Are they less likely to pay back the loan? The answer might be surprising. Over ninety-seven percent of microloans are paid back! So microloans are a very good way of helping people help themselves, and doing it with little risk.

GO ON →

Name: ______________________________ Date: ________

Now answer Numbers 1 through 10. Base your answers on "Small Loan, Big Impact."

1 Read this sentence from the article.

> **It was impossible for her to obtain a loan from a big bank; she knew she could never get the money from them.**

What word in the sentence helps the reader understand what *obtain* means?

Ⓐ impossible
Ⓑ knew
Ⓒ never
Ⓓ get

2 Read this sentence from the article.

> **So she applied for a microloan.**

The prefix *micro–* means "very small" or "involving something very small." Therefore, a *microbiologist* is probably someone who studies

Ⓕ wildlife.
Ⓖ farm animals.
Ⓗ various plants.
Ⓘ tiny forms of life.

3 What do the details in the first paragraph on page 206 have in common?

Ⓐ They all tell how microloans help the community.
Ⓑ They all tell how difficult microloans can be to pay back.
Ⓒ They all tell how microloans have improved people's lives.
Ⓓ They all tell how hard it is to make a living in developing countries.

GO ON →

Name: ______________________________ Date: __________

4. Read this sentence from the article.

When the person's business does well, it brings money into a community.

What point of view of the author does this evidence from the text support?

Ⓕ Microloans will be paid back faster if communities help.

Ⓖ Microloans can help communities as well as individuals.

Ⓗ Microloans should be given to communities, not just people.

Ⓘ A person who gets a microloan will often apply for another one.

5. Read this sentence from the article.

This makes a noticeable difference and helps other businesses sell or do more.

The suffix *-able* means *able to be.* Which answer choice uses *-able* in the same way as *noticeable*?

Ⓐ cable

Ⓑ enjoyable

Ⓒ stable

Ⓓ table

6. What text evidence supports the author's point that microloans are not very risky?

Ⓕ People use microloans to start small businesses.

Ⓖ Microloans can help people pay for an education.

Ⓗ Ninety-seven percent of microloans are paid back.

Ⓘ Microloans have helped people in Africa and Asia.

GO ON →

Name: ______________________________ Date: ________

❼ What evidence in the text supports the author's point that microloans help individuals?

Ⓐ Microloans are becoming more and more popular.

Ⓑ A microloan provides a small amount of money to people.

Ⓒ Families use microloans to send children to school.

Ⓓ People in the United States can use microloans.

❽ Read this sentence from the article.

Often, people who get microloans will repeatedly apply for loans to improve their businesses.

If *repeated* means "done again," what does *repeatedly* mean?

Ⓕ done over and over

Ⓖ done once more

Ⓗ done less often

Ⓘ not often done

❾ Read this sentence from the article.

The loans are becoming increasingly popular.

If *increasing* means "growing," what does *increasingly* mean?

Ⓐ quietly

Ⓑ slowly

Ⓒ less and less

Ⓓ more and more

❿ From text evidence, it is clear that the author believes

Ⓕ microloans help people, not communities.

Ⓖ lenders take a risk when they give microloans.

Ⓗ microloans can change people's lives for the better.

Ⓘ only people in developing countries use microloans.

GO ON →

Read the article "The Courage of Mum Bett" before answering Numbers 11 through 20.

The Courage of Mum Bett

Around the year 1742, a woman named Elizabeth was born a slave. She had no last name. She and her younger sister Lizzie grew up in the household of Pieter Hogeboom, a Dutch landowner. He lived in the Hudson Valley of New York State. Elizabeth and Lizzie were either sold or given by the Hogeboom family to the Ashley family of Sheffield, Massachusetts.

Elizabeth lived in the Ashley household for about thirty years. There are not many documents that give information about her early life. The facts are difficult to determine. Records state that she married and had a child. By that time, she was known as "Mum Bett," and her daughter was called "Little Bett." Her husband fought in the American Revolution. He was probably killed in battle.

John Ashley, the head of the Ashley household, was an important man in eighteenth-century Massachusetts. He was a lawyer and a judge. He was involved in writing the state constitution, which established the laws of the state. The constitution, adopted in 1780, included a statement called the Sheffield Declaration. It said, "Mankind in a State of Nature are equal, free, and independent of each other, and have a right to the undisturbed Enjoyment of their lives, their Liberty and Property."

No one knows just how Mum Bett learned about this statement. Some sources say she overheard a discussion about it when serving at the family table or working around the house. Others say she heard the Sheffield Declaration read aloud at the village meetinghouse. Either way, the statement made her think about the injustice of slavery.

GO ON →

No one is sure, either, what drove Mum Bett to act. One story claims that Mrs. Ashley discovered that Mum Bett's sister Lizzie had made a cake for herself. Furious, she tried to strike Lizzie with a hot shovel. Unafraid, Mum Bett pushed Lizzie aside. The shovel hit her own arm instead of Lizzie's, injuring and burning it.

Mum Bett left the Ashley house and refused to return. The Ashleys tried to use the law to bring her back. At that time, slavery was legal in Massachusetts. Mum Bett went to a lawyer named Theodore Sedgewick, who was known for his anti-slavery views. She asked him to help file a lawsuit for her freedom. Sedgewick agreed. Another slave, a man named Brom, joined in the lawsuit. Sedgewick sued for their freedom. Since the state constitution was now law, Sedgewick claimed that Ashley was acting unlawfully by enslaving Mum Bett.

The case was tried in 1781, and in August of that year, Sedgewick won the case. There is no record of what happened to Brom after the trial. The court fined Ashley, and Mum Bett was freed. Other similar cases were tried in Massachusetts, and finally, in 1783, slavery was outlawed in the state. Massachusetts was only the third state in the U.S. to ban slavery, and it did so more than eighty years before slavery was banned in the country as a whole.

Mum Bett took the last name Freeman and went to work as a paid servant for the Sedgewicks, staying with them until she was able to buy her own house. The family loved and relied on her. In an uprising called Shays' Rebellion, she defended the Sedgewicks' house against rebels who tried to enter and loot it. Holding a shovel and using her wits, she convinced the rebels to leave. Mum Bett died in 1829 and is buried in the Sedgewick family burial plot.

Mum Bett Freeman could not read or write. She never had the opportunity to become educated, but she had strong beliefs, and she was courageous. Without Mum Bett's daring and inspiring efforts, the Massachusetts law allowing slavery would have remained unchanged. Thousands of men and women would have continued living in slavery for years more.

GO ON →

Name: ______________________________ Date: ________

Now answer Numbers 11 through 20. Base your answers on "The Courage of Mum Bett."

11 Read this sentence from the article.

He was involved in writing the state constitution, which established the laws of the state.

Which word in the sentence helps the reader understand what *constitution* means?

Ⓐ involved

Ⓑ laws

Ⓒ state

Ⓓ writing

12 Read this sentence from the article.

Either way, the statement made her think about the injustice of slavery.

The prefix *in-* can mean "in" or "not." Which answer choice uses *in-* in the same way as *injustice*?

Ⓕ income

Ⓖ independence

Ⓗ infield

Ⓘ inhabit

13 What do the details in the next to last paragraph of the article have in common?

Ⓐ They all tell about the injustice of slavery.

Ⓑ They all tell about the laws of Massachusetts.

Ⓒ They all tell about the lawsuit that freed Mum Bett.

Ⓓ They all tell what Mum Bett did after she was freed.

GO ON →

Name: ______________________________ Date: ________

14 Read this sentence from the article.

Thousands of men and women would have continued living in slavery for years more.

Which point does this text evidence support?

Ⓕ Massachusetts should not have allowed slavery.

Ⓖ It is hard to find information on Mum Bett's early life.

Ⓗ Mum Bett's actions changed many people's lives.

Ⓘ Sedgewick was a very powerful man.

15 Read this sentence from the article.

Unafraid, Mum Bett pushed Lizzie aside.

The word *unafraid* suggests that Mum Bett was

Ⓐ brave.

Ⓑ fast.

Ⓒ strong.

Ⓓ wise.

16 Read this sentence from the article.

She never had the opportunity to become educated, but she had strong beliefs, and she was courageous.

Since *courage* means "bravery," what does *courageous* mean?

Ⓕ without bravery

Ⓖ with bravery

Ⓗ never brave

Ⓘ once brave

17 Based on the text evidence, the author most likely thinks that Mum Bett

Ⓐ was not patient.

Ⓑ was mostly lucky.

Ⓒ should be admired.

Ⓓ took unnecessary risks.

GO ON →

Name: ______________________________ Date: ________

18 What text evidence supports the author's point that Mum Bett was intelligent?

Ⓕ She married and had a child.

Ⓖ She worked for the Sedgewicks for many years.

Ⓗ She used the law of the time to gain her freedom.

Ⓘ She took the name "Freeman" when she was freed.

19 Read this sentence from the article.

Without Mum Bett's daring and inspiring efforts, the Massachusetts law allowing slavery would have remained unchanged.

A law that is *unchanged* is

Ⓐ harsh.

Ⓑ not fair.

Ⓒ the same.

Ⓓ different.

20 With which statement would the author most likely agree?

Ⓕ Mum Bett had a good life.

Ⓖ Mum Bett was very determined.

Ⓗ Massachusetts was a good place to live.

Ⓘ Massachusetts was slow to change its laws.

STOP

Name: ______________________________ Date: __________

21 How are the authors' points of view about their subjects similar? Use text evidence to support your answer.

Answer Key

Name: ______________________

Question	Correct Answer	Content Focus	CCSS	Complexity
1	D	Context Clues: Sentence Clues	L.5.4a	DOK 2
2	I	Prefixes and Suffixes	L.3.4b	DOK 1
3	C	Main Idea and Key Details	RI.5.2	DOK 1
4	G	Author's Point of View	RI.5.8	DOK 3
5	B	Prefixes and Suffixes	L.3.4b	DOK 1
6	H	Author's Point of View	RI.5.8	DOK 3
7	C	Author's Point of View	RI.5.8	DOK 3
8	F	Prefixes and Suffixes	L.3.4b	DOK 1
9	D	Prefixes and Suffixes	L.3.4b	DOK 1
10	H	Author's Point of View	RI.5.8	DOK 3
11	B	Context Clues: Sentence Clues	L.5.4a	DOK 2
12	G	Prefixes and Suffixes	L.3.4b	DOK 1
13	D	Main Idea and Key Details	RI.5.2	DOK 2
14	H	Author's Point of View	RI.5.8	DOK 3
15	A	Prefixes and Suffixes	L.3.4b	DOK 1
16	G	Prefixes and Suffixes	L.3.4b	DOK 1
17	C	Author's Point of View	RI.5.8	DOK 3
18	H	Author's Point of View	RI.5.8	DOK 3
19	C	Prefixes and Suffixes	L.3.4b	DOK 1
20	G	Author's Point of View	RI.6.6	DOK 3
21	see below	Author's Point of View	RI.5.8	DOK 3

Comprehension 3, 4, 6, 7, 10, 13, 14, 17, 18, 20	/10	%
Vocabulary 1, 2, 5, 8, 9, 11, 12, 15, 16, 19	/10	%
Total Weekly Assessment Score	/20	%

21 To receive full credit for the response, the following information should be included: Both authors have a positive view of their subjects. The author of the first article believes microloans have changed many people's lives, and the author of the second sees Mum Bett's actions as helping to free thousands of people from slavery.

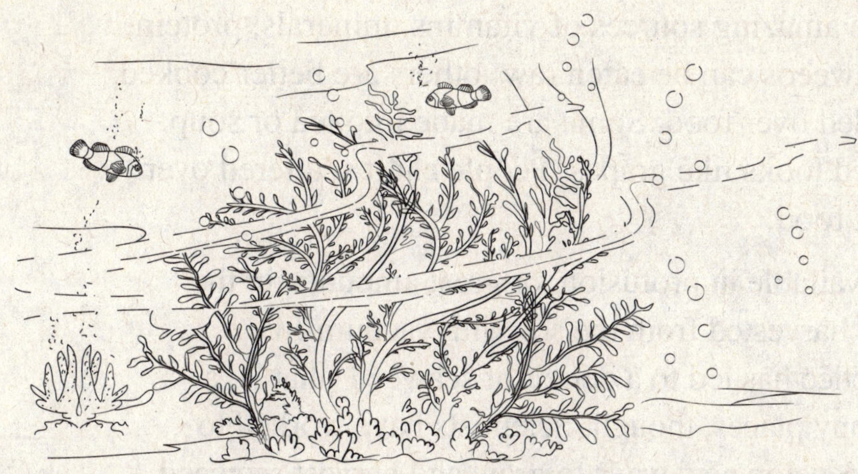

Read the article "Food of the Future" before answering Numbers 1 through 10.

Food of the Future

Anyone who has gone swimming in the ocean knows the feeling of seaweed as it brushes against you. It is a little slimy, a little icky. But seaweed is not just a weed. It is also a vegetable, just like broccoli and green beans are. Millions of people eat it. And millions more might find it on their dining room tables in the future.

In much of the United States, people do not eat seaweed. It has become popular in Hawaii and California, though. But in many Asian countries, in the British Isles, in Canada, and in the Caribbean, it has been a part of people's diet for a long time. In Scotland, for example, people have eaten a kind of seaweed called dulse for more than a thousand years! In fact, people who live on the coast have probably been eating seaweed since the earliest days of humans.

Most people in the U.S. have probably eaten seaweed in one form or another too. You might not even know you have eaten it! Agar agar, a jelly-like substance, is made from seaweed. This material is used to thicken many different kinds of foods, such as pies and puddings, ice cream, yogurt, and salad dressings.

GO ON →

Seaweeds are amazing sources of vitamins, minerals, protein, and fiber. Some seaweeds can be eaten raw; others are better cooked, or dried and sprinkled over food. Some are made into tea or soup. One kind of seaweed looks like grapes. People eat it scattered over salads or as a snack food.

Seaweed is available in profusion, or great amounts, in the ocean. Some of it is harvested from the sea with vacuum-like machines. This practice has led to a deficit of seaweed (that is, a shortage of it) in many places, though. Scientists have worked to persuade people to develop new ways to grow and harvest seaweed. Now, seaweed "farmers" grow different kinds of seaweeds in coastal waters. Some seaweeds are grown on ropes that rest in the water. Some kinds are grown on nets. In Canada, farmers grow seaweed onshore, in tanks, but this does not work for every kind of seaweed. Some seaweeds require the active movement of seawater to grow well.

Seaweed harvesters wash the vegetables with seawater. Some plants are dried in the sun; others are packed and sold fresh. Because seawater is salty, most kinds of seaweeds are salty too.

Seaweed has other uses besides providing nutrition for humans by giving them a healthful food. Some of it is dried and made into fertilizer, a material that improves soil. Because seaweed is so full of vitamins and minerals, it is great for soil, helping plants to grow faster and better. It can be added to animal feed to make it better for the animals. It can also be found in makeup, skin lotions, and bath products. And seaweed helps to give your toothpaste its gel-like smoothness.

Scientists have begun working on making seaweed into fuel. No one knows yet whether this experiment will work. If it does, seaweed could provide a great source of fuel. It grows more quickly than other plants used to make fuel and is less expensive.

Seaweed is easy to grow, and its cultivation—that is, the farming of it—does not take the place of other crops. Because of this, some people consider it the food of the future. Before too long, we could be seeing it on menus and supermarket shelves around the world.

GO ON →

Name: ______________________________ Date: ________

Now answer Numbers 1 through 10. Base your answers on "Food of the Future."

1 Read this sentence from the article.

Seaweed is available in profusion, or great amounts, in the ocean.

What does *profusion* mean in the sentence above?

Ⓐ less than enough

Ⓑ a very large quantity

Ⓒ just the right amount

Ⓓ an amount that changes

2 What paragraph on page 218 would the following detail best support?

Maybe someday our cars will be powered by seaweed.

Ⓕ paragraph 2

Ⓖ paragraph 3

Ⓗ paragraph 4

Ⓘ paragraph 5

3 Read this sentence from the article.

It grows more quickly than other plants used to make fuel and is less expensive.

What point of the author does the text evidence best support?

Ⓐ Seaweed has many different uses.

Ⓑ Seaweed could be a great source of fuel.

Ⓒ Seaweed will soon replace gasoline as a fuel.

Ⓓ Seaweed will never replace gasoline as a fuel.

GO ON →

Name: ________________________________ Date: ________

4 What text evidence supports the author's point that seaweed has been part of the human diet for a long time?

Ⓕ Seaweed can be used to help improve soil.

Ⓖ Seaweed is eaten in many places around the world.

Ⓗ In Canada, seaweed farmers grow seaweed onshore.

Ⓘ Dulse has been eaten in Scotland for more than a thousand years.

5 Read this sentence from the article.

This practice has led to a deficit of seaweed (that is, a shortage of it) in many places, though.

What does *deficit* mean in the sentence above?

Ⓐ crop

Ⓑ harvest

Ⓒ lack

Ⓓ waste

6 Read this sentence from the article.

Seaweed has other uses besides providing nutrition for humans by giving them a healthful food.

Which word in the sentence helps the reader understand what *nutrition* means?

Ⓕ food

Ⓖ giving

Ⓗ humans

Ⓘ seaweed

GO ON →

Name: ______________________________ Date: ________

7 Read this sentence from the article.

> **Seaweed is easy to grow, and its cultivation—that is, the farming of it—does not take the place of other crops.**

What does *cultivation* mean in the sentence above?

Ⓐ act of eating
Ⓑ act of growing
Ⓒ expense or cost
Ⓓ result of experiments

8 What text evidence supports the author's point that seaweed can be more than a health food?

Ⓕ Some seaweeds grow in coastal waters.
Ⓖ Some seaweeds are made into tea or soup.
Ⓗ Some seaweeds grow on ropes resting in water.
Ⓘ Some seaweeds are dried and made into fertilizer.

9 Read this sentence from the article.

> **Some seaweeds require the active movement of seawater to grow well.**

Act can mean "to do" and *-ive* means "tending to." Therefore, *active* seawater is

Ⓐ clear.
Ⓑ deep.
Ⓒ flowing.
Ⓓ salty.

10 From evidence in the text, you can tell that the author believes seaweed

Ⓕ tastes very good.
Ⓖ is cheap and easy to grow.
Ⓗ is becoming less common.
Ⓘ will never replace other foods.

GO ON →

Read the article "Desert Environments" before answering Numbers 11 through 20.

Desert Environments

Deserts cover about one fifth of Earth's surface. The terrain, or ground, of some deserts is sandy. Others have a rocky terrain. Yet all deserts have one major feature in common—lack of rainfall. Deserts are dry, desolate places. The desert landscape is harsh. It seems cruel and unforgiving. Few large animals live in deserts. Few trees grow there, and the ones that do are not like most forest trees. Forest trees generally grow tall and straight, but desert trees are short, and they often have amazing shapes. The winds that buffet them twist the trees into these shapes. The cactus is one plant that has adapted to survive in the desert. Cacti store water in their trunks. They have shallow roots that can take in any water that falls. Cactus leaves are often very thin, which gives them less exposure to the sun.

The temperature in deserts can be unbelievably hot or cold. The Sahara Desert in Africa gets very hot during the day, but at night the temperature goes down. Deserts like this are called "hot" deserts. In contrast, the Gobi Desert in Asia is always cold, as are the deserts at the South Pole. These are called "cold" deserts. They often get a lot of snow, and some get more rainfall than other kinds of deserts. There are also semidry deserts, such as the deserts in Utah and Montana and those in the Arctic. These have lower temperatures and more moisture. Finally, there are coastal deserts, which have warm days and cool nights. The soil is often salty, and there is more rainfall than in hot and semidry deserts.

GO ON →

Desert animals have special characteristics that allow them to adapt to their harsh settings. In hot deserts, some animals go on a quest for food early in the morning, the coolest time of the day. Early in the day roadrunners chase rattlesnakes, and coyotes hunt for ground squirrels. During the heat of the day, many animals are dormant, or motionless. Some hide under the ground, while others hide under rocks. At night, the temperature gets much cooler, and then the animals come out to find food. Scorpions and bats hunt for insects, and spiders as big as mice also hunt at night. In the driest deserts, animals might hibernate, or hide away, for months. They only come out when rain finally falls.

Animals in cold deserts have a different system. They hunt during the day when temperatures are slightly warmer. But the nights are very cold, and the animals take shelter.

Living conditions are harsh in a desert. Because food is never plentiful, most desert animals are small and skinny. How do desert animals survive with little or no food to eat? Some of them store fat in their bodies. For example, one type of desert lizard stores fat in its large tail; it uses this fat when food is scarce. This is similar to some types of forest bears who store fat in their bodies during the summer. In the winter, when they hibernate, they have a reduced need for food. However, they still need some food, and they get that food from their stored fat.

Deserts get very little rainfall. The driest deserts might get less than half an inch of moisture a year. Often this moisture is in the form of fog, not rain. When there is a rainstorm, pools of water form on the ground, and the animals drink as much as they can. Yet some desert animals do not drink at all. They get all the water they need from the food they eat. Amazingly, deserts are second only to rainforests in the number of different plant and animal species that live there!

GO ON →

Name: ______________________________ Date: ________

Now answer Numbers 11 through 20. Base your answers on "Desert Environments."

11 Read this sentence from the article.

The terrain, or ground, of some deserts is sandy.

What does *terrain* mean in the sentence above?

Ⓐ earth Ⓒ rocks

Ⓑ roads Ⓓ sand

12 Read this sentence from the article.

Because food is never plentiful, most desert animals are small and skinny.

What point in the article does the text evidence best support?

Ⓕ It is very difficult to live in a desert.

Ⓖ Most desert animals do not live long.

Ⓗ There are very few animals in a desert.

Ⓘ Most desert animals do not need to eat.

13 Read this sentence from the article.

The temperature in deserts can be unbelievably hot or cold.

What does the word *unbelievably* mean?

Ⓐ imagined often

Ⓑ imagined again

Ⓒ not able to imagine

Ⓓ one who cannot imagine

GO ON →

Name: ______________________________ Date: __________

14 What paragraph would the following detail best support?

Yet Earth's driest desert is a costal desert.

Ⓕ paragraph 1, page 222

Ⓖ paragraph 2, page 222

Ⓗ paragraph 3, page 223

Ⓘ paragraph 4, page 223

15 Read this sentence from the article.

During the heat of the day, many animals are dormant, or motionless.

What does the word *dormant* mean in the sentence above?

Ⓐ alive

Ⓑ fearful

Ⓒ slow

Ⓓ still

16 What evidence in the text supports the author's point that animals adapt to the desert?

Ⓕ Coastal deserts have salty soil.

Ⓖ Forest trees generally grow tall and straight.

Ⓗ Some animals hide underground during the heat of the day.

Ⓘ Living conditions are harsh in the desert.

GO ON →

Name: ________________________________ Date: ________

17 Read this sentence from the article.

> **In the driest deserts, animals might hibernate, or hide away, for months.**

Which word in the sentence helps the reader understand what *hibernate* means?

Ⓐ animals
Ⓑ desert
Ⓒ driest
Ⓓ hide

18 What text evidence supports the author's point that desert plants have adapted to their living conditions?

Ⓕ Soil is often salty in coastal deserts.
Ⓖ Food is never plentiful in the desert.
Ⓗ Many desert plants have shallow roots.
Ⓘ Some deserts are sandy and some are rocky.

19 Read these sentences from the article.

> **The desert landscape is harsh. It seems cruel and unforgiving.**

What word in the sentences helps the reader understand what *harsh* means?

Ⓐ cruel
Ⓑ desert
Ⓒ landscape
Ⓓ seems

20 From text evidence, it is clear that the author believes that

Ⓕ deserts are growing larger all over the earth.
Ⓖ deserts can be great places for people to live.
Ⓗ living in a desert requires special characteristics.
Ⓘ without regular rainfall, animals and plants cannot live.

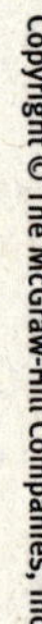

STOP

Name: ______________________________ Date: __________

21 Describe the unique characteristics of the plants presented in “Foods of the Future” and the plants and animals in “Desert Environments.” Use text evidence from both articles in your description.

Answer Key

Name: ______________________

Question	Correct Answer	Content Focus	CCSS	Complexity
1	B	Context Clues: Definitions and Restatements	L.5.4a	DOK 2
2	I	Main Idea and Key Details	RI.5.2	DOK 2
3	B	Author's Point of View	RI.5.8	DOK 3
4	I	Author's Point of View	RI.5.8	DOK 3
5	C	Context Clues: Definitions and Restatements	L.5.4a	DOK 2
6	F	Context Clues: Definitions and Restatements	L.5.4a	DOK 2
7	B	Context Clues: Definitions and Restatements	L.5.4a	DOK 2
8	I	Author's Point of View	RI.5.8	DOK 3
9	C	Prefixes and Suffixes	L.3.4b	DOK 1
10	G	Author's Point of View	RI.5.8	DOK 3
11	A	Context Clues: Definitions and Restatements	L.5.4a	DOK 2
12	F	Author's Point of View	RI.5.8	DOK 3
13	C	Prefixes and Suffixes	L.3.4b	DOK 1
14	G	Main Idea and Key Details	RI.5.2	DOK 2
15	D	Context Clues: Definitions and Restatements	L.5.4a	DOK 2
16	H	Author's Point of View	RI.5.8	DOK 3
17	D	Context Clues: Definitions and Restatements	L.5.4a	DOK 2
18	H	Author's Point of View	RI.5.8	DOK 3
19	A	Context Clues: Definitions and Restatements	L.5.4a	DOK 2
20	H	Author's Point of View	RI.6.6	DOK 3
21	see below	Comparing Across Texts	RI.5.9	DOK 2

Comprehension 2, 3, 4, 8, 10, 12, 14, 16, 18, 20	/10	%
Vocabulary 1, 5, 6, 7, 9, 11, 13, 15, 17, 19	/10	%
Total Weekly Assessment Score	/20	%

21 To receive full credit for the response, the following information should be included: Plants, like seaweed, in "Food of the Future" are an amazing source of vitamins, minerals, protein, and fiber. The plants and animals described in "Desert Environments" demonstrate characteristics that allow them to live in harsh desert environments.

Read the passage "Marisa's Secret" before answering Numbers 1 through 10.

Marisa's Secret

"Do you want to go to my house this afternoon to hang out and make cookies?" Lisa asked her best friend Marisa.

"Not today," Marisa said regretfully, "I have to be somewhere."

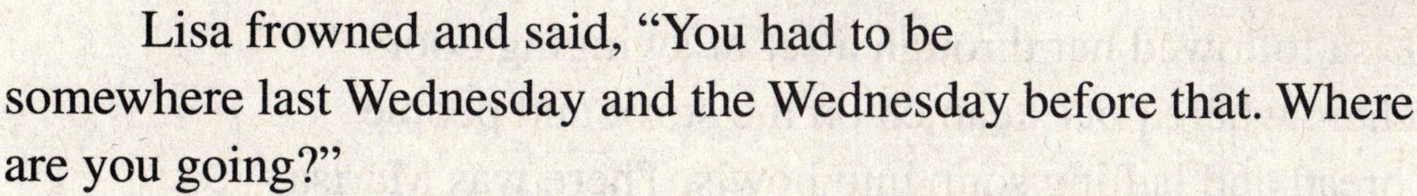

Lisa frowned and said, "You had to be somewhere last Wednesday and the Wednesday before that. Where are you going?"

"I just have to do this thing," Marisa replied, "and we can hang out tomorrow, okay?" Lisa knew that Marisa was keeping a secret, and the secret hung between them like a dark cloud. She watched Marisa walk over to the bus stop, and when the bus pulled in, Marisa climbed on board. The bus pulled away with a groan, and almost without thinking, Lisa ran to the bus stop herself. After a few minutes another bus pulled up, and she climbed on board and paid her fare.

The bus headed downtown, and Lisa watched the sidewalk like a hawk. After about ten minutes she saw Marisa walking past a row of run-down buildings, dirty and neglected, and she pulled the bell and jumped off the bus. She watched as Marisa stopped at a small storefront with a sign out front, pushed open the door, and disappeared inside. Lisa walked up to the storefront and stared at the sign, which said, "Soup Kitchen." What on earth was Marisa doing there? Lisa took a deep breath and then pushed open the door. Inside, she saw a big room lined with long tables, and at each table were a dozen or more people—men, women, and children. The room was crowded but not very noisy; people spoke quietly, and the air was perfumed with the scents of baking bread and roasting vegetables.

GO ON →

"Can I help you, dear?" a woman said to Lisa. "The line for food starts over there." She pointed to a line of people waiting patiently in front of a window.

"I am looking for a friend," Lisa explained, "Marisa Contes, do you know her?"

The woman smiled and said, "I am Amy Shu, and Marisa is one of my Wednesday regulars."

"But what does she do?" Lisa asked. "Does she eat here?"

"Come on back to the kitchen, and you can see for yourself," Mrs. Shu said. Lisa followed her through a set of swinging doors into a warm kitchen, where pots steamed on the stove and people worked cutting bread and ladling soup into bowls. There was Marisa, her hair in a net and a ladle in her hand. When she saw Lisa, she looked like she had seen a ghost.

"I followed you," Lisa admitted. "I am sorry, but I was so curious—I know it was wrong. What are you doing here?"

Marisa wiped her hands on a towel and said, "I never told you about my uncle Tomas, did I?" Lisa shook her head. "Well, I did not really know about him until this year, because we never saw him, and we never saw him because he had no address. He was homeless." Lisa was quiet, so Marisa went on. "It took him a long time, but he finally found a good job and got an apartment, and then he contacted us. It was great to see him doing so well! He told us how hard it had been, living without a real home, and how he ate a lot of his meals at soup kitchens—that is how he managed to keep going. So I thought I would try to help other people like him by working in a soup kitchen myself. It makes me really happy to help people like my uncle."

Lisa reached out and hugged her friend. "I think it is awesome," she said. "Hey, if I help out here too, will you introduce me to your uncle?"

GO ON →

Name: ______________________________ Date: ________

Now answer Numbers 1 through 10. Base your answers on "Marisa's Secret."

1 What message does the author want to give the reader?

Ⓐ Secrets can harm friendships.

Ⓑ Everyone has a secret relative.

Ⓒ Your closest friend can betray you.

Ⓓ Doing good can be its own reward.

2 Read this sentence from the passage.

Lisa knew that Marisa was keeping a secret, and the secret hung between them like a dark cloud.

Why does the author compare the secret to a dark cloud?

Ⓕ to describe exactly what the secret is

Ⓖ to show that the secret is something bad

Ⓗ to show that secrets can interfere with friendships

Ⓘ to show that the secret is something that happens at night

3 Which action by a character best describes the lesson of the passage?

Ⓐ Lisa follows Marisa on the bus.

Ⓑ Lisa invites Marisa to her house.

Ⓒ Marisa cannot go to Lisa's house.

Ⓓ Marisa works at the soup kitchen.

GO ON →

Name: ________________________________ Date: ________

4 Read this sentence from the passage.

After about ten minutes she saw Marisa walking past a row of run-down buildings, dirty and neglected, and she pulled the bell and jumped off the bus.

What word in the sentence tells you what *run-down* means?

Ⓕ buildings
Ⓖ neglected
Ⓗ pulled
Ⓘ row

5 Read this sentence from the passage.

The bus headed downtown, and Lisa watched the sidewalk like a hawk.

Why is the author comparing Lisa to a hawk?

Ⓐ to show that Lisa is watching carefully
Ⓑ to show that Lisa wishes she could fly
Ⓒ to show that Lisa has good eyesight
Ⓓ to show that Lisa notices a bird

6 Based on text evidence, what does Lisa think of Marisa's actions?

Ⓕ She is proud of her.
Ⓖ She is jealous of her.
Ⓗ She is angry with her.
Ⓘ She is unhappy with her.

7 Read this sentence from the passage.

When she saw Lisa, she looked like she had seen a ghost.

What feeling in Marisa does the author communicate by using the simile "she looked like she had seen a ghost"?

Ⓐ anxiety
Ⓑ fear
Ⓒ joy
Ⓓ shock

GO ON →

Name: ______________________________ Date: ________

8 Read this sentence from the passage.

"It makes me really happy to help people like my uncle."

What does this quote tell about the theme of the passage?

Ⓕ that everybody needs help from someone

Ⓖ that helping people can make you happy

Ⓗ that young people can do a lot of good

Ⓘ that soup kitchens help a lot of people

9 Read this sentence from the passage.

The room was crowded but not very noisy; people spoke quietly, and the air was perfumed with the scents of baking bread and roasting vegetables.

What does "the room was perfumed" mean?

Ⓐ The room smelled bad.

Ⓑ The room smelled good.

Ⓒ People were wearing perfume.

Ⓓ The room smelled like perfume.

10 Which sentence best supports the theme of the passage?

Ⓕ There was Marisa, her hair in a net and a ladle in her hand.

Ⓖ Lisa walked up to the storefront and stared at the sign, which said, "Soup Kitchen."

Ⓗ "So I thought I would try to help other people like him by working in a soup kitchen myself."

Ⓘ "It took him a long time, but he finally found a good job and got an apartment, and then he contacted us."

GO ON →

Read the story "To Honor a Hero" before answering Numbers 11 through 20.

To Honor a Hero

Martin sat quietly between his mother and his grandfather. The meeting hall was crowded with people who had come to pay their respects to a hero. Martin was confused; he had no idea who was being honored. He searched the smiling faces of many of the elderly people sitting around him. Some were as wrinkled as crumpled paper. But none of them looked much like a hero to him.

The speaker started his speech, saying, "Friends, we are here to honor a man who served the Navajo people and the United States of America. This was a man who enlisted in the Marines during World War II. He signed up as a Navajo Code Talker." The speaker looked around the audience. "Some of our youngsters may not know that many Navajos fought with the Marines in every battle in the Pacific Corridor from 1942 to 1945. Our men served in more than one invasion, and they were a crucial part of these attacks."

Martin's eyes wandered over the faces of the older men. Did some of them really play such an important role in a war? It hardly seemed possible; these were people he saw every day—his friends' grandparents, shopkeepers, the owner of the local diner.

Martin's shoulders began to sag with boredom. He had heard about World War II in school. It was part of the past, a closed book to Martin. What was so exciting about a war, anyway? People were always fighting. Even on reservation land where everyone lived and worked, people sometimes fought with each other.

GO ON →

Martin turned his attention again to the speaker. "The time has come," the man was saying, "to honor our Code Talkers, now that so many of them have passed on. These were the people who helped assure victory in the war by sending and receiving coded messages about troop actions and orders. They sent vital information about each battle location so the Allies could position themselves at the site of the action. No member of the enemy Axis forces could break the Navajo Code during the Battle of Iwo Jima, and six of our people worked without sleep until that battle was won."

The crowd murmured, and Martin leaned forward, paying attention. This was getting more interesting.

"A man we know only as a friend and neighbor was a Code Talker," said the speaker. "His valiant work in the war helped win it, and after the war, he came home to help his people on the reservation. He did not forget his home, and so he will not be forgotten."

The speaker closed his eyes and softly spoke the following poem in his native language.

What is a hero, my brothers, my sisters?
To find one, how long must you roam?
Is it an eagle that soars for freedom?
Is it the bear that defends its home?

A hero is both the eagle and bear,
One who will fight to protect.
And then return to the Navajo land
To show his love and respect.

Then a surprising thing happened: the speaker asked Martin's grandfather to rise, saying, "Let us honor one of our Code Talkers." Martin's grandfather slowly got up from his seat. He looked very serious, but his eyes were as bright as diamonds.

Martin glanced at his mom and saw that there were tears in her eyes. He felt a wave of pride break over him as he looked up at the man he thought he knew so well. His own grandfather—a hero!

GO ON →

Name: ______________________ **Date:** ________

Now answer Numbers 11 through 20. Base your answers on "To Honor a Hero."

11 What message does the author want to give the reader?

Ⓐ We don't always know who has behaved heroically.

Ⓑ Heroes should get prizes and honors.

Ⓒ Grandparents are all heroes.

Ⓓ Everybody is a hero.

12 Read these sentences from the passage.

He searched the smiling faces of many of the elderly people sitting around him. Some were as wrinkled as crumpled paper.

Why does the author compare faces to crumpled paper?

Ⓕ to show the color of the faces

Ⓖ to present the ages of the people

Ⓗ to describe the sounds that people made

Ⓘ to state that the people are without value

13 Which action by a character best describes the lesson of the passage?

Ⓐ The speaker describes the Navajo Code Talkers.

Ⓑ Martin's grandfather keeps his heroism a secret.

Ⓒ Martin is bored during the presentation.

Ⓓ Martin's mother has tears in her eyes.

GO ON →

Name: ______________________________ Date: ________

14 Read these sentences from the passage.

This was a man who enlisted in the Marines during World War II. He signed up as a Navajo Code Talker.

What word or words in the sentences tell you what *enlisted* means?

Ⓕ man

Ⓖ Navajo

Ⓗ signed up

Ⓘ World War II

15 Read this sentence from the passage.

It was part of the past, a closed book to Martin.

The author compares the past to a closed book to show that Martin

Ⓐ is not a very good reader.

Ⓑ has not learned any history.

Ⓒ does not care about the past.

Ⓓ has difficulty learning about the past.

16 Which sentence best supports the theme of the passage?

Ⓕ "Some of our youngsters may not know that many Navajos fought with the Marines in every battle in the Pacific Corridor from 1942 to 1945."

Ⓖ "They sent vital information about each battle location so the Allies could position themselves at the site of the action."

Ⓗ Even on reservation land where everyone lived and worked, people sometimes fought with each other.

Ⓘ "He did not forget his home, and so he will not be forgotten."

GO ON →

Name: ______________________________ Date: ________

17 Read this sentence from the passage.

He looked very serious, but his eyes were as bright as diamonds.

What does "his eyes were as bright as diamonds" mean?

Ⓐ anxiety
Ⓑ embarrassment
Ⓒ joy
Ⓓ sorrow

18 Read this sentence from the passage.

His own grandfather—a hero!

What does this sentence tell about the story's theme?

Ⓕ People in your family are heroes.
Ⓖ Even the shyest person can be a hero.
Ⓗ Heroes can be found in surprising places.
Ⓘ Even elderly people can behave heroically.

19 Read this sentence from the passage.

He felt a wave of pride break over him as he looked up at the man he thought he knew so well.

"A wave of pride" suggests a feeling that is

Ⓐ balanced.
Ⓑ slight.
Ⓒ overwhelming.
Ⓓ unpleasant.

20 How does Martin's attitude change during the passage?

Ⓕ from feeling surprised to feeling worried
Ⓖ from feeling confused to feeling unhappy
Ⓗ from feeling proud to feeling embarrassed
Ⓘ from feeling bored to feeling proud

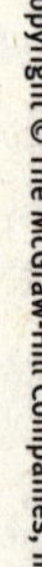

STOP

Read the passage "Camp Pennacook" before answering Numbers 1 through 10.

Camp Pennacook

Eleven-year-old Henry lived in Manchester, New Hampshire, with his mom, two sisters, and grandmother. Their apartment was small for five people, and the building was on one of the busiest streets in the city. Henry didn't have a bedroom and slept on the couch. One day his teacher, Ms. Jeffers, asked him if he would like to go to a boys' camp in the summer. She had talked to Henry's mom, who said he could go to Camp Pennacook if he wanted. It was on an island in Lake Winnipesaukee. The camp would last a month, and there would be swimming, boating, hiking, and other activities. Henry knew about camps from his neighbor James and said yes.

On June 22, Henry met a group of other campers at a dock and got on a boat that would take them to the island. After a short trip, they reached their destination. Camp Pennacook was different from the city, with trees everywhere. Trees even surrounded the cabin where Henry would live with his teammates. At first Henry was shy. Then, Nathan, whose cot was next to his, offered to share his video game during leisure time, an hour in the evening that did not have anything scheduled for the campers. Henry had a new friend.

That night the boys had a chance to get acquainted at a hot dog and hamburger cookout. Henry sat with Nathan and Clark, another boy from his cabin, during the camp sing-along. The boys went back to their cabins early because they had their first swimming lesson in the morning.

GO ON →

Henry did not know how to swim and was nervous about the lesson. When the boys got to the beach, he stepped slowly into the shallow water. It was cold but not icy. The instructor taught him how to float using a swim board. When it was time to go to his work project, Henry did not want the swimming lesson to end.

Every boy in camp spent one hour a day working on a project. Henry's team was assigned the boathouse where they would scrub down boats and take out trash. Team members worked like busy bees except for Eric, who was not doing his share. Henry almost got into a fight with Eric because it was not fair for him not to help. Then he remembered the commitment he made when he was accepted at Camp Pennacook. He would live up to his responsibility and try hard to get along with his teammates. He walked away to avoid trouble.

After the work hour, they went to see the ropes challenge course. The ropes were high! Henry could not imagine climbing to the top, but he remembered that he had agreed to try everything. He would climb a little way up the first time, and he could climb higher each day.

In the afternoon, Henry went to the arts and crafts room in the lodge. He had always liked to draw, so he chose the painting class. Later in thc afternoon, the boys chose a sports team. It could be softball, basketball, or soccer. For Henry, the sport was not a difficult choice. He signed up for the softball team.

The boys followed a routine. Every day began with swimming. Then they worked on their projects. Later they practiced with their sports team. During the month, the cabin group went on a three-day hike in the mountains. First, they took a course in survival skills. The boys learned how to put out a campfire and tell direction from the sun's position. After three days sleeping in a tent, cooking over a fire, and hiking miles over a rough trail, Henry felt he could rely on his outdoor skills.

At the end of the month, Henry sadly said good-bye to all his new friends. He had pride in his skills and new self-respect for his own abilities. He hoped he could return next summer.

GO ON →

Name: ______________________________ Date: ________

Now answer Numbers 1 through 10. Base your answers on "Camp Pennacook."

1 What text evidence shows that the setting of Henry's home and the setting of Camp Pennacook are unalike?

Ⓐ He signed up for the softball team.

Ⓑ Later they practiced with their sports team.

Ⓒ He had always liked to draw, so he chose the painting class.

Ⓓ Camp Pennacook was different from the city, with trees everywhere.

2 Read these sentences from the passage.

Henry's team was assigned the boathouse where they would scrub down boats and take out trash. Team members worked like busy bees except for Eric, who was not doing his share.

Why is the author comparing the team members and bees?

Ⓕ to point out what fun the boys had

Ⓖ to show how hard the boys worked

Ⓗ to describe the color of their uniforms

Ⓘ to explain what the team's job involved

3 What is the theme of this passage?

Ⓐ City life and country life are very different.

Ⓑ The best part of camp is making friends.

Ⓒ Self-respect can result from trying new things.

Ⓓ All eleven-year-olds should go to summer camp.

GO ON →

Name: ______________________________ Date: ________

4 Read these sentences from the passage.

On June 22, Henry met a group of other campers at a dock and got on a boat that would take them to the island. After a short trip, they reached their destination.

What does *destination* mean in the sentences above?

Ⓕ landing place
Ⓖ starting point
Ⓗ deserted island
Ⓘ fate and fortune

5 What is one way the camp is different from Henry's neighborhood?

Ⓐ The camp is less crowded.
Ⓑ There is less to do at camp.
Ⓒ Henry has his own room at camp.
Ⓓ There are no other boys in Henry's neighborhood.

6 Read this sentence from the passage.

Then, Nathan, whose cot was next to his, offered to share his video game during leisure time, an hour in the evening that did not have anything scheduled for the campers.

What does *leisure* mean in the sentence above?

Ⓕ lesson
Ⓖ meal
Ⓗ relaxation
Ⓘ visiting

7 How are the three-day hike and first days in camp different?

Ⓐ On the hike, the boys sleep in tents.
Ⓑ The boys have relaxation time only on the hike.
Ⓒ There is a cookout only on the first night in camp.
Ⓓ Henry does not have to try to get along with others on the hike.

GO ON →

Name: ______________________________ Date: __________

8 Read these sentences from the passage.

> **The instructor taught him how to float using a swim board. When it was time to go to his work project, Henry did not want the swimming lesson to end.**

What does *instructor* mean in the sentences above?

Ⓕ friend

Ⓖ speaker

Ⓗ student

Ⓘ teacher

9 What word best describes both the beach and the hike in the mountains?

Ⓐ mountainous

Ⓑ outdoors

Ⓒ perilous

Ⓓ sandy

10 Read these sentences from the passage.

> **Then he remembered the commitment he made when he was accepted at Camp Pennacook. He would live up to his responsibility and try hard to get along with his teammates.**

What does *commitment* mean in the sentences above?

Ⓕ mark

Ⓖ problem

Ⓗ promise

Ⓘ speech

GO ON →

Read the passage "Books for Uganda" before answering Numbers 11 through 20.

Books for Uganda

Last year, Ms. Perry, who taught fifth grade in America, had read about the need for volunteers at a rural school in Africa. She applied and was accepted. Now it was summer break, and she was in Uganda, a country in Africa, a long way from her home in Minneapolis. She was staying with Mr. Omara, a teacher at the school, and his family.

When Mr. Omara showed her the school, she could not believe how many students were packed into the classroom. Students were seated on benches behind long tables and on the floor. It was overcrowded. She guessed there were ninety to a hundred students in one classroom! Mr. Omara asked a question, and the students responded from everywhere. Their voices came together and grew quickly louder like mushrooms sprouting up after a rain. Everyone paid close attention to Mr. Omara.

Mr. Omara explained that Ms. Perry could best help by working with a small group of students as they practiced writing and speaking English. From her conversations with them, she learned about their lives. Ritah, Joseph, and Winnie got up at 5 AM and walked half a mile each way to collect water from the well. Then, they walked to school. Before classes they had to do some cleanup in the room. After classes, they had more chores to do at home. They did their homework by candlelight.

During her month in rural Uganda, Ms. Perry learned that not only did schools need pens and paper, but books. Five students in a class shared one textbook. Mr. Omara explained that textbooks had to match the curriculum and be bought in Uganda. Yet many storybooks in English were needed for reading practice.

GO ON →

When Ms. Perry returned to Minneapolis, she met her new students as they got off the buses on the first day of school. Her class of 25 students looked small. She had much to tell them about the Ugandan school she had visited. After she finished, Jackson said, “The school needs supplies and books. We could collect these and send them to the school.”

“That’s a great idea for a project,” Victoria said. “How can we get started?”

Ms. Perry said, “Remember, we will need money for shipping expenses. If everyone lists their ideas for the project and funding them, we will talk about your ideas on Friday.”

On Friday, everyone was eager to share ideas. Eva had found a Web site that listed books needed in Uganda. Ms. Perry suggested they focus on fiction, or storybooks about made-up people and events. It would help students practice their skills in reading English. Logan pointed out that drop-off boxes for books could be placed in the front hall of the school and in the cafeteria, where everyone would see them during lunchtime. Molly suggested publicity. They could make posters to get their information to the public. Ian said his parents had too many books on their bookshelves and were talking about giving some away. His idea was to collect books from families and neighbors and sell them in the shopping mall one weekend to make money.

Molly drew a poster decorated with some colorful books. It said, “Bring your books to Parkside School for our book drive. From November 1 through November 15, we are collecting books to send to a school in Uganda. We need picture books and especially the books listed below.” She printed the titles of the recommended books.

At the very bottom, a line said, “We are selling used books for adult readers to pay for our shipping charges. Stop by Vernon Mall on November 13 or 14. You may see a book or two you want to buy, or you can donate a book in good condition for us to sell.”

Everyone in Ms. Perry’s class agreed. This was going to be a fun project!

GO ON →

Name: ______________________________ Date: ________

Now answer Numbers 11 through 20. Base your answers on "Books for Uganda."

11 What text evidence shows that there are two settings in this passage?

Ⓐ Eva had found a Web site that listed books needed in Uganda.

Ⓑ It would help students practice their skills in reading English.

Ⓒ They could make posters to get their information to the public.

Ⓓ When Ms. Perry returned to Minneapolis, she met her new students as they got off the buses on the first day of school.

12 What is the theme of this passage?

Ⓕ Collecting books is a lot of work.

Ⓖ Classmates can learn from books.

Ⓗ Helping others makes people feel good.

Ⓘ Traveling is the best way to spend a holiday.

13 Read these sentences from the passage.

It was overcrowded. She guessed there were ninety to a hundred students in one classroom!

What does *overcrowded* mean in the sentences above?

Ⓐ too hot

Ⓑ too full

Ⓒ too small

Ⓓ too damaged

GO ON →

Name: ______________________________ Date: ________

14 Read this sentence from the passage.

Their voices came together and grew quickly louder like mushrooms sprouting up after a rain.

What does "like mushrooms sprouting up after a rain" mean?

Ⓕ Someone needed to take notes.

Ⓖ Not all the responses were practical.

Ⓗ The voices were all quite wonderful.

Ⓘ Many were answering at the same time.

15 How are the school in Uganda and the school in America different?

Ⓐ Students in Uganda never use pens and paper.

Ⓑ Classrooms in Uganda have more students in a room.

Ⓒ Only students in Minneapolis need textbooks to learn.

Ⓓ In Minneapolis, there are more students in each classroom.

16 Read this sentence from the passage.

Ms. Perry suggested they focus on fiction, or storybooks about made-up people and events.

Which word in the sentence helps the reader understand what *fiction* means?

Ⓕ events

Ⓖ focus

Ⓗ made-up

Ⓘ people

GO ON →

Name: ______________________________ Date: ________

17 Read this sentence from the passage.

Logan pointed out that drop-off boxes for books could be placed in the front hall of the school and in the cafeteria, where everyone would see them during lunchtime.

What does *cafeteria* mean in the sentence above?

Ⓐ fast-food place
Ⓑ fine-dining restaurant
Ⓒ outdoor stand
Ⓓ self-service place

18 Read these sentences from the passage.

Molly suggested publicity. They could make posters to get their information to the public.

What does *publicity* mean in the sentence above?

Ⓕ advertising
Ⓖ people
Ⓗ readers
Ⓘ support

19 What sentence tells you the setting for selling used books will differ from the setting for collecting children's books?

Ⓐ Stop by Vernon Mall on November 13 or 14.

Ⓑ We need picture books and especially the books listed below.

Ⓒ They could make posters to get their information to the public.

Ⓓ When Ms. Perry returned to Minneapolis, she met her new students as they got off the buses on the first day of school.

20 How are the classrooms in Minneapolis and Uganda alike?

Ⓕ Neither is overcrowded.

Ⓖ Both are places of learning.

Ⓗ Neither is a large enough room.

Ⓘ Both have desks for every student.

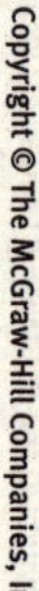

STOP

Name: ______________________ Date: __________

21 Compare and contrast the settings in "Camp Pennacook" and "Books for Uganda." Provide text evidence to explain your answer.

Answer Key Name: ______________________

Question	Correct Answer	Content Focus	CCSS	Complexity
1	D	Character, Setting, Plot: Compare and Contrast	RL.5.3	DOK 2
2	G	Simile	L.5.5a	DOK 2
3	C	Theme	RL.5.2	DOK 3
4	F	Context Clues: Comparison	L.5.4a	DOK 2
5	A	Character, Setting, Plot: Compare and Contrast	RL.5.3	DOK 3
6	H	Context Clues: Comparison	L.5.4a	DOK 2
7	A	Character, Setting, Plot: Compare and Contrast	RL.5.3	DOK 3
8	I	Context Clues: Comparison	L.5.4a	DOK 2
9	B	Character, Setting, Plot: Compare and Contrast	RL.5.3	DOK 3
10	H	Context Clues: Comparison	L.5.4a	DOK 2
11	D	Character, Setting, Plot: Compare and Contrast	RL.5.3	DOK 2
12	H	Theme	RL.5.2	DOK 3
13	B	Context Clues: Comparison	L.5.4a	DOK 2
14	I	Simile	L.5.5a	DOK 2
15	B	Character, Setting, Plot: Compare and Contrast	RL.5.3	DOK 3
16	H	Context Clues: Comparison	L.5.4a	DOK 2
17	D	Context Clues: Comparison	L.5.4a	DOK 2
18	F	Context Clues: Comparison	L.5.4a	DOK 2
19	A	Character, Setting, Plot: Compare and Contrast	RL.5.3	DOK 3
20	G	Character, Setting, Plot: Compare and Contrast	RL.5.3	DOK 3
21	see below	Character, Setting, Plot: Compare and Contrast	RL.5.3	DOK 3

Comprehension 1, 3, 5, 7, 9, 11, 12, 15, 19, 20	/10	%
Vocabulary 2, 4, 6, 8, 10, 13, 14, 16, 17, 18	/10	%
Total Weekly Assessment Score	/20	%

21 To receive full credit for the response, the following information should be included: The settings of "Camp Pennacook" are an American city and a summer camp for boys in the state of New Hampshire, while the settings of "Books for Uganda" are a classroom in Uganda and an American classroom. The outdoor setting in "Camp Pennacook" is new to the boys at camp, and the school in rural Uganda is new to Ms. Perry and very different from her classroom in Minneapolis.

Read the passage "The New Village" before answering Numbers 1 through 10.

The New Village

"I am going to the store, Uncle Moti," Mina said to her uncle. "Do you want to come along? You have not seen much of the neighborhood yet, and I could introduce you to some people."

Uncle Moti shook his head. "No thank you, Mina," he said, "it is just too loud and crowded for me out there. Everyone is always on the go, while I am used to the peace and quiet of our village. I have to admit the city frightens and confuses me. I get panicky out there, like a frightened child."

Mina sat on the sofa next to her uncle. "Tell me about the village, Uncle Moti," she said. "Would I like it there?"

Uncle Moti laughed. "Without a doubt, you would find it dull at first—the loudest sound is usually birdsong, or sometimes a truck backfiring. You can hear the sound of the water in the canal and the bells that hang around the goats' necks. The people I meet on the street are all people I know, and we stop and talk or go to the tea shop and have tea. There are not many shops, but the shopkeepers know all their customers. Everyone is friendly and has a smile for everyone else."

"It sounds really nice," Mina said, "and really different—in some ways. But I think maybe it is not different in every way. I really wish you would come with me, and I could show you why I say that."

Uncle Moti sighed and got up, saying, "All right, Mina, I will go, and you can show me what you mean."

GO ON →

Out on the street, cars zoomed by, some of them honking. People shouted to each other, and kids ran up and down the street playing. Uncle Moti looked very nervous at all the noise and activity, and Mina took his hand.

"Look, Uncle," she said, "there is my friend Nate and his brother, and coming down the street is my teacher from last year, Ms. Sanchez." Mina waved to Nate, who waved back, and then called hello to her teacher. Then she led her uncle down the street to the store, where she greeted the shopkeeper. "Hi, Ms. Franklin, this is my Uncle Moti, who has come here from India to live."

"Hello, Uncle Moti, and welcome to the United States!" the woman replied, smiling. "And what can I get for you today?" Mina handed Ms. Franklin her shopping list, and they went through the little store collecting the items.

When they left the little store, a horn honked, making Uncle Moti jump. Someone pushed by them, bumping into the grocery bag Uncle Moti carried. "Hey, Mr. Watkins, watch your step!" Mina cried.

The man called back, "Sorry, sorry!" as he hurried on.

"Look, Uncle Moti," Mina said, pointing ahead of them at a tree that grew up from the sidewalk, surrounded by a little iron fence. On the lowest branch of the tree was a little sparrow, and as they drew closer they could hear it chirp.

"Over here, Uncle," Mina instructed, taking her uncle's arm and leading him across the street. A sign over a door read "Navid's Tea Shop," and Uncle Moti broke into a big smile. He and Mina went in and took a seat at a table, setting down the grocery bag in an empty chair. They ordered tea, and Uncle Moti sighed happily.

"Well, I see what you were trying to show me, Mina," he said. "This neighborhood is your village, and now it will be mine too. It has friends, kind shopkeepers, birds, and even a tea shop. I think that once I get used to it, I could be very happy here."

GO ON →

Name: ______________________________ Date: __________

Now answer Numbers 1 through 10. Base your answers on "The New Village."

1 Read this sentence from the passage.

He and Mina went in and took a seat at a table, setting down the grocery bag in an empty chair.

What does the idiom "took a seat" mean?

Ⓐ stood up

Ⓑ sat down

Ⓒ moved a chair

Ⓓ carried away a chair

2 What text evidence shows that Mina's neighborhood and Uncle Moti's village are similar?

Ⓕ "I have to admit the city frightens and confuses me."

Ⓖ "It has friends, kind shopkeepers, birds, and even a tea shop."

Ⓗ Someone pushed by them, bumping into the grocery bag Uncle Moti carried.

Ⓘ "Over here, Uncle," Mina instructed, taking her uncle's arm and leading him across the street.

3 How are Mina and Uncle Moti the same?

Ⓐ Neither of them likes the city.

Ⓑ They are from the same village.

Ⓒ They both love peace and quiet.

Ⓓ They both like to see friends on the street.

GO ON →

Name: ______________________________ Date: ________

4 Read this sentence from the passage.

"I get panicky out there, like a frightened child."

What word in the sentence tells you what *panicky* means?

Ⓕ child

Ⓖ frightened

Ⓗ out

Ⓘ there

5 Read this sentence from the passage.

"Without a doubt, you would find it dull at first—the loudest sound is usually birdsong, or sometimes a truck backfiring."

What does "without a doubt" mean?

Ⓐ full of doubt

Ⓑ suspicious

Ⓒ certainly

Ⓓ boldly

6 What text evidence shows that Mina is calmer than Uncle Moti?

Ⓕ Uncle Moti looked very nervous at all the noise and activity, and Mina took his hand.

Ⓖ A sign over a door read "Navid's Tea Shop," and Uncle Moti broke into a big smile.

Ⓗ Mina waved to Nate, who waved back, and then called hello to her teacher.

Ⓘ "Look, Uncle," she said, "there is my friend Nate and his brother, and coming down the street is my teacher from last year, Ms. Sanchez."

GO ON →

Name: ________________________________ Date: __________

7. Read this sentence from the passage.

   "Hey, Mr. Watkins, watch your step!" Mina cried.

   What does "watch your step" mean?

   Ⓐ Look at your feet.

   Ⓑ Walk more quickly.

   Ⓒ Look out for the stairs.

   Ⓓ Be careful where you are walking.

8. Read this sentence from the passage.

   "Everyone is always on the go, while I am used to the peace and quiet of our village."

   What does the idiom "on the go" mean?

   Ⓕ going home

   Ⓖ working hard

   Ⓗ moving quickly

   Ⓘ stopping and going

9. What word best describes both Mina and Uncle Moti?

   Ⓐ bored

   Ⓑ energetic

   Ⓒ friendly

   Ⓓ timid

10. The story suggests that Uncle Moti will become more like Mina in that he will

   Ⓕ start to do the shopping.

   Ⓖ become friends with Mina's friends.

   Ⓗ become willing to go out in the neighborhood.

   Ⓘ tell people when he's displeased by their actions.

GO ON →

Read the story "All in a Day's Work" before answering Numbers 11 through 20.

All in a Day's Work

Dr. Schwartz studied the elements of soil and plant life. Because of her work, she spent a great deal of time looking for specimens. She searched the woods, looking under rocks, on leaves, and in the soil for interesting plants to use in her experiments.

One day she found some algae, a slimy plantlike life form, in a dirty, murky pond. She carefully placed the algae in a plastic bag. Then she picked some mushrooms off a tree. Finally, before ending her search for that day, she scooped some soil from the ground. The soil contained bacteria that she needed to complete her research.

Back in her quiet, peaceful lab, Dr. Schwartz first performed tests on the soil she had collected. She cleaned up as she went along, leaving everything orderly and neat. She was just about to start her experiments on the algae when a co-worker, Dr. Rao, threw open the door to her lab. He shouted, "We need you to look at our latest experiment. Come to my lab!"

"I don't think I can get away right now," Dr. Schwartz said, her hands full of tubes and dirt. "I will be happy to take a look at your experiment later today—or maybe tomorrow, when I am done with this."

"Just for a few moments," he pleaded wildly. "Something awful has occurred!"

"Not again!" said Dr. Schwartz, wiping the dirt off her hands and following Dr. Rao down the hall. "What is it this time?" she asked him.

GO ON →

"Our mixture was dormant, like a sleeping baby," Dr. Rao explained as they walked quickly down the hall. "It was inactive, but—" He paused as he opened the door, and Dr. Schwartz peered inside.

"Oh, my," said Dr. Schwartz, taken aback but speaking in a matter-of-fact tone. "It is definitely not inactive anymore." The mixture had erupted all over the lab! Thick slime was shooting out of beakers, like a volcano exploding all over. The slime hung from the ceiling and covered the floor. As they watched, the green goo seemed to spread, quickly moving over desks and blocking the sun that streamed in the windows.

"I am just an observer," Dr. Schwartz said, "and I am not conducting this experiment. But if worse comes to worst, we could be in danger. We had better get out of here."

Dr. Schwartz, Dr. Rao, and the other people who had been working in his lab backed out of the room and slammed the door behind them. They stood in the hallway arguing, trying to decide what to do. Dr. Rao was hopping from one foot to the other. Only Dr. Schwartz, who was thinking hard, was quiet.

At last Dr. Schwartz spoke, saying, "We have to do something before it slimes the entire building. We are working against the clock here. I have an idea that I think may work. Let me handle this." She hurried to her lab and was back in a matter of seconds, clutching a bag. Then she opened the door to Dr. Rao's lab and threw in the contents of the bag, which was full of dirt.

She smiled as she observed the slime being scrubbed away. The soil seemed to clean the slime from the room, destroying the green stuff that had dirtied the walls and floor. Dr. Rao and the others watched in amazement. Dr. Schwartz explained, "The soil I'm studying appears to have anti-slime properties. I discovered the soil in an area that had no algae—not a single one was to be found. But I never expected that my discovery would come in handy so soon." Then she turned to leave and said, "Well, back to work for me."

GO ON →

Name: ______________________________ Date: ________

Now answer Numbers 11 through 20. Base your answers on "All in a Day's Work."

11 What word best describes Dr. Schwartz and Dr. Rao?

Ⓐ artists
Ⓑ professors
Ⓒ scientists
Ⓓ workers

12 Read this sentence from the passage.

"Oh, my," said Dr. Schwartz, taken aback but speaking in a matter-of-fact tone.

What does the idiom "taken aback" mean?

Ⓕ working hard
Ⓖ pulled backwards
Ⓗ suddenly surprised
Ⓘ showing one's true feelings

13 How are Dr. Schwartz and Dr. Rao different?

Ⓐ Dr. Schwartz is calmer than Dr. Rao.
Ⓑ Dr. Schwartz is louder than Dr. Rao.
Ⓒ Dr. Schwartz is braver than Dr. Rao.
Ⓓ Dr. Schwarz is not as smart as Dr. Rao.

14 Read this sentence from the passage.

"Our mixture was dormant, like a sleeping baby," Dr. Rao explained as they walked quickly down the hall.

What word in the sentence tells you what *dormant* means?

Ⓕ explained
Ⓖ mixture
Ⓗ quickly
Ⓘ sleeping

GO ON →

Name: ______________________ Date: __________

15 Read this sentence from the passage.

"But if worse comes to worst, we could be in danger."

What does the idiom "if worse comes to worst" mean?

Ⓐ if the worst thing happens

Ⓑ the worst thing has happened

Ⓒ nobody knows what will happen next

Ⓓ things are worse than you could imagine

16 What text evidence shows that Dr. Rao is excitable?

Ⓕ "Just for a few moments," he pleaded wildly.

Ⓖ Dr. Rao and the others watched in amazement.

Ⓗ She smiled as she observed the slime being scrubbed away.

Ⓘ "I don't think I can get away right now," Dr. Schwartz said.

17 Read this sentence from the passage

"We are working against the clock here."

What does the idiom "We are working against the clock" mean?

Ⓐ We are too late.

Ⓑ We have a limited time.

Ⓒ We have to stop working.

Ⓓ We do not have time to work.

GO ON →

Name: ______________________________ Date: ________

18 What text evidence shows that the two labs are different?

Ⓕ He paused as he opened the door, and Dr. Schwartz peered inside.

Ⓖ She cleaned up as she went along, leaving everything orderly and neat.

Ⓗ He shouted, "We need you to look at our latest experiment. Come to my lab!"

Ⓘ Then she opened the door to Dr. Rao's lab and threw in the contents of the bag, which was full of dirt.

19 Read this sentence from the passage.

"But I never expected that my discovery would come in handy so soon."

What does the idiom "come in handy" mean?

Ⓐ be useful

Ⓑ be held up

Ⓒ come inside

Ⓓ be handed around

20 This passage suggests that

Ⓕ Dr. Schwartz is nicer than Dr. Rao.

Ⓖ Dr. Schwartz is older than Dr. Rao.

Ⓗ Dr. Schwartz is more careful than Dr. Rao.

Ⓘ Dr. Schwartz is more intelligent than Dr. Rao.

STOP

Name: ______________________ Date: __________

21 How do Mina and Dr. Schwartz both help other people? Use text evidence to support your answer.

Answer Key

Name: ______________________

Question	Correct Answer	Content Focus	CCSS	Complexity
1	B	Idioms	L.5.5b	DOK 2
2	G	Character, Setting, Plot: Compare and Contrast	RL.5.3	DOK 2
3	D	Character, Setting, Plot: Compare and Contrast	RL.5.3	DOK 3
4	G	Context Clues: Comparison	L.5.4a	DOK 2
5	C	Idioms	L.5.5b	DOK 2
6	F	Character, Setting, Plot: Compare and Contrast	RL.5.3	DOK 2
7	D	Idioms	L.5.5b	DOK 2
8	H	Idioms	L.5.5b	DOK 2
9	C	Character, Setting, Plot: Compare and Contrast	RL.5.3	DOK 3
10	H	Character, Setting, Plot: Compare and Contrast	RL.5.3	DOK 3
11	C	Character, Setting, Plot: Compare and Contrast	RL.5.3	DOK 3
12	H	Idioms	L.5.5b	DOK 2
13	A	Character, Setting, Plot: Compare and Contrast	RL.5.3	DOK 3
14	I	Context Clues: Comparison	L.5.4a	DOK 2
15	A	Idioms	L.5.5b	DOK 2
16	F	Character, Setting, Plot: Compare and Contrast	RL.5.3	DOK 2
17	B	Idioms	L.5.5b	DOK 2
18	G	Character, Setting, Plot: Compare and Contrast	RL.5.3	DOK 3
19	A	Idioms	L.5.5b	DOK 2
20	H	Character, Setting, Plot: Compare and Contrast	RL.5.3	DOK 3
21	see below	Character, Setting, Plot: Compare and Contrast	RL.5.3	DOK 3

Comprehension 2, 3, 6, 9, 10, 11, 13, 16, 18, 20	/10	%
Vocabulary 1, 4, 5, 7, 8, 12, 14, 15, 17, 19	/10	%
Total Weekly Assessment Score	/20	%

21 To receive full credit for the response, the following information should be included: Mina and Dr. Schwartz both work calmly with others. Mina calms her uncle, and Dr. Schwartz calms Dr. Rao and the others in the lab.

Read the article "From Enemy to Friend" before answering Numbers 1 through 10.

From Enemy to Friend

Wolves and dogs are closely related. After all, most scientists believe that dogs' ancestors were wolves. Over time, wolves became tame enough to live with humans and help them. The change from wolf to dog was, it is believed, mostly a result of careful breeding. Early humans allowed only the friendliest wolf pups to remain near them. This ensured that, over time, the wolves that stayed with groups of humans became tamer and tamer.

As wolves were influenced by their relationship with humans, they slowly became what we know today as dogs. Eventually, they arrived at the point where they were useful in ways besides just warning people of danger. They became adept at protecting and herding sheep and other animals. Their ancestors would, instead, have made a meal of them. This ability made dogs very useful. However, although they are quite similar, wolves and dogs are also quite different.

Wolves are wild animals that live in packs, or groups. They eat only meat. They find their food for themselves by hunting. The most common noise they make is a howl. They may also bark, growl, yelp, and whine, but these sounds are much less common than howling. All wolves look very much alike, although their colors vary. They are large, slender, powerful animals with long legs and tails.

GO ON →

Wolves are quite wary of people; they don't trust them. They prefer to keep their distance from humans. They will make every effort to avoid them. They attack people only on rare occasions, usually when they are startled.

Dogs, on the other hand, are tame. They have been influenced by people for many, many years. This has made them quite different from wolves. For one thing, dogs eat vegetables and grains as well as meat products. They are much more likely to bark than to howl. Their sizes range from gigantic animals that are much larger than wolves to tiny animals that can sit comfortably in a cereal bowl. Large dogs are not only taller than wolves, they are much heavier. Their appearances can vary as much as their sizes. Many look nothing like a wolf. However, the main difference is found in dogs' relationship with humans, whom they usually prefer to be near. The main effect of this is that most dogs are friendly to people. Some show hostility, but almost always only to strangers. This willingness to be friendly is especially true if they do not feel threatened or are not protecting their property. Although most dogs are no smarter than wolves, they can certainly be trained more easily. Dogs can be taught to do many more things than a wolf can be taught to do, including complicated tricks. They can be easily trained to obey hand signals. They rarely hunt prey to eat and depend on their owners to supply them with food. This reliance on people just adds to the closeness of the relationship.

Wolves and dogs both pant to stay cool. They both can hear and smell very well, and they both can run silently. They even have the same number of teeth: 42. However, no matter how similar wolves and dogs may seem to be, a wolf can never be made into a pet. No one can tame a wolf so that it can be counted on to be gentle. Wolves are, by nature, suspicious. This makes them untrustworthy. They are also worthless as guard animals because they are shy. Domestic animals, such as cats and small dogs, are in more danger from wolves than humans are, but small children can also be in danger. The Big Bad Wolf may exist only in fairy tales, but real wolves can be as much of a threat, especially if they are not understood.

GO ON →

Name: ______________________________ Date: ________

Now answer Numbers 1 through 10. Base your answers on "From Enemy to Friend."

1 The author shows the relationship between wolves and dogs by

Ⓐ telling how their habitats are similar.

Ⓑ listing the ways they developed over time.

Ⓒ stating the fierce rivalries between them.

Ⓓ comparing and contrasting their characteristics.

2 Read this sentence from the article.

Wolves are quite wary of people; they don't trust them.

What does *wary* mean in the sentence above?

Ⓕ accepting

Ⓖ suspicious

Ⓗ terrified

Ⓘ unaware

3 In the second paragraph on page 265, the author compares the first herding dogs to

Ⓐ wolves.

Ⓑ guard dogs.

Ⓒ the humans they helped.

Ⓓ modern-day herding dogs.

GO ON →

Name: ______________________________ Date: ________

4 Read these sentences from the article.

The main effect of this is that most dogs are friendly to people. Some show hostility, but almost always only to strangers.

What does *hostility* mean in the sentences above?

Ⓕ affection
Ⓗ gratitude
Ⓖ fear
Ⓘ unfriendliness

5 One of the ways in which wolves and dogs are most similar is that both

Ⓐ are similar sizes.
Ⓑ can hear quite well.
Ⓒ hunt for their meals.
Ⓓ have long legs and tails.

6 What text evidence supports the author's view that wolves can be dangerous?

Ⓕ Wolves make good hunters.
Ⓖ Wolves are such good guards.
Ⓗ Wolves look so much like dogs.
Ⓘ Wolves have suspicious natures.

7 According to text evidence, the major difference between wolves and dogs is their

Ⓐ appearance.
Ⓑ intelligence.
Ⓒ ability to learn.
Ⓓ reaction to people.

GO ON →

Name: ______________________ Date: ________

8 Read these sentences from the article.

Early humans allowed only the friendliest wolf pups to remain near them. This ensured that, over time, the wolves that stayed with groups of humans became tamer and tamer.

What does *ensured* mean in the sentences above?

Ⓕ made sure

Ⓖ made unsure

Ⓗ made confident

Ⓘ made it unlikely

9 Read these sentences from the article.

They became adept at protecting and herding sheep and other animals. Their ancestors would, instead, have made a meal of them. This ability made dogs very useful.

What does *adept* mean in the sentences above?

Ⓐ fast

Ⓑ hungry

Ⓒ skillful

Ⓓ trusting

10 Read these sentences from the article.

They rarely hunt prey to eat and depend on their owners to supply them with food. This reliance on people just adds to the closeness of the relationship.

What word in the sentences is the best clue to the meaning of *reliance*?

Ⓕ depend

Ⓖ food

Ⓗ hunt

Ⓘ relationship

GO ON →

Read the article "Marvels of Engineering" before answering Numbers 11 through 20.

Marvels of Engineering

It's hard to imagine two more different structures than the Eiffel Tower and Hoover Dam. For one thing, the Eiffel Tower is in Paris, France. Hoover Dam is on the border between Nevada and Arizona. The Eiffel Tower is elegant and delicate looking. Hoover Dam looks like a huge slab of concrete. The Eiffel Tower was made of many individual parts and then put together. The concrete for Hoover Dam was poured at the site, right where the dam would be. The Eiffel Tower was built for a fair and was not intended to remain in place for long. Hoover Dam was built to allow water to be used in desert country and to create electricity. Everyone expected it to remain in place for many, many years.

Even though these two structures are so different, there are similarities. Each required great effort to complete; each also necessitated the involvement of many workers. The workers on each faced many challenges and difficulties. Each was built in a series of steps. Each is huge but was built quickly, considering the amount of labor involved.

All of the Eiffel Tower's parts were made in a factory near Paris. Each piece had to be the right size and shape. Smaller parts were put together. The small parts were then joined to form a larger piece. These large pieces were put together at the site of the tower.

GO ON →

Bolts held together the pieces made at the factory. At the tower, these bolts were pulled out and replaced with hot rivets. When the rivets cooled, they shrank, which held the pieces firm. Teams of people worked to take out the bolts and put in the rivets.

The Hoover Dam was built to replace one that had been washed away, but it was built in a new place. First the water that flowed through the Colorado River had to be diverted. Four tunnels were blasted through rock to cause the water to go in new directions. Then the river's canyon walls had to be cleared. From great heights, workers dangled from ropes. With only air below their feet, they prepared the area for great concrete walls. Far underneath them, the area for the foundation was cleared of mud and loose rock. When this was all finished, tons of wet concrete were poured into a gigantic form. For thirty months, concrete was poured. Finally the work was done. Across the Colorado River stood a dam 700 feet tall. When the water was allowed to rush through tunnels, it passed through giant rotary engines. As their parts whirled, they created electricity.

Making electricity and using water to irrigate dry land were both practical purposes for Hoover Dam. The Eiffel Tower had no original purpose but to be beautiful. The man who designed it, Gustave Eiffel, did not want it to be torn down. He hated the idea of his great creation being destroyed, so he looked for a practical use for it. He thought it might be used to study the weather. Or, it might be used as a radio station. Given that it was more than a thousand feet tall, it was a perfect place for a radio antenna. This would allow the French army to keep in contact across the whole country. Soon, a radio station was built on the tower. A practical use for it had been found. That helped the tower survive, and now no one can imagine Paris without it.

Both the Eiffel Tower and Hoover Dam are popular tourist attractions. They are majestic sights. Everyone who sees them is amazed. And each, to this day, is considered a marvelous example of engineering skill.

GO ON →

Name: ______________________________ Date: ________

Now answer numbers 11 through 20. Base your answers on "Marvels of Engineering."

11 In this article, the author discusses the Eiffel Tower and Hoover Dam by

Ⓐ presenting the history of their building.

Ⓑ showing the talents of their builders.

Ⓒ detailing the problems overcome in their building.

Ⓓ comparing and contrasting their features.

12 Read this sentence from the article.

The concrete for Hoover Dam was poured at the site, right where the dam would be.

What does *site* mean in the sentence above?

Ⓕ factory

Ⓖ location

Ⓗ situation

Ⓘ wall

13 Read these sentences from the article.

From great heights, workers dangled from ropes. With only air below their feet, they prepared the area for great concrete walls.

What does *dangled* mean in the sentences above?

Ⓐ dropped

Ⓑ hung

Ⓒ jumped

Ⓓ rose

GO ON →

Name: ______________________________ Date: ________

14 What is the purpose of the first paragraph of the article?

Ⓕ to tell where the two structures are

Ⓖ to show just how different the two structures are

Ⓗ to show what is meant by "marvels of engineering"

Ⓘ to show how alike two very different structures are

15 What is a major similarity between the Eiffel Tower and Hoover Dam?

Ⓐ their height

Ⓑ how they were built

Ⓒ what they are made of

Ⓓ the effort needed to complete them

16 What is different about the original purposes of each structure?

Ⓕ The tower was built to last forever; the dam was built to be temporary.

Ⓖ The tower was built to be decorative; the dam was built for practical uses.

Ⓗ The tower was built to increase tourism; the dam was built to discourage tourism.

Ⓘ The tower was built to give people something to look at; the dam was built to give people work to do.

17 According to text evidence, the author views the Eiffel Tower and Hoover Dam as being

Ⓐ admirable.

Ⓑ unnecessary.

Ⓒ delicate in appearance.

Ⓓ important for communication.

GO ON →

Name: ______________________________ Date: ________

18 Read these sentences from the article.

First the water that flowed through the Colorado River had to be diverted. Four tunnels were blasted through rock to cause the water to go in new directions.

What does *diverted* mean in the sentences above?

Ⓕ dried up

Ⓖ stopped from flowing

Ⓗ stopped by a new dam

Ⓘ turned aside to a new course

19 Read these sentences from the article.

When the water was allowed to rush through tunnels, it passed through giant rotary engines. As their parts whirled, they created electricity.

Which word in the sentences is the best clue to the meaning of *rotary*?

Ⓐ giant

Ⓑ rush

Ⓒ parts

Ⓓ whirled

20 Read these sentences from the article.

They are majestic sights. Everyone who sees them is amazed.

What does *majestic* mean in the sentences above?

Ⓕ bold

Ⓖ interesting

Ⓗ magnificent

Ⓘ ordinary

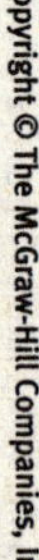

STOP

Name: ______________________________ Date: __________

21 Depending on the purpose of their writing, authors choose a certain text structure to help them give their readers information. On the lines below, compare and contrast the particular text structures the authors used in these articles. Do you think they suited the authors' purposes? Use text evidence to support your answer.

Answer Key

Name: ______________________

Question	Correct Answer	Content Focus	CCSS	Complexity
1	D	Text Structure: Compare and Contrast	RI.5.3	DOK 2
2	G	Context Clues: Comparison	L.5.4a	DOK 2
3	A	Compare and Contrast	RI.5.3	DOK 2
4	I	Context Clues: Paragraph Clues	L.5.4a	DOK 2
5	B	Compare and Contrast	RI.5.3	DOK 2
6	I	Author's Point of View	RI.5.8	DOK 2
7	D	Compare and Contrast	RI.5.3	DOK 2
8	F	Context Clues: Paragraph Clues	L.5.4a	DOK 2
9	C	Context Clues: Paragraph Clues	L.5.4a	DOK 2
10	F	Context Clues: Paragraph Clues	L.5.4a	DOK 2
11	D	Text Structure: Compare and Contrast	RI.5.3	DOK 2
12	G	Context Clues: Comparison	L.5.4a	DOK 2
13	B	Context Clues: Paragraph Clues	L.5.4a	DOK 2
14	G	Compare and Contrast	RI.5.3	DOK 3
15	D	Compare and Contrast	RI.5.3	DOK 3
16	G	Compare and Contrast	RI.5.3	DOK 3
17	A	Author's Point of View	RI.5.8	DOK 2
18	I	Context Clues: Paragraph Clues	L.5.4a	DOK 2
19	D	Context Clues: Paragraph Clues	L.5.4a	DOK 2
20	H	Context Clues: Paragraph Clues	L.5.4a	DOK 2
21	see below	Comparing Across Texts	RI.5.9	DOK 4

Comprehension 1, 3, 5, 6, 7, 11, 14, 15, 16, 17	/10	%
Vocabulary 2, 4, 8, 9, 10, 12, 13, 18, 19, 20	/10	%
Total Weekly Assessment Score	/20	%

21 To receive full credit for the response, the following information should be included: Using these particular text structures allowed the authors to tell how wolves and dogs are alike and how they're different and also how the Eiffel Tower and Hoover Dam are alike and different. The text structures used did suit the authors' purposes.

Read the article "The Birth of the Movies" before answering Numbers 1 through 10.

The Birth of the Movies

Why do we love the movies? There is something magical about watching a story play out on a screen as we sit in the darkness. We love westerns, cartoons, horror films, action movies, and love stories. Many of the films we watch are filled with special effects. We might watch them in 3-D or admire their wild car chases or glorious landscapes. But when movies began, films were much simpler and more basic.

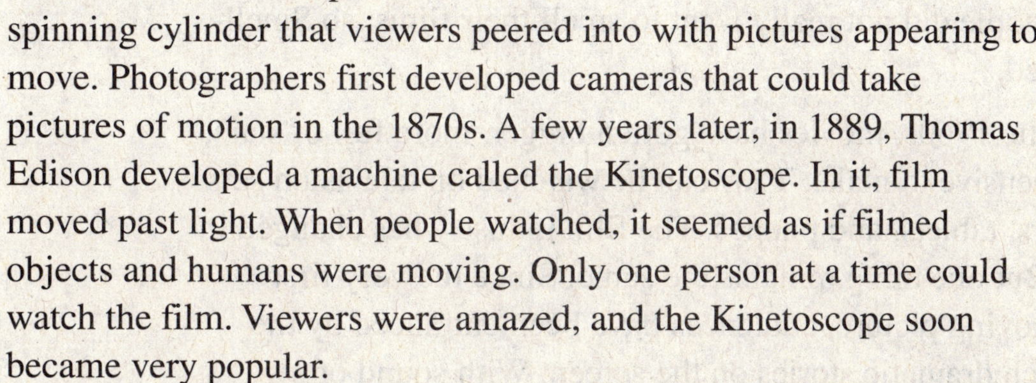

In the 1830s, inventors created machines that spun around like wheels. They had pictures on them. Viewing the pictures as they cycled around made it look as if the images were moving. Next came the zoetrope. This was a spinning cylinder that viewers peered into with pictures appearing to move. Photographers first developed cameras that could take pictures of motion in the 1870s. A few years later, in 1889, Thomas Edison developed a machine called the Kinetoscope. In it, film moved past light. When people watched, it seemed as if filmed objects and humans were moving. Only one person at a time could watch the film. Viewers were amazed, and the Kinetoscope soon became very popular.

In France in 1895, the Lumiere brothers created a machine that could take movies and show them, too. Now groups of viewers could watch films at the same time. Thomas Edison and others soon realized that movies could tell stories. By the early 1900s, the first animated movie and the first western had been made. Comedies were especially popular. People loved to laugh at the movies. By 1909, there were about 9,000 movie theaters in America.

GO ON →

Films were very short in the early 1900s, and there were no such things as movie stars. The performers were unknown. But that did not last long. Moving picture companies organized into film studios. They began promoting actors and actresses, who quickly became stars. Audiences were thrilled by pictures of and articles about the theatrical people they saw up on the screen.

At that point, movies were silent, accompanied only with music and sometimes with written titles. Filmmakers had been trying to figure out how to use sound with film for years. The technology was complicated. Thomas Edison had produced a machine that included sound, but he was not able to get the sound to work correctly with the images on film. Finally, in 1927, Warner Brothers Studio produced the first film with sound, *The Jazz Singer*. Other films with sound quickly followed. In 1935, color films were first produced. Now films began to look like the movies we know today.

In 1952, film studios introduced 3-D films, movies that, when viewed with special glasses, look as if they were three-dimensional. Eight years later studios brought viewers "Smell-O-Vision," which allowed audiences to smell the scents that were in the movies. Apparently people did not really want to smell their films, so Smell-O-Vision failed.

Since the 1960s, movies have gotten bigger, more full of stars, and more expensive to make. They can be watched on television sets and computers, tablets, and phones. The film industry has changed in many ways. But one thing remains the same. Since the very first days of the moving picture, audiences have been entranced by the ability to watch dramatic stories on the screen. With sound or without, in color or black and white, movies have created joy and amazement in viewers for more than a hundred years.

GO ON →

Name: ______________________________ Date: ________

Now answer Numbers 1 through 10. Base your answers on "The Birth of the Movies."

1 Read these sentences from the article.

> **Viewing the pictures as they cycled around made it look as if the images were moving.**

The word *cycled* comes from a Greek root, *kyklos,* which means "wheel." Therefore, a *cyclone* is likely to move

Ⓐ very quickly.

Ⓑ only over land.

Ⓒ faster than a car.

Ⓓ in a circular motion.

2 Read the following sentence from the article.

> **The technology was complicated.**

The word *technology* comes from a Greek root, *techne,* which means "skill." This suggests that a *technician* is someone who

Ⓕ is a scientist.

Ⓖ works very hard.

Ⓗ has special abilities.

Ⓘ wants to please others.

3 Going to the movies became a social activity because

Ⓐ movie theaters became very large.

Ⓑ people could view films in groups.

Ⓒ people liked going to films with sound.

Ⓓ people enjoyed looking through the zoetrope.

GO ON →

Name: ______________________________ Date: ________

4 Read these sentences from the article.

Comedies were especially popular. People loved to laugh at the movies.

Which word in the sentences helps the reader understand what *comedies* are?

Ⓕ especially

Ⓖ laugh

Ⓗ loved

Ⓘ popular

5 Because the technology of matching sound with film was complicated,

Ⓐ only Thomas Edison could do it.

Ⓑ films were silent until 3-D was developed.

Ⓒ people preferred silent films until the 1950s.

Ⓓ it took over 20 years to develop movies with sound.

6 According to the article, Thomas Edison's invention of film that moved past light has the effect of

Ⓕ matching film to sound.

Ⓖ making films a social event.

Ⓗ making filmed objects visible.

Ⓘ making things appear to be moving.

GO ON →

Name: ______________________________ Date: ________

7 Read this sentence from the article.

Since the very first days of the moving picture, audiences have been entranced by the ability to watch dramatic stories on the screen.

The origin of *dramatic* is the Greek word *dramatikos,* meaning "having to do with plays." This suggests that *dramatic* relates to providing

Ⓐ a history.
Ⓑ an opinion.
Ⓒ a performance.
Ⓓ a suggestion.

8 Because film studios promoted actors and actresses, the actors and actresses

Ⓕ became stars.
Ⓖ made animated films.
Ⓗ produced better movies.
Ⓘ worked on stage.

9 Read this sentence from the article.

Photographers first developed cameras that could take pictures of motion in the 1870s.

The word *photographers* comes from two Greek roots, *photo* and *graph. Graph* means "write." What is the most likely meaning of *photo*?

Ⓐ dark
Ⓑ light
Ⓒ moon
Ⓓ pen

10 According to the author, movies are popular because

Ⓕ they are great social events.
Ⓖ films have color and sound.
Ⓗ comedians often appear in them.
Ⓘ there is something magical about them.

GO ON →

Read the article "Up, Up, and Away!" before answering Numbers 11 through 20.

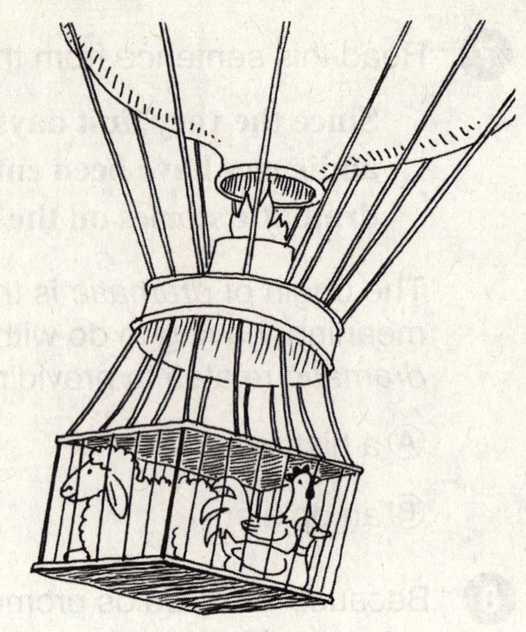

Up, Up, and Away!

More than a century before the Wright brothers' famous plane flight took place, a different type of object rose into the sky. It was a balloon filled with heated air. The year was 1783, and the place was France. Two brothers named Montgolfier launched the very first hot-air balloon. It was made of four huge pieces of fabric and paper, held together by almost 2,000 buttons.

The balloon stayed in the air about ten minutes. There were no humans on board because that would have been too dangerous. Instead, the aerial passengers were a sheep, a duck, and a rooster. After this historic event, interest in balloons grew quickly. Inventors began competing to see who could make the safest balloon and take the longest flight. Some people continued to work on balloons filled with heated air, while others developed balloons filled with hydrogen. That gas is lighter than air.

A few months after the flight of the Montgolfier balloon, another first in balloon history took place. A Frenchman named Jacques Charles launched a beautiful balloon made of silk. It was filled with hydrogen. Charles's balloon looked lovely as the gas lifted it in the air.

In November of that same year, the Montgolfier brothers again made history. A giant balloon they had constructed carried humans into the air for the first time. One of the aeronauts was a French science teacher who had helped with the Montgolfier flight of the animals. His companion was a French nobleman. The two men sailed over Paris for 25 minutes. The mechanism that heated the air and inflated the balloon was a fire of burning straw. It was a wonderful flight until the balloon caught on fire. Luckily, no one was hurt.

GO ON →

The first balloon flight in the United States traveled from Philadelphia, Pennsylvania, to New Jersey in 1793. George Washington was one of the spectators. He watched as the anchored balloon was released so that it could soar into the air. Balloons had officially entered into United States history.

While the first hot-air balloons were used for adventure, people soon saw that they could be used for military purposes, such as delivering messages across long distances. During the Civil War and in World War I, balloons were used for communication and transportation. In World War II, they served another purpose as well. Wires were strung between balloons, forming a trap that military planners hoped would stop enemy airplanes.

Soon there was nearly an epidemic of hot-air balloonists trying to see how far up they could soar. In 1932, balloonists went into the stratosphere, over 52,000 feet up. Their cabin had to be pressurized so they could endure the trip. Since then, balloonists have been going ever farther into the sky. In 1988, a record was set: 65,000 feet upward. That is over 10 miles high!

More recently, balloons have been used to travel long distances. In 1978, a balloon called the Double Eagle crossed the Atlantic Ocean. The balloon was filled with helium and carried three passengers. In 1991, a hot-air balloon crossed the Pacific Ocean. It reached speeds of up to 245 miles an hour! Later that year, two men completed a balloon flight around the world. It was a thrilling feat. Another record was set the following year, when two balloonists spent over 144 hours in the air, flying from Bangor, Maine, to Morocco.

Today, many hot-air balloons are used for science and studying the weather. They often carry thermometers and other weather-measuring devices. So, while hot-air balloons often are used for fun, they still are used for serious purposes as well.

GO ON →

Name: ________________________________ Date: __________

Now answer Numbers 11 through 20. Base your answers on "Up, Up, and Away!"

11 The balloon mentioned in the fourth paragraph caught on fire because

Ⓐ the air was too hot.

Ⓑ the balloonist used an explosive.

Ⓒ the wind was blowing very hard.

Ⓓ the air was heated by burning straw.

12 Read this sentence from the article.

Instead, the aerial passengers were a sheep, a duck, and a rooster.

The word *aerial* comes from a Greek root, *aero,* which means "air." This suggests that an *aerial* passenger is

Ⓕ falling.

Ⓖ jumping.

Ⓗ in the sky.

Ⓘ in a basket.

13 What were the effects of the epidemic of soaring balloonists?

Ⓐ balloons reaching record heights

Ⓑ more and more balloon disasters

Ⓒ less interest in balloon travel

Ⓓ balloons being used in wars

GO ON →

Name: ______________________________ Date: ________

14 Read these sentences from the article.

> **Some people continued to work on balloons filled with heated air, while others developed balloons filled with hydrogen. That gas is lighter than air.**

Which word in the sentences helps the reader understand what *hydrogen* is?

Ⓕ air

Ⓖ balloon

Ⓗ gas

Ⓘ lighter

15 Read these sentences from the article.

> **The mechanism that heated the air and inflated the balloon was a fire of burning straw.**

The Greek root of *mechanism* is *mech,* which means "machine." Therefore, a *mechanic* would be likely to work with

Ⓐ animals.

Ⓑ engines.

Ⓒ plants.

Ⓓ water.

16 Because hydrogen is lighter than air, balloonists

Ⓕ decided to stop using hydrogen.

Ⓖ tried to find other gases to use.

Ⓗ preferred to use hot air in their balloons.

Ⓘ used hydrogen to make their balloons rise.

GO ON →

Name: ______________________________ Date: ________

17 Read this sentence from the article.

Soon there was nearly an epidemic of hot-air balloonists trying to see how far up they could soar.

The origin of *epidemic* is a Greek word meaning "visiting" and the Greek root *dem* meaning "people." This suggests that an *epidemic*

Ⓐ affects no one.
Ⓑ affects many.
Ⓒ is easily fixed.
Ⓓ is hard to find.

18 According to the article, advances in ballooning resulted in

Ⓕ the end of World War II.
Ⓖ the development of airplanes.
Ⓗ a way to measure temperature.
Ⓘ a balloon flight around the world.

19 Read this sentence from the article.

They often carry thermometers and other weather-measuring devices.

The word *thermometer* comes from two Greek roots, *therm* and *meter. Meter* means "measure." What is the most likely meaning of *therm*?

Ⓐ disease
Ⓑ heat
Ⓒ shape
Ⓓ size

20 Besides for adventure, how have balloons been used?

Ⓕ They were viewed by George Washington.
Ⓖ They have been admired as being beautiful.
Ⓗ They have been helpful in science and in war.
Ⓘ They have been used to cure all types of illnesses.

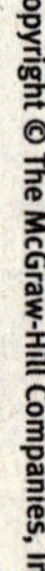

STOP

Name: ______________________ Date: __________

21 According to the articles, how has technology changed over time? Use text evidence from both articles to support your answer.

Answer Key

Name: ______________________________

Question	Correct Answer	Content Focus	CCSS	Complexity
1	D	Greek Roots	L.5.4b	DOK 1
2	H	Greek Roots	L.5.4b	DOK 1
3	B	Text Structure: Cause and Effect	RI.5.5	DOK 3
4	G	Context Clues: Paragraph Clues	L.5.4a	DOK 2
5	D	Text Structure: Cause and Effect	RI.5.5	DOK 3
6	I	Text Structure: Cause and Effect	RI.5.5	DOK 2
7	C	Greek Roots	L.5.4b	DOK 1
8	F	Text Structure: Cause and Effect	RI.5.5	DOK 2
9	B	Greek Roots	L.5.4b	DOK 1
10	I	Main Idea and Key Details	RI.5.2	DOK 2
11	D	Text Structure: Cause and Effect	RI.5.5	DOK 3
12	H	Greek Roots	L.5.4b	DOK 1
13	A	Text Structure: Cause and Effect	RI.5.5	DOK 2
14	H	Context Clues: Paragraph Clues	L.5.4a	DOK 2
15	B	Greek Roots	L.5.4b	DOK 1
16	I	Text Structure: Cause and Effect	RI.5.5	DOK 2
17	B	Greek Roots	L.5.4b	DOK 1
18	I	Text Structure: Cause and Effect	RI.5.5	DOK 3
19	B	Greek Roots	L.5.4b	DOK 1
20	H	Main Idea and Key Details	RI.5.2	DOK 1
21	see below	Comparing Across Texts	RI.5.9	DOK 4

Comprehension 3, 5, 6, 8, 10, 11, 13, 16, 18, 20	/10	%
Vocabulary 1, 2, 4, 7, 9, 12, 14, 15, 17, 19	/10	%
Total Weekly Assessment Score	/20	%

21 To receive full credit for the response, the following information should be included: Like other technologies, both movies and hot-air balloons have become more advanced and complex in terms of what they can do.

Read the article "The First Rock Star" before answering Numbers 1 through 10.

The First Rock Star

Florence Bascom was born in Massachusetts in 1862. She was the daughter of a professor and a suffragist (someone who worked for women's right to vote). Her parents supported both the life of the mind and women's rights. So it might not seem unlikely that she became the first female geologist. But the path she took to her life's work was not an easy one.

Florence Bascom's love of geology began during a car trip she took with her father and a geologist friend of his, Edward Orton. In 1877, Bascom enrolled at the University of Wisconsin. Her father had recently taken the position of university president. Women had only been allowed to enroll there since 1875. She was not permitted to take many of the classes the university offered. Her hours in the library were limited. Still, Bascom graduated with first a bachelor's degree and then a master's degree from the university in 1887. Two geologists, Roland Irving and Charles Van Hise, helped her in her studies. She learned new ways of analyzing rocks and earth from them.

Florence Bascom wanted to go on with her studies. Though she had faced difficulties at Wisconsin, her father was the school's president. She had it easier there than she might have had elsewhere.

GO ON →

She wanted to go to Johns Hopkins University to study for her doctorate, an even more advanced degree. A geology professor named George H. Williams was pioneering the use of microscopes to study geology at Johns Hopkins. She wanted to work with him. Johns Hopkins, however, had never allowed a woman in its Ph.D. program before. It took seven months for a committee to agree to allow Bascom to attend classes there. They would not permit her to enroll officially. And the university told her that she would have to sit behind a screen in her classes so she would not disturb the male students. That seems unbelievable now!

This announcement did not stop Bascom, though. In 1892 she was secretly entered into the Johns Hopkins Ph.D. program. The paper she wrote to get her degree was brilliant, and she received her Ph.D. in 1893. It was the first Ph.D. Johns Hopkins University ever gave to a woman. One other woman had previously finished her studies for a Ph.D. there, but the university refused to give her the degree. Bascom's was the second Ph.D. in geology ever awarded to a woman from an American university.

After accepting a teaching post at Bryn Mawr, a women's college, Bascom founded the Department of Geology there. At first, geology was not considered an important science at Bryn Mawr. Bascom had to work in a storage space in the building that housed the other sciences. She created a large collection of minerals and rocks. She also focused on teaching numerous young women who wanted, like her, to become geologists. Under her influence, many Bryn Mawr graduates went on to work as mineralogists.

Bascom's specialty was the rock formations that created mountains. The studies she did and the papers she wrote were a vital contribution to understanding the geology of the Piedmont area. Florence Bascom was elected the first female Fellow of the Geological Society of America. Eventually she became the vice-president of the organization. She worked for the United States Geological Survey, the first woman ever to do so. Her successes were astonishing at the time. She deserves much credit for opening the door for generations of female scientists.

GO ON →

Name: ______________________________ Date: ________

Now answer Numbers 1 through 10. Base your answers on "The First Rock Star."

1 Read this sentence from the article.

So it might not seem unlikely that she became the first female geologist.

The word *geologist* comes from the root *geo*, which means "earth." This suggests that a *geological* report tells about

Ⓐ rocks and minerals.
Ⓑ animal life.
Ⓒ plant life.
Ⓓ the sea.

2 Read this sentence from the article.

A geology professor named George H. Williams was pioneering the use of microscopes to study geology at Johns Hopkins.

The word *microscope* comes from two Greek roots, *micro* and *scope. Micro* means "tiny." What is the most likely meaning of *scope?*

Ⓕ distant
Ⓖ see
Ⓗ sound
Ⓘ touch

3 Read these sentences from the article.

The studies she did and the papers she wrote were a vital contribution to understanding the geology of the Piedmont area.

The word *vital* comes from a Latin root, *vit,* which means "life." This suggests that a person with a great deal of *vitality* is quite

Ⓐ energetic.
Ⓑ irritating.
Ⓒ jolly.
Ⓓ large.

GO ON →

Name: ______________________________ Date: ________

4 From text evidence, the reader can tell that the author views Florence Bascom as

Ⓕ someone who does not give up.

Ⓖ someone who does not care.

Ⓗ someone who is friendly.

Ⓘ someone who is shy.

5 Read this sentence from the article.

She deserves much credit for opening the door for generations of female scientists.

The origin of *credit* is the Latin root *cred,* meaning "believe." This suggests that a *credible* excuse is one that seems

Ⓐ silly.

Ⓑ made up.

Ⓒ frightening.

Ⓓ likely to be true.

6 Read this sentence from the article.

This announcement did not stop Bascom, though.

Which view of the author does this text evidence support?

Ⓕ Florence Bascom worked harder than the men in her classes.

Ⓖ Florence Bascom was more intelligent than her classmates.

Ⓗ Nothing would keep Florence Bascom from succeeding.

Ⓘ Florence Bascom was tired of the unfairness she faced.

GO ON →

Name: ______________________________ Date: ________

7 What text evidence supports the view that Bascom had an important role in science history?

Ⓐ It took seven months for a committee to agree to allow Bascom to attend classes there.

Ⓑ She deserves much credit for opening the door for generations of female scientists.

Ⓒ In 1892 she was secretly entered into the Johns Hopkins Ph.D program.

Ⓓ In 1877, Bascom enrolled at the University of Wisconsin.

8 Read this sentence from the article.

She also focused on teaching numerous young women who wanted, like her, to become geologists.

The origin of *numerous* is the Latin root *numer,* which means "number." *Numerous* means

Ⓕ good.

Ⓖ kind.

Ⓗ many.

Ⓘ smart.

9 Text evidence shows the author believes that

Ⓐ people used to respect female scientists.

Ⓑ it was once easier to become a geologist.

Ⓒ women had more career choices in Bascom's day.

Ⓓ women were not treated equally in Bascom's day.

10 Florence Bascom had to sit behind a screen because

Ⓕ she was very shy.

Ⓖ she wanted to study in secret.

Ⓗ it was not legal for her to be there.

Ⓘ officials thought she might disturb the male students.

GO ON →

Read the article "Roald Amundsen, Polar Explorer" before answering Numbers 11 through 20.

Roald Amundsen, Polar Explorer

Roald Amundsen had long dreamed of being the first European to reach the North Pole. Unfortunately, Robert E. Peary got there first. As a result, Amundsen abandoned the idea of an expedition to the North Pole. He began planning one to the South Pole instead. He kept this plan secret because he did not want Robert Falcon Scott's team to know what he was doing. Scott also was planning an expedition to the South Pole, and Amundsen did not want him to know that he had competition. Amundsen did not even tell the men on his own ship where they were going until the night before they left.

The South Pole is a much more extreme environment than the North Pole. The average year-round temperature there is minus fifty-six degrees. At the North Pole, the average temperature is zero degrees. There are mountains located at the South Pole that rise far above sea level, while the North Pole does not have mountains. There are no native human groups at the South Pole, and very few animals live there.

Amundsen's ship, the *Fram*, left Norway on August 9, 1910. It was eight weeks after the departure of Robert Scott's team. Amundsen's expedition was already behind. But the team was incredibly well organized. On board were 97 Greenland sled dogs.

GO ON →

Amundsen believed that sled dogs would be more effective than the ponies and tractors with motors that Scott used to pull his sledges. The *Fram* also carried a hut and various supplies. There was enough food to last the crew for two years. The supplies included lamps, tools, and medicines for the treatment of injuries and illnesses.

Four months later, the *Fram* reached the Ross Ice Shelf in Antarctica. The men built their base camp at the Bay of Whales. The team members would need supplies and shelter along the route to the South Pole. They set up depots, or storage places for supplies, along the way. The labor was difficult and demanding. The men had to finish their tasks as fast as they could. Amundsen put them on a strict schedule, regulating their work hours. He even instructed them on what to eat to ensure they stayed healthy. They were in a race against time. The long, dark nights of winter would begin in April. Then the sun would not rise at all. Amundsen also worried about Scott's team reaching the South Pole before him.

On September 8, the team of eight men started off over the dangerous ice. They rode in sledges that were pulled by 86 dogs. One man stayed behind to watch over their base camp. Frigid weather set in, so the team made a run for the nearest depot. The weather was so cold that the team could not proceed. They had to return to the base camp. As soon as the weather improved, a smaller group started out again. Amundsen and four other men struggled through blizzards and over glaciers. They were determined to beat Scott's expedition, despite the delay that the terrible weather had caused.

Finally, on December 14, 1911, Amundsen and his men reached the South Pole. Many of the men had frostbite on their hands and faces, but all were alive. The team members planted the Norwegian flag in the frozen ground to claim their victory over Scott. Without Amundsen's organization and leadership skills, the team probably would have suffered loss of life and possibly failed entirely.

GO ON →

Name: ________________________________ Date: ________

Now answer Numbers 11 through 20. Base your answers on "Roald Amundsen, Polar Explorer."

11 What text evidence supports the author's point that the South Pole was dangerous?

Ⓐ average temperatures about minus fifty-six degrees

Ⓑ mountains rising above sea level

Ⓒ few animals living there

Ⓓ sleds pulled by 86 dogs

12 Read this sentence from the article.

> **There are mountains located at the South Pole that rise far above sea level, while the North Pole does not have mountains.**

The Latin root of *located* is *loc,* which means "place." This suggests that if you choose the *locale* for a party, you pick

Ⓕ when it will be.

Ⓖ where it will be.

Ⓗ who it will be for.

Ⓘ what food will be served.

13 From text evidence, it is clear that the author believes that

Ⓐ Amundsen's group was braver than Scott's.

Ⓑ Amundsen's actions almost ruined the expedition.

Ⓒ Amundsen's leadership helped the group succeed.

Ⓓ the weather was not bad when Scott's group set out.

GO ON →

Name: ______________________________ Date: ________

14 Read this sentence from the article.

The *Fram* also carried a hut and various supplies.

The Latin root of *various* is *var,* which means "different." This suggests that a *variety* is a

Ⓕ new thing.

Ⓖ real thing.

Ⓗ mixture of things.

Ⓘ request for things.

15 Which word from the article meaning "to be enough for the needs of" is a homograph for the word defined below?

following all the rest; final

Ⓐ last

Ⓑ left

Ⓒ plan

Ⓓ result

16 Text evidence shows the author's belief that Roald Amundsen

Ⓕ was very determined.

Ⓖ had a scientific mind.

Ⓗ did not like to be bored.

Ⓘ thought the Antarctic was beautiful.

GO ON →

Name: ______________________________ Date: ________

17 Read this sentence from the article.

The weather was so cold that the team could not proceed.

The origin of *proceed* is the Latin root *ceed,* meaning "go." Knowing this suggests that a victory *procession* is a

Ⓐ banner.
Ⓑ parade.
Ⓒ song.
Ⓓ speech.

18 Read this sentence from the article.

Amundsen put them on a strict schedule, regulating their work hours.

What point from the article does this text evidence support?

Ⓕ The men were lazy.
Ⓖ Amundsen liked to work.
Ⓗ The men hated Amundsen.
Ⓘ Amundsen was organized.

19 Read this sentence from the article.

The team members planted the Norwegian flag in the frozen ground to claim their victory over Scott.

The word *claim* comes from the Latin root *claim*, which means "shout." Knowing this suggests that someone who *proclaims* the truth

Ⓐ is lying.
Ⓑ says it loudly.
Ⓒ says it firmly.
Ⓓ uses a low voice.

20 Amundsen's men had to turn back at first because

Ⓕ they ran out of needed food.
Ⓖ the weather was so cold.
Ⓗ the dogs were too weak.
Ⓘ Scott had won the race.

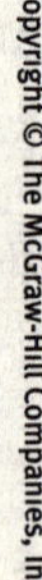

STOP

Name: ______________________ Date: __________

21 Use text evidence to compare and contrast the accomplishments of Florence Bascom and Roald Amundsen. Then explain how the authors of both articles view their subjects.

Answer Key

Name: ____________________

Question	Correct Answer	Content Focus	CCSS	Complexity
1	A	Root Words	L.5.4b	DOK 1
2	G	Greek Roots	L.5.4b	DOK 1
3	A	Root Words	L.5.4b	DOK 1
4	F	Author's Point of View	RI.5.8	DOK 2
5	D	Root Words	L.5.4b	DOK 1
6	H	Author's Point of View	RI.5.8	DOK 2
7	B	Author's Point of View	RI.5.8	DOK 2
8	H	Root Words	L.5.4b	DOK 1
9	D	Author's Point of View	RI.5.8	DOK 2
10	I	Cause and Effect	RI.5.3	DOK 2
11	A	Author's Point of View	RI.5.8	DOK 2
12	G	Root Words	L.5.4b	DOK 1
13	C	Author's Point of View	RI.5.8	DOK 3
14	H	Root Words	L.5.4b	DOK 1
15	A	Homographs	L.5.5c	DOK 1
16	F	Author's Point of View	RI.5.8	DOK 2
17	B	Root Words	L.5.4b	DOK 1
18	I	Author's Point of View	RI.5.8	DOK 2
19	B	Root Words	L.5.4b	DOK 1
20	G	Cause and Effect	RI.5.3	DOK 2
21	see below	Comparing Across Texts	RI.5.9	DOK 4

Comprehension 4, 6, 7, 9, 10, 11, 13, 16, 18, 20	/10	%
Vocabulary 1, 2, 3, 5, 8, 12, 14, 15, 17, 19	/10	%
Total Weekly Assessment Score	/20	%

21 To receive full credit for the response, the following information should be included: Both authors admire their respective subjects and provide details that point to the determination and abilities of Bascom and Amundsen.

Read the passage "Joining Forces for Freedom" before answering Numbers 1 through 10.

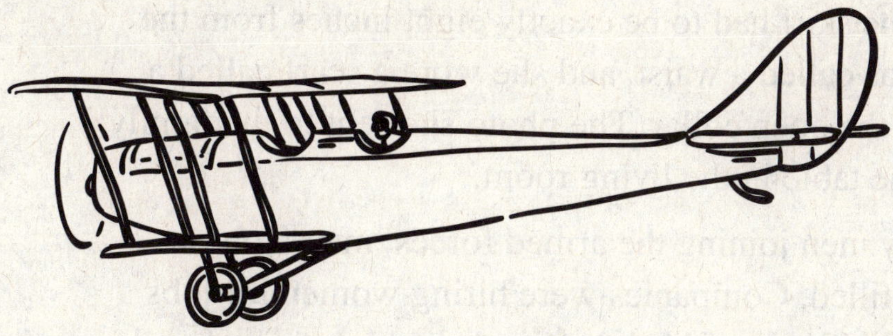

Joining Forces for Freedom

The year was 1918. Emma lived in Buffalo, New York. One day in April almost a year before, her dad came home from work with a newspaper under his arm. The headline said, "PRESIDENT CALLS FOR WAR DECLARATION." Dad explained that Germany was trying to take over other countries and attacking ships, including American ships. President Wilson had asked Congress to declare war and join forces with Germany's enemies. America had a duty to fight for freedom.

Along with many of the men where he worked, Dad joined the U.S. Army to fight in World War I. He went to training camp and then was sent to France. Emma knew Mom missed him and was sad, even though her mother did not say it aloud. Emma was proud her dad was helping the cause of freedom.

Mom missed Aunt Edith too. Aunt Edith was Mom's younger sister and had lived with them as long as Emma could remember. When Aunt Edith was eighteen, she got a job as a switchboard operator for the telephone company. Then, for the first time in American history, women were allowed to join the U.S. Navy because of the Naval Act of 1916. It said "all persons" who were able to provide "useful service" could be in the Navy. When America entered the war, telephone operators, chauffeurs, and truck drivers were needed. Aunt Edith wanted to serve her country. She signed up and moved to Washington, D.C., where she shared an apartment with other young women.

GO ON →

Aunt Edith wrote home often. She was proud of her uniform, a navy blue jacket with gold buttons and navy blue skirt. She said that the bottom of the skirt had to be exactly eight inches from the floor. Her blouse was called a waist, and she wore a scarf called a neckerchief around the open collar. The photo she sent to the family was displayed on the table in the living room.

With so many men joining the armed forces, many jobs at home needed to be filled. Companies were hiring women for jobs that men usually held. Some of Mom's friends had jobs. The family needed money, so Dad's mom agreed to help care for Emma if Mom got a job. Mom saw ads for jobs at the Curtiss Company, a corporation that made airplanes at a plant outside the city of Buffalo. The company was at the end of the streetcar line.

Mom applied for and got a job. When she came home after the first day at the factory, she told Emma about the company. Company workers made two kinds of aircraft: flying boats and training planes. Flying boats were aircraft that could land on water, and training planes were light aircraft not closed-in at the top.

To manufacture the aircraft, different departments carried out the various steps. One department worked with machines, another with the wood used for the frames of airplanes, and other departments assembled the craft and finished it. Mom was an inspector. Each part had to be carefully checked with tools that measured very short lengths and small diameters. Every bolt and screw had to match exactly the length and width shown on the plans. The job was important because lives of pilots who flew the planes depended on careful attention to detail. Mom enjoyed her work at the factory.

In August, 1918, the family received a letter from Dad. He had fought in a battle but was fine. Then, in November of 1918, the German Kaiser, or emperor, gave up his rule. The fighting stopped on November 11, and Dad wrote that he was coming home. The family was so happy and ready to see him. Mom wanted to keep working but was not sure it would be possible because the men returning from war would want their old jobs back.

GO ON →

Name: ______________________________ Date: ________

Now answer Numbers 1 through 10. Base your answers on "Joining Forces for Freedom."

1 What is the theme of this passage?

Ⓐ Attention to details is an important habit.

Ⓑ People working together can accomplish much.

Ⓒ The actions of the past affect the events of the future.

Ⓓ Working hard is considered to be its own reward.

2 Which words from the passage are homophones?

Ⓕ aloud, allowed

Ⓖ company, corporation

Ⓗ eight, waist

Ⓘ flew, flying

3 How are Dad and Aunt Edith alike?

Ⓐ They want to stay in Buffalo.

Ⓑ They wear U.S. Navy uniforms.

Ⓒ They want to serve their country.

Ⓓ They fight overseas in World War I.

4 Which word from the passage is a homophone for the word defined below?

useless spending; something worthless

Ⓕ ads

Ⓖ blouse

Ⓗ join

Ⓘ waist

GO ON →

Name: ______________________ Date: ________

5 What does the passage suggest about freedom?

Ⓐ Freedom is worth fighting for.

Ⓑ Not all people believe in freedom.

Ⓒ The American flag stands for freedom.

Ⓓ Young people do not have the same freedom as adults.

6 Which word from the passage is a homophone for the word defined below?

past tense of *win*

Ⓕ day

Ⓖ back

Ⓗ for

Ⓘ one

7 Read this quotation.

The cost of freedom is always high, but Americans have always paid it. —John F. Kennedy

What idea from the passage does this quote support?

Ⓐ Americans are willing to fight to be free.

Ⓑ Aunt Edith was proud of her Navy uniform.

Ⓒ Women who worked during the war often enjoyed their jobs.

Ⓓ Emma's mom knew that Dad needed to do what he was doing.

GO ON →

She wondered how many other children had to work. She read that Illinois had passed a law in 1897. It provided that no one under fourteen years old could work for wages. People must be ignoring the law if students as young as George were working to make money. Anna believed that anyone who was not yet sixteen should be in school. It was a right they should have in America in 1909. She wanted to do something to help.

A friend gave Anna a photo essay by Lewis W. Hine. Like Anna, Hine had trained to be a teacher. He noticed that children were employed in dangerous and unhealthy jobs, and he wanted to show the need for change. He left teaching to become a photographer for the National Child Labor Committee.

His photographs of working children were taken across America, from the coal mines of Pennsylvania to fishing docks in Mississippi and cotton mills in Massachusetts. In the coal mines, children as young as eight years old separated coal from clay, soil, and slate. Sometimes they worked twelve hours a day in a room thick with coal dust. In a cotton mill in Georgia, boys and girls had to climb onto a frame in order to reach and replace empty bobbins. A bobbin is a kind of reel for holding thread. Other photos pictured boys tending furnaces in factories and children as young as five picking cotton in Texas. In Colorado, children worked in beet fields. Accidents happened because the children had to use a sharp knife to cut off the top of a beet. Seeing the photos made Anna's head throb and her heart beat in pain and sadness. She wanted to find a way to make a difference.

A teacher at her school told Anna about Jane Addams, who, along with Ellen Star, had started a settlement house to help immigrants. Other reformers had joined Addams and Star. They worked to improve conditions for working people. The site, or location, of Hull House was not far from Anna's school in Chicago. Anna wrote Jane Addams saying she would like to volunteer at Hull House. She offered to tutor children or adult immigrants in reading. Anna hoped she could contribute to helping people get the education they needed for better jobs and lives.

GO ON →

Name: ______________________________ Date: ________

Now answer Numbers 11 through 20. Base your answers on "Voices for Change."

11 What message about society does the passage provide?

Ⓐ People need to work to make money.

Ⓑ If something seems wrong, work to make it better.

Ⓒ A person who wants to help children is a good person.

Ⓓ In the past, children as young as five years old worked hard jobs.

12 What text evidence best states the author's message?

Ⓕ Anna loved teaching fifth grade.

Ⓖ George did not think he could come to school any more.

Ⓗ Anna wanted to find a way to make a difference.

Ⓘ In a cotton mill in Georgia, boys and girls had to climb onto a frame in order to reach and replace empty bobbins.

13 Which word from the passage is a homophone for the word defined below?

to form letters on a surface with an instrument, such as a pen

Ⓐ essay

Ⓑ grade

Ⓒ right

Ⓓ route

GO ON →

Name: ______________________ Date: ________

14 What word best describes Anna Johnson and Lewis Hine?

Ⓕ photographers
Ⓖ readers
Ⓗ reformers
Ⓘ tutors

15 Which word from the passage is a homophone for the word defined below?

not imagined or made up; actual

Ⓐ job
Ⓑ pain
Ⓒ reel
Ⓓ site

16 Which words from the passage are homophones?

Ⓕ beat, beet
Ⓖ beat, throb
Ⓗ class, school
Ⓘ mines, mills

17 Read these sentences from the passage.

Anna wrote Jane Addams saying she would like to volunteer at Hull House. She offered to tutor children or adult immigrants in reading. Anna hoped she could contribute to helping people get the education they needed for better jobs and lives.

How do these lines support the theme?

Ⓐ They prove that Anna was an excellent teacher.
Ⓑ They show that Anna was a friend of Jane Addams.
Ⓒ They show that Anna decided to act to correct an injustice.
Ⓓ They suggest that learning to read leads to better jobs and better lives.

GO ON →

Name: ______________________________ Date: ________

18 Read these sentences from the passage.

Anna realized this job was much harder than a paper route. She deeply worried about George and the brevity of his education.

The root of *brevity* is *brev,* meaning "short," as in *abbreviation.* This suggests that *brevity* means

Ⓕ briefness.

Ⓖ end.

Ⓗ lack.

Ⓘ uselessness.

19 What is the theme of this passage?

Ⓐ People can make a difference.

Ⓑ It takes courage to be a reformer.

Ⓒ Everyone should be paid a fair wage.

Ⓓ Look to your friends in a time of trouble.

20 Which word from the passage is a homophone for the word defined below?

vision

Ⓕ frame

Ⓖ lives

Ⓗ site

Ⓘ stay

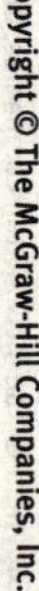

STOP

Name: ______________________________ Date: ________

21 Compare the ways Emma's mom in "Joining Forces for Freedom" and Anna Johnson in "Voices for Change" respond to the challenges of their times. Use clear text evidence from both articles to support your comparison.

Answer Key

Name: ______________________

Question	Correct Answer	Content Focus	CCSS	Complexity
1	B	Theme	RL.5.2	DOK 3
2	F	Homophones	L.5.4a	DOK 1
3	C	Character, Setting, Plot: Compare and Contrast	RL.5.3	DOK 3
4	I	Homophones	L.5.4a	DOK 1
5	A	Theme	RL.5.2	DOK 3
6	I	Homophones	L.5.4a	DOK 1
7	A	Theme	RL.5.2	DOK 3
8	I	Root Words	L.5.4b	DOK 1
9	B	Theme	RL.5.2	DOK 3
10	G	Homophones	L.5.4a	DOK 1
11	B	Theme	RL.5.2	DOK 3
12	H	Theme	RL.5.2	DOK 3
13	C	Homophones	L.5.4a	DOK 1
14	H	Character, Setting, Plot: Compare and Contrast	RL.5.3	DOK 3
15	C	Homophones	L.5.4a	DOK 1
16	F	Homophones	L.5.4a	DOK 1
17	C	Theme	RL.5.2	DOK 3
18	F	Root Words	L.5.4b	DOK 1
19	A	Theme	RL.5.2	DOK 3
20	H	Homophones	L.5.4a	DOK 1
21	see below	Comparing Across Texts	RL.5.9	DOK 4

Comprehension 1, 3, 5, 7, 9, 11, 12, 14, 17, 19	/10	%
Vocabulary 2, 4, 6, 8, 10, 13, 15, 16, 18, 20	/10	%
Total Weekly Assessment Score	/20	%

21 To receive full credit for the response, the following information should be included: In "Joining Forces for Freedom," Emma's mom takes a job in a factory to help her country when workers are needed during World War I. In "Voices for Change," Anna Johnson becomes concerned about child labor when she learns some children have to work to help support their families and volunteers at Hull House. Both women take action because of their beliefs.

Read the passage "New Country, New School" before answering Numbers 1 through 10.

New Country, New School

Vlad lived in Moscow, a big city in Russia, until he was ten years old. Then his father received a letter from Uncle Igor, who was living in Alexandria, Virginia. Like his father, Uncle Igor was a chemist. He wrote that there were jobs for trained chemists in the Washington, D.C. area where he lived and wanted Vlad's father to move to America. He said that life was good in his adopted country.

Vlad's mother was hardworking and ambitious. She said, "If we don't make this move now, we never will do it. Now is the time to make a change."

Vlad didn't want to leave his chess players club, Saturday gymnastics classes, and friends. Yet the decision was made. His parents packed for the move.

Uncle Igor and Aunt Irina, who were friendly and not at all cold, met them at the airport. Vlad and his parents would stay with them until they found a place of their own. In Russia, Vlad and his parents shared a tiny apartment in a high-rise building with Vlad's grandparents because it was customary to live with relatives.

Uncle Igor and Aunt Irina lived in a townhouse where Vlad had his own room on the lower level. When Vlad saw the room, he was enthusiastic and said, "Wow! This is big. It's great!"

Vlad's parents enrolled him at Jefferson School nearby so that he wouldn't miss any time. They hoped to find a place in the area so Vlad wouldn't have to change schools again. Vlad was nervous on his first day, but the teacher, Ms. Chin, made him feel very welcome.

GO ON →

She introduced him to the class. She said they were studying Russia, and Vlad could give them firsthand information. Vlad did not understand all of her words, but she smiled and seemed kind.

At lunch, Anthony motioned for him to sit at his table in the cafeteria. Even though Anthony and the others spoke no Russian, and Vlad knew only a few English words, they communicated by signaling with their hands. Vlad would point to a food on someone's tray, and Anthony would say the English word. Then Vlad repeated the word. By the end of the lunch break, Vlad had a few new words in his vocabulary and new friends as well.

Vlad's parents took a class to learn to speak better English. His father got a job as a chemist, and his mother took a position on the staff of a hospital. After a few months, all three were becoming familiar with their new life in America. Mother thought they had taken advantage of Uncle Igor and Aunt Irina's generosity long enough and needed to get a place of their own. On a Saturday, they went looking for an apartment. The typical apartments in Alexandria were larger than apartments in Moscow, and they found a nice one that day.

Vlad was happy to be able to stay at Jefferson School. His parents said he could join a gymnastics club where he could continue improving his skills. He was enjoying his new friends and learning the language. He also liked sharing information about Russia. During class, he showed photographs of Moscow. His mother made *blinis,* which are thin pancakes, and filled them with the traditional smoked salmon and sour cream. He took them to share with classmates.

Vlad's favorite activity was the chess club that met after school. He was teaching interested classmates how to play chess. They said it was a good game and that they never would have learned if Vlad hadn't taught them. Vlad realized that he could make new friends by expressing his interest in American customs and sharing his Russian culture with his new friends.

GO ON →

Name: ______________________ **Date:** ________

Now answer Numbers 1 through 10. Base your answers on "New Country, New School."

1. What point does the passage communicate about people?

Ⓐ Vlad was a typical ten-year-old Russian boy.

Ⓑ Americans always welcome people from other countries.

Ⓒ Gymnastics is an important sport in Russia and in America.

Ⓓ People adjust to change by learning new things and making new friends.

2. Read these sentences from the passage.

Vlad's mother was hardworking and ambitious. She said, "If we don't make this move now, we never will do it. Now is the time to make a change."

The use of *ambitious* instead of *hopeful* emphasizes that Vlad's mother is

Ⓕ famous.

Ⓖ forceful.

Ⓗ wealthy.

Ⓘ unconcerned.

3. What text evidence shows that the settings are different?

Ⓐ Vlad lived in Moscow, a big city in Russia, until he was ten years old.

Ⓑ His father got a job as a chemist, and his mother took a position on the staff of a hospital.

Ⓒ The typical apartments in Alexandria were larger than apartments in Moscow, and they found a nice one that day.

Ⓓ His mother made *blinis,* which are thin pancakes, and filled them with the traditional smoked salmon and sour cream.

GO ON →

Name: ______________________________ Date: ________

4 What is the theme of this passage?

Ⓕ Reaching out helps us get along with others.

Ⓖ Every culture has special foods that others may enjoy.

Ⓗ School is the same anywhere you go.

Ⓘ Food is the universal language.

5 Which word from the passage has a negative connotation when it is used to describe a person?

Ⓐ cold

Ⓑ enthusiastic

Ⓒ interested

Ⓓ trained

6 Read this sentence from the passage.

In Russia, Vlad and his parents shared a tiny apartment in a high-rise building with Vlad's grandparents because it was customary to live with relatives.

The use of *customary* instead of *common* suggests that sharing an apartment in this way is

Ⓕ necessary.

Ⓖ done infrequently.

Ⓗ the result of habits.

Ⓘ the result of traditions.

GO ON →

Name: ______________________________ Date: ________

7. What text evidence best states the author's message?

Ⓐ Like his father, Uncle Igor was a chemist.

Ⓑ "If we don't make this move now, we never will do it."

Ⓒ The typical apartments in Alexandria were larger than apartments in Moscow, and they found a nice one that day.

Ⓓ Vlad realized that he could make new friends by expressing his interest in American customs and sharing his Russian culture with his new friends.

8. Which word from the passage has a positive connotation?

Ⓕ generosity

Ⓖ information

Ⓗ letter

Ⓘ nervous

9. Which action by a character best describes the lesson of the passage?

Ⓐ Vlad's mother encourages the family to move.

Ⓑ Vlad teaches some of his classmates how to play chess.

Ⓒ Uncle Igor and Aunt Irina meet the family at the airport.

Ⓓ Vlad's mother accepts a position on the staff of a nearby hospital.

10. Which word from the passage is a homophone for the word defined below?

something used for slowing or stopping motion

Ⓕ break

Ⓖ learn

Ⓗ packed

Ⓘ staff

GO ON →

Read the passage "Getting Along with Grandma" before answering Numbers 11 through 20.

Getting Along with Grandma

Sam and his friends Robert and Scott had formed a jazz band and were practicing at Sam's house. Robert played the keyboard, Scott the drums, and Sam the bass guitar. Sam's young brother, Guy, pestered them and asked silly questions because he wanted attention.

Finally, Sam said, "Guy, just go to your own room. You are annoying us."

Guy's expression turned into a pout, and Sam was hoping he would not cry when Mom came into the room. She said, "I have some great news. Guy and Sam, your grandmother is coming from Thailand to live with us."

A few days later, Mom said to the boys, "Guy will have to share Sam's room. We must make your grandmother feel welcome by giving her a room. You boys can get along if you try."

The boys each agreed to try, and that weekend, Guy moved into Sam's room. Guy had enough toys and games to fill the room, and Sam wondered if the arrangement would work. Yet he was determined to try. Sam told Guy which of his things he could use, but Guy paid no attention. First, he took Sam's baseball and left it at the park. Then he carelessly knocked Sam's soccer trophy off its base. Sam asked his dad to talk to Guy. Dad suggested that they put tape down the middle of the room to separate it into two parts. Each boy would have his half and could not touch anything on the other side. The system worked.

GO ON →

Mom, Dad, and the boys went to the airport to meet Grandma. She had a nice smile and gave them many hugs. At home, May, the boys' older sister, had prepared a special Thai dinner in Grandma's honor. It was pad thai, a family favorite made with rice noodles and shrimp. Grandma spoke English well and enjoyed telling them about her life in Thailand. She explained that she had loved the dinner but would like to try some American food soon and learn some American customs.

A few days later, Robert and Scott came over to practice and started tuning their instruments. When Mom came from the kitchen and asked them not to play because Grandma was taking a nap, the boys were disappointed.

On Saturday afternoon, Dad was working, Mom was taking Guy to the dentist, and Sam had soccer practice. Mom asked May to please stay home to keep Grandma company. May had planned on a long bike ride with friends but agreed to stay home instead. It was not going to be as easy as she had hoped to have Grandma with them.

The next time Robert and Scott came to practice, Grandma came into the room and asked if she could listen. The boys looked at each other. Then Sam said, "Grandma, we don't mind, but you may not like our music. It's loud, and it has a strong beat."

Grandma explained that she wanted to hear some American music and would like to hear them play. She stayed through the practice session. Afterwards she clapped and said they had real talent. She wanted to be invited to their first performance on a stage.

Mom asked May and Sam to stay with Guy and Grandma on Saturday night. Immediately, Grandma spoke up, "May and Sam don't need to stay home because Guy and I will watch out for each other. He will take care of me, and I will take care of him."

Mom asked, "Are you sure, Mother? You didn't come here to work."

Grandma said, "I'm sure. You are helping me, and I want to help you. Besides, being with Guy is fun, not work."

GO ON →

Name: ______________________________ Date: ________

Now answer Numbers 11 through 20. Base your answers on "Getting Along with Grandma."

11 What do you learn from the passage about getting along with people?

Ⓐ It is very difficult to change one's ways.

Ⓑ Children must respect older family members.

Ⓒ People who help others receive help in return.

Ⓓ The only way to share a space is to divide it in two.

12 Which words from the passage are homophones?

Ⓕ base, baseball

Ⓖ bass, base

Ⓗ cry, try

Ⓘ bike, ride

13 What caused problems between Sam and Guy when they started to share a room?

Ⓐ Sam was selfish about his belongings.

Ⓑ The room wasn't large enough for two boys.

Ⓒ Guy was not responsible about Sam's belongings.

Ⓓ The boys did not stay out of each other's side of the room.

GO ON →

Name: ______________________________ Date: ______

14 Read the following sentence from the passage.

Sam's young brother, Guy, pestered them and asked silly questions because he wanted attention.

Which word has a connotation most similar to *pestered*?

Ⓕ angered

Ⓖ bothered

Ⓗ disappointed

Ⓘ welcomed

15 What text evidence best supports the lesson in the passage?

Ⓐ "Guy will have to share Sam's room."

Ⓑ She stayed through the practice session.

Ⓒ It was not going to be as easy as she had hoped to have Grandma with them.

Ⓓ "May and Sam don't need to stay home because Guy and I will watch out for each other."

16 Which word from the passage has a negative connotation?

Ⓕ jazz

Ⓖ many

Ⓗ pout

Ⓘ strong

17 What is the theme of this passage?

Ⓐ Grandparents should live with their families.

Ⓑ Getting along means meeting others halfway.

Ⓒ It is easy for members of a family to get along.

Ⓓ Practicing something will lead to mastery.

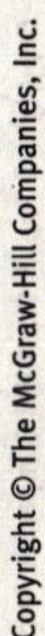

GO ON →

Name: ______________________________ Date: ________

18 Read this sentence from the passage.

> **Then he carelessly knocked Sam's soccer trophy off its base.**

The connotation of the word *carelessly* suggests that Guy was acting in

Ⓕ a mean way.

Ⓖ a selfish way.

Ⓗ an angry way.

Ⓘ a thoughtless way.

19 Which word from the passage has a positive connotation?

Ⓐ arrangement

Ⓑ attention

Ⓒ clapped

Ⓓ practice

20 How does this old proverb from Thailand support the message of the passage?

> **When you enter a town where people wink, wink as they do.**

Ⓕ When you travel, pay attention to people's eyes.

Ⓖ If you want to be accepted in another country, follow the customs.

Ⓗ If you are in a new country, be sure to tell people about your own customs.

Ⓘ When you travel, keep your eyes open at all times to see as much as possible.

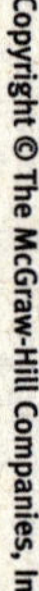

STOP

Name: ______________________________ Date: ________

21 Compare how Vlad in "New Country, New School" and Sam in "Getting Along with Grandma" meet the challenge of getting along with new people. Give clear text evidence from the stories to explain your response.

Answer Key Name: ______________________________

Question	Correct Answer	Content Focus	CCSS	Complexity
1	D	Theme	RL.5.2	DOK 3
2	G	Connotation and Denotation	L.5.5	DOK 2
3	C	Character, Setting, Plot: Compare and Contrast	RL.5.3	DOK 2
4	F	Theme	RL.5.2	DOK 3
5	A	Connotation and Denotation	L.5.5	DOK 2
6	I	Connotation and Denotation	L.5.5	DOK 2
7	D	Theme	RL.5.2	DOK 3
8	F	Connotation and Denotation	L.5.5	DOK 2
9	B	Theme	RL.5.2	DOK 3
10	F	Homophones	L.5.4a	DOK 1
11	C	Theme	RL.5.2	DOK 3
12	G	Homophones	L.5.4a	DOK 1
13	C	Character, Setting, Plot: Problem and Solution	RL.4.3	DOK 2
14	G	Connotation and Denotation	L.5.5	DOK 2
15	D	Theme	RL.5.2	DOK 3
16	H	Connotation and Denotation	L.5.5	DOK 2
17	B	Theme	RL.5.2	DOK 3
18	I	Connotation and Denotation	L.5.5	DOK 2
19	C	Connotation and Denotation	L.5.5	DOK 2
20	G	Theme	RL.5.2	DOK 3
21	see below	Comparing Across Texts	RL.5.9	DOK 4

Comprehension 1, 3, 4, 7, 9, 11, 13, 15, 17, 20	/10	%
Vocabulary 2, 5, 6, 8, 10, 12 14, 16, 18, 19	/10	%
Total Weekly Assessment Score	/20	%

21 To receive full credit for the response, the following information should be included: In "New Country, New School," Vlad joins Anthony's table in the cafeteria and begins to learn a new language in order to communicate with his classmates. In "Getting Along with Grandma," Sam works to get along with Guy for his family's sake. Both Vlad and Guy share something from their own culture. Vlad shows photos of Moscow and brings *blinis* to school. Sam and his friends play jazz for Grandma.

Read the article "Watch Out for the Octopus!" before answering Numbers 1 through 10.

Watch Out for the Octopus!

There are a lot of deadly animals in the world. Some are poisonous. That is, they use poison as a defense. If you touch them, you might absorb the poison through your skin. Others are venomous. They use their poison to attack. What are some of the deadliest animals out there?

One truly deadly animal is the puffer fish. It does not look dangerous, but its skin and organs are poisonous to humans. Oddly, people like to eat the puffer fish. Cooks who work with it have to have a special license. It is supposed to be delicious—as long as you don't take a bite of those parts of it that might be fatal! Puffer fish could be the last meal you ever have. The stonefish is a poisonous fish. It is covered with sharp spines where it stores its poison. If you step on it–watch out! It uses its spines to keep away predators.

The exotic poison dart frog is found in the jungles of South and Central America. These tiny frogs are unusually colorful. Their beauty is sinister, though. Their skin is so poisonous that if enemies touch or try to eat it, they will quickly die.

Snakes, of course, are known for being venomous. The taipan is called the world's most venomous snake. It lives in Australia. Its venom is said to be four hundred times stronger than that of the next most venomous snake. Luckily, the taipan is very shy and secretive.

GO ON →

It is rarely seen by humans. King cobras are the longest venomous snakes, growing to more than eighteen feet in length. They live in East and Southeast Asia and have been known to kill full-grown elephants. The faint-banded sea snake is another deadly snake, though it rarely bites. When it does bite, it does not always release its poison. It is found in the Indian Ocean.

Some animals have very venomous stings. Scorpions, with their sharp tails, are among them. The death starker scorpion has a strong, painful poison. It is found in North Africa and the Middle East. Many spiders, too, are venomous. The Brazilian wandering spider is one; it is especially dangerous because it moves around a lot. It might be found in someone's shoe or under a bed. In the United States, black widow spiders and brown recluse spiders are the most common venomous spiders, but they do not match the danger of the Brazilian wandering spider or the funnel-web spider of Australia. Like scorpions, venomous spiders use their poison to get food.

You might not think of an octopus as being venomous, but the blue-ringed octopus certainly is. It is small and brightly colored, and it can move very quickly. It lives in the waters around Asia and Australia, and its sting is both painful and dangerous. The waters off Japan, the Philippines, Australia, and Hawaii are home to the animal that is considered the world's most venomous. It is the box jelly, a fearsome creature with long tentacles that are full of poison. Like the blue-ringed octopus, the box jelly uses its poison to stun and kill other animals, which it then eats.

There are poisonous and venomous animals almost everywhere in the world. That is why it is usually a good idea to be careful if you see an unfamiliar animal—especially an unfamiliar snake, spider, jellyfish, scorpion, fish, or octopus!

GO ON →

Name: ______________________________ Date: __________

Now answer Numbers 1 through 10. Base your answers on "Watch Out for the Octopus!"

1 According to the article, poisonous animals are different from venomous animals because poisonous animals use poisons in order to

Ⓐ move quickly.

Ⓑ defend themselves.

Ⓒ find their food easily.

Ⓓ hide from predators.

2 Read these sentences from the article.

It is supposed to be delicious—as long as you don't take a bite of those parts of it that might be fatal! Puffer fish could be the last meal you ever have.

What does *fatal* mean in the sentences above?

Ⓕ deadly

Ⓖ delicious

Ⓗ fragile

Ⓘ physical

3 What is the effect of the puffer fish's poison?

Ⓐ It stuns or kills its prey.

Ⓑ It kills those who eat it.

Ⓒ It is absorbed through the skin.

Ⓓ It is strong enough to kill an elephant.

GO ON →

Name: ______________________ Date: ________

4 How does the author show the relationship between certain kinds of animals and humans?

Ⓕ Poisonous animals never harm humans.

Ⓖ People and animals together help sustain nature.

Ⓗ Animal bites must be treated promptly with medicine.

Ⓘ Animals can be dangerous, and people need to be careful.

5 The poison dart frog is deadly because

Ⓐ its skin is poisonous.

Ⓑ it has a poisonous bite.

Ⓒ it has poisonous spines.

Ⓓ its tentacles are full of poison.

6 Read these sentences from the article.

The exotic poison dart frog is found only in the jungles of South and Central America. These tiny frogs are unusually colorful.

What does *exotic* mean in the sentences above?

Ⓕ charming

Ⓖ common

Ⓗ lively

Ⓘ unusual

7 What text evidence best explains what the article is about?

Ⓐ People should be afraid of all animals.

Ⓑ Animals can be deadly to other animals.

Ⓒ Brightly-colored animals are often poisonous.

Ⓓ Animals use poison to defend themselves and get food.

GO ON →

Name: ______________________________ Date: ________

8 Read these sentences from the article.

Their beauty is sinister, though. Their skin is so poisonous that if enemies touch or try to eat it, they will quickly die.

What does *sinister* mean in the sentence above?

Ⓕ false

Ⓖ harmless

Ⓗ pretend

Ⓘ threatening

9 Read these sentences from the article.

Luckily, the taipan is very shy and secretive. It is rarely seen by humans.

The use of *secretive* instead of *mysterious* suggests that the taipan tries to

Ⓐ be dangerous.

Ⓑ remain hidden.

Ⓒ confuse people.

Ⓓ be misunderstood.

10 Read these sentences from the article.

The waters off Japan, the Philippines, Australia, and Hawaii are home to the animal that is considered the world's most venomous. It is the box jelly, a fearsome creature with long tentacles that are full of poison.

What does *fearsome* mean in the sentences above?

Ⓕ beautiful

Ⓖ frightening

Ⓗ spectacular

Ⓘ weird

GO ON →

Read the article "Animal Communities" before answering Numbers 11 through 20.

Animal Communities

In human communities, people work together. Working together helps us obtain food and shelter, raise children, and enjoy a higher quality of life. When each person contributes to a community, the community functions better. A society needs many different kinds of workers in order to do well. Animals also live in varied communities. In fact, nature gives most creatures a social instinct that serves a number of purposes.

Many lions work together in well-organized groups. The females do the hunting. They work in teams to trap their prey. Because of this, the lions can surround an animal and cut off its escape. Wolves also hunt in teams. They have a strong social order. They follow a leader and obey rules for the good of the pack.

Naturalist Dr. Regis Ferriere notes that some insect species exist cooperatively. An example is the relationship between ants and aphids. The ants watch over groups of aphids on grasses as if they were herds of cattle, and from time to time, the ants "milk" the aphids of sugar droplets. In turn, the ants protect the aphids from predators.

Bees, ants, and wasps have special jobs in their communities. For example, a queen and worker bees and other bees live in a beehive. The worker bees serve the queen so the queen can lay eggs. If the queen did not lay enough eggs, the busy hive would become vacant. In an ant community, soldier ants are protectors for the colony. In bee and wasp communities, females take on the job of providing defense.

GO ON →

Baboons and antelopes often eat together to protect one another. Baboons have excellent eyesight, and the antelopes have a keen sense of smell. Together they function as a warning system. Cattle and birds work in much the same way. The birds eat the insects that the cattle stir up, and in turn, the birds make a lot of warning noises and fly off if they sense danger. Thus, their combined efforts benefit both the birds and the cattle.

Crocodiles and birds called plovers help each other in a unique way. Crocodiles have very sharp teeth. They often have tiny, harmful animals attached to their teeth. The plover will pick the animals out of a crocodile's teeth, getting food for itself while helping to clean the crocodile's teeth.

On the African plains, the honeyguide bird looks for honey. When it finds a beehive, it cannot open it. The ratel, or honey badger, comes to the rescue. It tears open the beehive, which the honeyguide has found for it, and exposes the honey so both can eat.

In the desert, mongooses and hornbills (a type of bird) help each other out. There are few trees or other shelters available. Both mongooses and hornbills are very exposed to predators. The groups take turns guarding. They use warning cries to tell when predators sneak up. A predator's ambush is difficult when so many are watching and warning.

Another example of two very different animals helping each other can be found in warm oceans. The remora is a fish that cannot swim well. However, the form of its head allows it to attach itself to large sharks. So it gets from one place to another in the ocean by getting rides from sharks. In turn, the remora cleans the shark of small animals that hurt it.

As you can see, there are certain basic similarities between human and animal societies. We have many of the same needs, after all. We must depend on one another to help all survive.

GO ON →

Name: ______________________________ Date: ________

Now answer Numbers 11 through 20. Base your answers on "Animal Communities."

11 Read these sentences from the article.

In an ant community, soldier ants are protectors for the colony. In bee and wasp communities, females take on the job of providing defense.

What does *protectors* mean in the sentences above?

Ⓐ defenders
Ⓑ helpers
Ⓒ planners
Ⓓ producers

12 Read this sentence from the article.

Baboons have excellent eyesight, and the antelopes have a keen sense of smell.

The use of *keen* instead of *good* suggests that the antelopes' sense of smell is

Ⓕ ordinary.
Ⓖ very good.
Ⓗ the best there is.
Ⓘ a little better than average.

13 Read these sentences from the article.

The worker bees serve the queen so the queen can lay eggs. If the queen did not lay enough eggs, the busy hive would become vacant.

What does *vacant* mean in the sentences above?

Ⓐ complete
Ⓑ dead
Ⓒ empty
Ⓓ full

GO ON →

Name: ______________________________ Date: ______

14 Based on text evidence, which of the following pairs of effects are caused by the relationship between crocodiles and plovers?

Ⓕ food to eat and clean teeth

Ⓖ ability to move and clean skin

Ⓗ locating food and being able to get it

Ⓘ safety from attack and a warning system

15 How does the author show the relationship between human and animal communities?

Ⓐ Living in communities helps both humans and animals to survive.

Ⓑ Animals first inhabit an area; then humans follow.

Ⓒ Humans can learn to settle disputes by observing animal behavior.

Ⓓ Humans and animals form communities for different reasons.

16 Read these sentences from the article.

They use warning cries to tell when predators sneak up. A predator's ambush by a predator is difficult when so many are watching and warning.

What does *ambush* mean in the sentences above?

Ⓕ rush

Ⓖ disturbance

Ⓗ surprise attack

Ⓘ dangerous attack

GO ON →

Name: ______________________________ Date: ________

17 What text evidence best explains what the article is about?

Ⓐ Animals and people can help each other.

Ⓑ People need protection just as animals do.

Ⓒ Animals are better at helping other animals than people are.

Ⓓ Animals, like people, often work together to help one another.

18 All of the following are identified in the article as causes for animal cooperation EXCEPT the need

Ⓕ to find food.

Ⓖ for company.

Ⓗ for protection.

Ⓘ for cleanliness.

19 Read these sentences from the article.

There are few trees or other shelters available. Both mongooses and hornbills are very exposed to predators.

What does *exposed* mean in the sentences above?

Ⓐ delightful

Ⓑ delicious

Ⓒ enclosed

Ⓓ visible

20 What is the effect of the remora on the shark?

Ⓕ It feeds the shark.

Ⓖ It cleans the shark.

Ⓗ It protects the shark.

Ⓘ It helps the shark move.

STOP

Name: ________________________ Date: __________

21 How have venomous animals and those that cooperate with other animals adapted to survive? Use clear text evidence from both articles to support your answer.

Answer Key Name: ___________________________

Question	Correct Answer	Content Focus	CCSS	Complexity
1	B	Text Structure: Cause and Effect	RI.5.3	DOK 2
2	F	Context Clues: Paragraph Clues	L.5.4a	DOK 2
3	B	Cause and Effect	RI.5.3	DOK 2
4	I	Text Structure: Cause and Effect	RI.5.3	DOK 2
5	A	Cause and Effect	RI.5.3	DOK 2
6	I	Context Clues: Paragraph Clues	L.5.4a	DOK 2
7	D	Main Idea and Key Details	RI.5.2	DOK 2
8	I	Context Clues: Paragraph Clues	L.5.4a	DOK 2
9	B	Connotation and Denotation	L.5.5	DOK 2
10	G	Context Clues: Paragraph Clues	L.5.4a	DOK 2
11	A	Context Clues: Paragraph Clues	L.5.4a	DOK 2
12	G	Connotation and Denotation	L.5.5	DOK 2
13	C	Context Clues: Paragraph Clues	L.5.4a	DOK 2
14	F	Text Structure: Cause and Effect	RI.5.3	DOK 2
15	A	Text Structure: Cause and Effect	RI.5.3	DOK 2
16	H	Context Clues: Paragraph Clues	L.5.4a	DOK 2
17	D	Main Idea and Key Details	RI.5.2	DOK 3
18	G	Cause and Effect	RI.5.3	DOK 2
19	D	Context Clues: Paragraph Clues	L.5.4a	DOK 2
20	G	Cause and Effect	RI.5.3	DOK 2
21	see below	Comparing Across Texts	RI.5.9	DOK 4

Comprehension 1, 3, 4, 5, 7, 14, 15, 17, 18, 20	/10	%
Vocabulary 2, 6, 8, 9, 10, 11, 12, 13, 16, 19	/10	%
Total Weekly Assessment Score	/20	%

21 To receive full credit for the response, the following information should be included: Both venomous animals and animals that cooperate have developed ways to defend themselves and find food.

Name: ______________________ Date: ________

7 According to the article, what can be done with uneaten food?

Ⓐ Uneaten food can be thrown in landfills.

Ⓑ Uneaten food can be composted with worms.

Ⓒ The students can take all the uneaten food home.

Ⓓ The students can be forced to eat all of their food.

8 Which words from the article have almost the same meaning?

Ⓕ assemble, construct

Ⓖ garbage, compost

Ⓗ scraps, supplies

Ⓘ richer, bigger

9 Which words from the article are most OPPOSITE in meaning?

Ⓐ plants, soil

Ⓑ meat, dairy

Ⓒ trash, landfill

Ⓓ moisture, dry

10 Which paragraph does the following key detail best support?

It does not take long to fill a bottle with water from home.

Ⓕ Paragraph 2

Ⓖ Paragraph 3

Ⓗ Paragraph 4

Ⓘ Paragraph 5

GO ON →

Read the article "Kind Actions" before answering Numbers 11 through 20.

Kind Actions

We are all affected by the actions of those around us. Your class would most likely have a positive reaction if your teacher announced a delightful surprise, such as ice cream, as a treat for all students. You may think that only adults are able to influence others, but this is not true. Anyone can improve another person's life with his or her actions. We all can take time to help others in need.

A simple way to help others is to spend time with them. Some residents of nursing homes may be lonely and in need of a friend. You could get permission to visit a nursing home. If your parents give their consent, you could talk with some residents. They might like to hear about your life and what you like to do. Or, they might like to have someone listen to their stories. Talking and listening are gifts that do not cost any money. They can make a big difference in the life of someone who is lonely.

Some people need help doing tasks that they are unable to do for themselves. You may know someone who could use help with chores around the house. A great gesture is offering to help without expecting any money in return. Performing the tasks in a dependable way will be a big help.

GO ON →

There might be opportunities to help people in your community that you may not know personally. You can donate your time by helping out at a soup kitchen, which is a place that provides free meals for those in need. These are staffed by volunteers, so any help is welcome. There are many tasks that need to be done. Do not be discouraged by the smallness of tasks such as serving food, washing dishes, and cleaning up tables. They are of great importance to those who run the soup kitchens. Without help, soup kitchens are unable to provide meals for those who need them.

Sometimes, people are in need of things instead of time. When the weather turns colder, some people in your community may be in need of extra blankets or coats. The solution to this problem does not have to be expensive. With the help of others, you could organize a collection of an assortment of coats and blankets that are no longer needed. If you hold this drive at your school or in your neighborhood, you should get a variety of coat sizes and blanket types. Collections like this can be held at any time of the year. Many people like to clean out closets in the spring time, so this might be a good time to gather coats that have been outgrown.

While cleaning out closets or looking for coats and blankets, you may want also to look for toys or books that are no longer used. If they are in good shape, you could consider donating them. Thrift shops sell these items, and the profits benefit the organization. You could also donate them to a homeless shelter. Non-profit organizations that care for children may also be able to use these items. There are many places that would gladly accept things in good condition that you no longer need.

Sharing time and unused items with others in need are actions that can have a positive effect on those around us. These are just a few ways that you could impact your community. Many other opportunities exist. Gather a group of your friends and see if you can find a way to make a difference in your school or community. You will be glad that you took action.

GO ON →

Name: ______________________________ Date: __________

Now answer Numbers 11 through 20. Base your answers on "Kind Actions."

11 According to the article, which of the following is a solution for helping people who are lonely?

Ⓐ visiting with them

Ⓑ helping with chores

Ⓒ giving them warm blankets

Ⓓ volunteering at a soup kitchen

12 Read the sentence from the article.

> **Your class would most likely have a positive reaction if your teacher announced a delightful surprise, such as ice cream, as a treat for all students.**

Which word has the OPPOSITE meaning of *delightful?*

Ⓕ delicious

Ⓖ horrible

Ⓗ lightweight

Ⓘ wonderful

13 How does the author show the relationship between people in need and the actions of others?

Ⓐ Individuals cannot solve all social needs.

Ⓑ People in need today are fewer than in the past.

Ⓒ People in need can be helped by others' kind deeds.

Ⓓ Poverty is caused by ignoring the needs of others.

14 Which words have almost the same meaning?

Ⓕ simple, positive

Ⓖ talking, listening

Ⓗ consent, permission

Ⓘ opportunities, volunteers

GO ON →

Name: ______________________________ Date: ________

15 Read this sentence from the article.

> **Performing the tasks in a dependable way will be a big help.**

Which word has almost the same meaning as *dependable* as used in the sentence above?

Ⓐ bossy

Ⓑ free

Ⓒ generous

Ⓓ reliable

16 How does cleaning out closets help others?

Ⓕ It comforts a lonely person.

Ⓖ It raises money to help people.

Ⓗ It provides them with a needed meal.

Ⓘ It can be a way to locate unused coats or toys.

17 Which of the following is a problem that is solved by soup kitchens?

Ⓐ Some people have too many toys.

Ⓑ Some people do not have warm coats.

Ⓒ Some people do not have enough books.

Ⓓ Some people are not able to afford a meal.

GO ON →

Name: ______________________________ Date: ________

18 Which words from the article are most OPPOSITE in meaning?

Ⓕ donate, sell

Ⓖ items, things

Ⓗ simple, dependable

Ⓘ tasks, chores

19 Read these sentences from the article.

With the help of others, you could organize a collection of an assortment of coats and blankets that are no longer needed. If you hold this drive at your school or in your neighborhood, you should get a variety of coat sizes and blanket types.

What does *assortment* mean in the sentences above?

Ⓐ copy

Ⓑ donation

Ⓒ mixture

Ⓓ test

20 According to the article, who performs much of the work at soup kitchens?

Ⓕ employees

Ⓖ volunteers

Ⓗ professional chefs

Ⓘ the people eating the meals

STOP

Name: ______________________ Date: __________

21 According to both articles, how can our actions affect our environment and the people in our communities? Support your answers with clear text evidence from the articles.

Answer Key

Name: ____________________

Question	Correct Answer	Content Focus	CCSS	Complexity
1	D	Problem and Solution	RI.5.3	DOK 2
2	H	Synonyms and Antonyms	L.5.5c	DOK 2
3	C	Text Structure: Problem and Solution	RI.5.5	DOK 2
4	F	Context Clues: Paragraph Clues	L.5.4a	DOK 2
5	D	Synonyms and Antonyms	L.5.5c	DOK 2
6	H	Problem and Solution	RI.5.3	DOK 2
7	B	Problem and Solution	RI.5.3	DOK 2
8	F	Synonyms and Antonyms	L.5.5c	DOK 1
9	D	Synonyms and Antonyms	L.5.5c	DOK 1
10	G	Main Idea and Key Details	RI.5.2	DOK 2
11	A	Problem and Solution	RI.5.3	DOK 2
12	G	Synonyms and Antonyms	L.5.5c	DOK 2
13	C	Text Structure: Problem and Solution	RI.5.5	DOK 2
14	H	Synonyms and Antonyms	L.5.5c	DOK 1
15	D	Synonyms and Antonyms	L.5.5c	DOK 2
16	I	Problem and Solution	RI.5.3	DOK 2
17	D	Problem and Solution	RI.5.3	DOK 2
18	F	Synonyms and Antonyms	L.5.5c	DOK 1
19	C	Context Clues: Paragraph Clues	L.5.4a	DOK 2
20	G	Main Idea and Key Details	RI.5.2	DOK 2
21	see below	Comparing Across Texts	RI.5.9	DOK 4

Comprehension 1, 3, 6, 7, 10, 11, 13, 16, 17, 20	/10	%
Vocabulary 2, 4, 5, 8, 9, 12, 14, 15, 18, 19	/10	%
Total Weekly Assessment Score	/20	%

21 To receive full credit for the response, the following information should be included: We can choose to use reusable packaging for our lunches and compost uneaten food. We can clean out our closets and donate unwanted blankets to those who need them.

Read the passage "Becoming a Musician" before answering Numbers 1 through 10.

Becoming a Musician

With frustration, I stared at the open pages of the piano music book. The musical notes mocked me as I tried to read them and play at the same time. My brain seemed unable to tell my fingers which keys to play next. The resulting song sounded nothing like the familiar tune I was supposedly playing. I closed the book and ended my practice session.

I started taking piano lessons because of my Uncle Sahil. He is a wonderful pianist, and any piano he touches welcomes his attention. Before I began taking lessons, I dreamed of a day when I would be able to play like Uncle Sahil. I begged my parents until they agreed to let me take lessons. The first few months of lessons with my piano teacher, Ms. Wong, were fun and I practiced every day to learn the basics. The trouble began once I was ready to progress to more complicated music.

I could not play the more advanced music as well as I wanted to. At the end of each lesson, I would leave Ms. Wong's house with a new song to learn for the week. The melody would be fresh in my head, because Ms. Wong would play the song for me before I left. When I tried to play the same song at home, it sounded nothing like it was supposed to. I would practice for a while, but I felt as though I never made any improvement. The piano was no longer my friend, and I dreaded practicing.

GO ON →

My parents talked with me about my piano lessons. My mother explained that the lessons were very expensive and that I would not be allowed to continue them if I did not practice daily. The thought of not taking lessons saddened me, and I frowned at the idea. My father saw my frown and suggested that I talk with Uncle Sahil about his experiences learning how to play the piano.

"Kalinda, you will find that many things in life take hard work to accomplish," my father said. "If you give up when things are difficult, you will not succeed at much."

I thought about my father's words later that night as I lay in bed. I knew that working hard was important, but working hard took a lot of effort! I decided to call Uncle Sahil in the morning and ask for his advice.

When I called Uncle Sahil, I explained my difficulty with piano lessons and asked if he had any advice. Uncle Sahil paused before answering, and then replied, "Kalinda, do you know that I almost quit playing the piano when I was young? Then I decided that I loved music so much that I wanted to keep playing. I practiced before and after school. I still spend at least an hour every day playing the piano. You have to dedicate yourself in order to do well. If you commit to the music, you will learn to play like me."

This shocked me because I did not know that Uncle Sahil almost quit playing and that he still spent so much time practicing. The beautiful music did not happen by accident and was the result of hard work. I decided that I would spend more time practicing because I wanted to be able to play well. For the next six months, I worked as hard as I could on my music. I was pleased to find out that the harder I worked, the better I became.

Finally, I was ready to do something that I had dreamed about. Uncle Sahil and I were going to play a duet together at my piano recital. As we drove to the auditorium on the night of the recital, the stars winked encouragingly at me. I smiled back at them and felt proud of what I had accomplished.

GO ON →

Name: ______________________________ Date: ________

Now answer Numbers 1 through 10. Base your answers on "Becoming a Musician."

1 When Kalinda is practicing at the beginning of the passage, why does she stare at the music in frustration?

Ⓐ She does not know how to read music.

Ⓑ She is having difficulty playing the song.

Ⓒ She does not like the song she is trying to play.

Ⓓ She is being interrupted by noises in her house.

2 Read this sentence from the passage.

> **The musical notes mocked me as I tried to read them and play at the same time.**

What does "the musical notes mocked me" mean in the sentence above?

Ⓕ Kalinda felt as though the notes were making fun of her.

Ⓖ Kalinda's family laughed at her when she made mistakes.

Ⓗ The music sounded like laughter while Kalinda was playing.

Ⓘ The notes copied exactly what Kalinda did as she tried to play.

3 Who is the narrator of the story?

Ⓐ Kalinda

Ⓑ Kalinda's father

Ⓒ Uncle Sahil

Ⓓ someone outside the story

GO ON →

Name: ______________________ Date: ________

❹ Read this sentence from the passage.

He is a wonderful pianist, and any piano he touches welcomes his attention.

What does "welcomes his attention" mean in the sentence above?

Ⓕ The piano is happy to see Uncle Sahil.

Ⓖ Uncle Sahil asks the piano if he can play.

Ⓗ Pianos respond well to Uncle Sahil's skill.

Ⓘ Uncle Sahil never ignores a piano that he passes.

❺ Read this sentence from the passage.

The piano was no longer my friend, and I dreaded practicing.

Why is the author comparing a piano to a friend?

Ⓐ Kalinda used to have a piano for a friend.

Ⓑ The piano told Kalinda that they were not friends.

Ⓒ All of Kalinda's friends had pianos in their houses.

Ⓓ Kalinda used to have good feelings about her piano.

❻ When Kalinda learns about Uncle Sahil's experiences when he was younger, she feels

Ⓕ angry.

Ⓖ confused.

Ⓗ frustrated.

Ⓘ surprised.

GO ON →

Name: ______________________________ Date: ________

7 At the end of the story, how does Kalinda feel about hard work?

Ⓐ She does not see the value of hard work.

Ⓑ She does not want to work hard on her music.

Ⓒ She wishes that she could work as hard as Uncle Sahil.

Ⓓ She sees that hard work has made her a better musician.

8 Which words from the passage have almost the same meaning?

Ⓕ time, work

Ⓖ melody, tune

Ⓗ beautiful, pleased

Ⓘ advice, improvement

9 Read this sentence from the passage.

> **As we drove to the auditorium on the night of the recital, the stars winked encouragingly at me.**

Why does the author make the stars seem human?

Ⓐ to compare the stars to blinking lights

Ⓑ to suggest that the stars can support people

Ⓒ to show that Kalinda feels positively about herself

Ⓓ to explain why the light coming from stars seems to flash

10 What message about life does the passage communicate?

Ⓕ You can still fail even if you work hard.

Ⓖ There is no replacement for hard work.

Ⓗ Music brings people together.

Ⓘ Everyone loves music.

GO ON →

Read the three poems before answering Numbers 11 through 20.

Morning

Canoes are dancing near the shore.
The sun is smiling down.
The morning is a gentle hand
That wipes away my frown.

The Wind

The wind is cold and strong and cruel
It tells me just what I must do.
I wear my mittens and my hat.
Well, I ask, now, wouldn't you?

Unsatisfied, it gives a roar
Of great displeasure and demands
I put on more and more and more
By grabbing me with ice-cold hands.

And so I turn and back I go
To find a scarf and warmer socks.
It claims it must come in with me.
I keep it out with chains and locks.

GO ON →

Autumn

The breezes kiss the treetops as they pass
And make the leaves fall softly to the ground.
The branches tremble slightly but no more;
A gentle sighing is their only sound.

The leaves invite me then to romp and play
Among their red and yellow colors bright.
I rake them all into a pile and jump,
Until the day is chased away by night.

I find it odd that autumn comes so late,
For one finds so much freshness every day.
The air is crisp and clear and full of hope.
"A new beginning now!" the breezes say.

GO ON →

Name: ______________________________ Date: ________

Now answer Numbers 11 through 20. Base your answers on the poems.

11 In "Morning," how does the speaker feel about the day ahead?

Ⓐ bored

Ⓑ eager

Ⓒ impatient

Ⓓ worried

12 Read this line from "Morning."

The sun is smiling down.

What does the speaker mean by saying that the sun is smiling?

Ⓕ The weather is very hot.

Ⓖ The weather is pleasantly warm.

Ⓗ The sun looks like a person's face.

Ⓘ The sun is casting curved shadows.

13 In "The Wind," what does the personification of the wind suggest about it?

Ⓐ It is helpful.

Ⓑ It has the ability to react.

Ⓒ It can be influenced by people.

Ⓓ It could change at any moment.

14 In "The Wind," the speaker's feelings about the wind suggest that he or she thinks of it as a

Ⓕ bully.

Ⓖ teacher.

Ⓗ police officer.

Ⓘ concerned parent.

GO ON →

Name: ______________________________ Date: ________

15 What text evidence in "The Wind" supports the speaker's statement that the wind is cruel?

Ⓐ It makes a roaring noise.

Ⓑ It tells the speaker what to do.

Ⓒ It tries to go inside with the speaker.

Ⓓ It grabs the speaker with ice-cold hands.

16 Read this line from "Autumn."

The breezes kiss the treetops as they pass

What does the speaker mean by saying that the breezes "kiss" the treetops?

Ⓕ The breezes show affection.

Ⓖ The breezes are soft and mild.

Ⓗ The breezes will soon be going away.

Ⓘ The breezes have missed the treetops.

17 What is a theme that all three poems share?

Ⓐ People are affected by the weather.

Ⓑ The weather can be hard to live with.

Ⓒ Everyone complains about the weather.

Ⓓ The weather changes from season to season.

GO ON →

Name: ______________________________ Date: ________

18 Read this line from "Autumn."

The leaves invite me then to romp and play

What does the speaker mean by saying that the leaves "invite" him or her to play?

Ⓕ The colors of the leaves are attractive.

Ⓖ Playing in the leaves seems appealing.

Ⓗ The speaker doesn't want to have to do any work.

Ⓘ The noise the leaves makes sounds like an invitation.

19 Read this line from "Autumn."

Among their red and yellow colors bright.

Which word means most nearly the OPPOSITE of *bright* as it is used in the sentence above?

Ⓐ dull

Ⓑ green

Ⓒ sparkling

Ⓓ unintelligent

20 Why does the speaker in "Autumn" find it unusual that autumn comes so late?

Ⓕ It is a windy time of year.

Ⓖ It is a colorful time of the year.

Ⓗ It is a time for making a fresh start.

Ⓘ It is a time for staying outside until night.

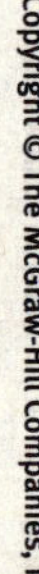

STOP

Name: ______________________________ Date: ________

21 Compare the points of view in the three poems. What is similar about them? What is different? Support your ideas with clear text evidence from the poems.

Answer Key Name: ____________________

Question	Correct Answer	Content Focus	CCSS	Complexity
1	B	Point of View	RL.5.6	DOK 3
2	F	Personification	RL.5.4	DOK 2
3	A	Point of View	RL.5.6	DOK 2
4	H	Personification	RL.5.4	DOK 2
5	D	Personification	RL.5.4	DOK 2
6	I	Point of View	RL.5.6	DOK 2
7	D	Point of View	RL.5.6	DOK 2
8	G	Synonyms and Antonyms	L.5.5c	DOK 1
9	C	Personification	RL.5.4	DOK 2
10	G	Theme	RL.5.2	DOK 3
11	B	Point of View	RL.5.6	DOK 2
12	G	Personification	RL.5.4	DOK 2
13	B	Personification	RL.5.4	DOK 2
14	F	Point of View	RL.5.6	DOK 2
15	D	Point of View	RL.5.6	DOK 2
16	G	Personification	RL.5.4	DOK 2
17	A	Theme	RL.5.2	DOK 3
18	G	Personification	RL.5.4	DOK 2
19	A	Synonyms and Antonyms	L.5.5c	DOK 2
20	H	Point of View	RL.5.6	DOK 2
21	see below	Comparing Across Texts	RL.5.9	DOK 4

Comprehension 1, 3, 6, 7, 10, 11, 14, 15, 17, 20	/10	%
Vocabulary 2, 4, 5, 8, 9, 12, 13, 16, 18, 19	/10	%
Total Weekly Assessment Score	/20	%

21 To receive full credit for the response, the following information should be included: The points of view are alike in that all the speakers view elements of nature as if they were human, using personification throughout. For example, the sun smiles; the wind grabs; the breezes speak. The points of view are different in that the speakers have different feelings about their subjects. In the first and third poems, the speakers' points of view are positive and appreciative. The speaker says the morning wipes away his or her frown in the first poem. The speaker says that everything is fresh in the third poem. In the second poem, the speaker's point of view is that the wind is cold and cruel.